Evidence-Based Policy

A Realist Perspective

Ray Pawson

SAGE Publications

Los Angeles • London • New Delhi • Singapore

SAGE Publications Ltd
1 Oliver's Yard
55 City Road
London EC1Y 1SP

SAGE Publications Inc.
2455 Teller Road
Thousand Oaks, California 91320

SAGE Publications India Pvt Ltd
B1/I 1 Mohan Cooperative Industrial Area
Mathura Road, New Delhi 110 044
India

SAGE Publications Asia-Pacific Pte Ltd
33 Pekin Street #02-01
Far East Square
Singapore 048763

British Library Cataloguing in Publication data

A catalogue record for this book is available from
the British Library

ISBN: 978-1-4129-1059-0 (hbk)
ISBN: 978-1-4129-1060-6 (pbk)

Library of Congress Control Number 2005905987

Typeset by C&M Digitals (P) Ltd., Chennai, India
Printed on paper from sustainable resources
Printed in Great Britain by Athenaeum Press, Gateshead

To Wendy

Contents

Preface

Choosing a title for a book is always an agony – just as difficult as naming one's children (mine, incidentally, are called Rhino and Rosebud). On this occasion I have ended up with a rather prosaic effort. It may be of interest to lift the cover on the reject pile, however, for this will give the reader a useful first glimpse of the content. The sub-title, the 'realist' bit, was straightforward enough. We academics love our symbols and totems, and everything I have written is in the name of realist methodology. So there's some dogged consistency to start with, though I should make clear from the outset that my understanding of realism does not square entirely with that of all other members of the tribe.

It was the main title, the 'evidence-based policy' banner, that was more troublesome. The problem with the term, and it is quite a big one, is that there is no such thing as evidence-based policy. Evidence is the six-stone weakling of the policy world. Even its most enthusiastic advocates are inclined to prefer the phrase 'evidence-informed policy' as a way of conveying a more authentic impression of research's sway. But that's a horrible expression, all thin-lipped, prissy and politically correct. My thoughts thus turned to a version with a bit more flair, whilst retaining the *savoir-faire* about the limited compass of evidence. What about 'evidence *au fait* policy'? Rather good, but maybe not. What about 'evidence *for* policy'? Also good, but rather enigmatic. What about 'evidence *enlightened* policy'? Well, this one is decidedly accurate and chimes beautifully with the argument to come. But I'm afraid it sounds somewhat ethereal and what I'm after is something a bit more down to earth.

One way of resolving the dilemma was simply to acknowledge it: *Evidence-Based Policy or Policy-Based Evidence: The Realist Resolution*. This permits the big problem – the four-hundred pound brute called politics – to surface. It also allows me to steal the rather waggish inversion of evidence-based policy to policy-based evidence already used by a couple of authors. What they have in mind is that the only empirical evidence that actually surfaces in policy-making is cherry-picked and rose-tinted. But I'm uncomfortable with all this, for the simple reason that I'm on the side of the rationalists. Evidence-based policy may be a weakling but he is my weakling and I want to make the best of him. So, having gone all round the houses, I ended up with plain old 'evidence-based policy'.

Anyway, that is the explanation and now you are in the know. The book is called *Evidence-Based Policy: A Realist Perspective* but remember that what you are about to read is – *The Best We Can Do By Way of Evidence-Based Policy: A Realist in One Sense of the Term Perspective.*

Books about research methods, for that is what this is, can be a mite dry, so I want to begin with the emotion of it all. You have been charged with synthesizing all the evidence relevant to Policy X. What does it actually feel like to conduct the review?

To find out I recommend that you trace the following steps. Take a flight to Venice and please try to arrive around one hour before dusk. Take a short walk to the harbour and board a water taxi. This is the rather functional name given to the silky, mahogany launch that will carry you to the island. I'm afraid that you and your partner must travel without fellow passengers, so the fare will be considerably more than your no-frills plane ticket. But, trust me, I have to capture the atmosphere perfectly. You are now speeding across the lagoon and before you, beneath the ochre sky, stands the black profile of Venice. Francesco, the skipper, who will be just as sleek as his craft, will enter the Canale Grande from the west. Now you are there, gliding along its entire sweep. The bustle of the day is over and surely by now you are getting the feeling. You are Canaletto. You are Titian. You are Veronese. Or, perhaps, you are Byron or Browning. Just maybe, you are Casanova.

Ask Francesco to drop you at the moorings at the Accademia. You are in the Dorsoduro, the most magical of the six Sestieri. Now you must hurry, for it's getting dark and I've still not described the entire sensation. Down the Rio Foscarini. Left at Calle Forner. You are now at the bridge over the Rio di San Vio, the prettiest of the little canals of Venice. Look behind you. In the window of the art shop is a very striking print by David Dalla Venezia. He has painted your portrait. There you are in free fall, arms and legs flying like a puppet. Not so much enlightened as blinded. All around you is the literature – anonymous, flapping, mocking – resisting all efforts to tame it. Now, *this* is what it feels like to carry out a systematic review. For those of you unable to make the trip, *l'artista* has kindly allowed it to be reproduced on the cover.

Whilst I hope its arguments are novel, and notwithstanding my attempt to produce a page-turner, the book follows the conventional academic drill – ground is cleared, principles are embraced, critiques are flourished, claims are made, claims are substantiated, arguments are illustrated, and conclusions are drawn. *Chapter 1* identifies the main vehicle for evidence-based policy. Current hopes are pinned on rigorous 'systematic reviews', which attempt to synthesize the entirety of evidence on existing interventions. *Chapter 2* assembles the platform upon which I want to build. Realist methodology is introduced, both as a philosophy of social inquiry and as a tool for dissecting the workings of social interventions. *Chapter 3* is a critical interlude examining 'meta-analysis', currently the dominant model for research synthesis. It is charged with providing mistaken answers to misplaced questions. *Chapter 4* is the pivot of the book, introducing a new model of systematic review. The principles and practice of 'realist synthesis' are set down at length. *Chapter 5* is the first of three providing illustrations of realist synthesis. The evidence on the

USA's sex offender registration and community notification programme (Megan's Law) is reviewed in order to show how and how much the success of complex interventions depends on the efficacy of each step in a long implementation chain. *Chapter 6* offers a review of youth mentoring programmes. The purpose is to show how realist synthesis can fine-tune understanding of the inner workings of programmes. *Chapter 7* is a realist synthesis of 'naming and shaming' interventions. The aim is to compare the same initiative in action in very different policy spheres in order to demonstrate the contextual sensitivity of a key weapon of public policy. *Chapter 8* returns to the big picture. Does this dose of realism about the nature of the evidence base change expectations about its capacity to infiltrate the policy process?

From this brief glimpse ahead, it can be seen that the book enters a huge imbroglio about a big issue. Also, by their very nature, systematic reviews are extensive in coverage and extended in the telling. Moreover, and wretchedly, methodologists are prone to bloated prose, using terms like epistemology and incommensurability in explaining themselves. The net result is that the book kept bursting its covers in the writing. Fortunately another mammoth idea, the world wide web, comes to the rescue. The book is served by its own website at www.leeds.ac.uk/realistsynthesis and here the reader will find full versions of two of the reviews and several papers that go off at tangents, albeit very interesting tangents, from the main line of argument.

> 📖 Points at which this supplementary material is most helpful are signalled like this in the main text. ⭐

At this point acknowledgements are due but, before I reveal the support of comrades, it should be pointed out that all the speechifying, all the overblown justifications and all loitering errors are my very own work. Three colleagues, in particular, have coloured the pages. The tapestry in the text is created by Lesley Grayson, who pinpointed the sources and laced the prose. The Romany in the text follows from Annette Boaz's zeal for leading me up all of policy's garden paths. The high voltage in the text draws on the human dynamism of Trish Greenhalgh. Thanks are also due to other members of the indomitable Queen Mary team – Alan Gomersall, Bill Solesbury, Fay Sullivan and Ken Young. Other partners in the evidential grime have been Gill Harvey, Kieran Walshe and Andrew Long. Two ex-poachers, Mike Kelley and Mike Fisher, proved highly tolerant gamekeepers. Nicoletta Stame, Frans Leeuw and Elliot Stern continue to be my international knowledge brokers. This time, there are no words in the text from Nick Tilley, but the invisible hand is conspicuous. Appreciation also goes to Marta Bolognani for the *bellissimissima* translation. And at the end of the line, gracious thanks go to Patrick Brindle for leaving well enough alone.

Finally, I should acknowledge the all-important financial stanchions. Methodological work is rather slow-burning and I have been surprised, surprised and surprised again that it finds funding. This work was supported directly by a fellowship at the ESRC UK Centre for Evidence-Based Policy and Practice at Queen Mary, University of London; through an award from the ESRC Research Methods Programme; and via a project funded jointly by the NHS Service Delivery Organisation and the Canadian Health Service Research Foundation. Backing for related projects from the Health Development Agency and the Social Care Institute for Excellence is also recorded with gratitude.

Ray Pawson
Leeds

'the rare occurrence of the expected ...'

WILLIAM CARLOS WILLIAMS
From 'At Kenneth Burke's Place'

1

Evidence-Based Policy: The Promise of Systematic Review

How does 'evidence' speak to 'power'? What do you get if you cross 'research' with 'realpolitik'? Where lies the ground between the 'ivory tower' and 'corridors of power'? What hope is there for nuptials between 'knowing' and 'doing'?

The answer to all these questions has coalesced in a new millennium big idea called evidence-based policy and, in the pages to follow, I am going to attempt to assess the state of this union between the realms of evidence and policy. The story I am going to tell is neither one of the root incompatibility of star-crossed lovers, nor one in which policy-makers and researchers all live happily ever after. Evidence-based policy is much like all trysts, in which hope springs eternal and often outweighs expectancy, and for which the future is uncertain as we wait to know whether the partnership will flower or pass as an infatuation.

The conflation of these two intellectual tides is itself a curiosity. We are more used to, and perhaps more comfortable with, the notion that decisions of state (or indeed of the street corner) are a matter for political conviction. Over the centuries the basis for such authority has changed as divine right and moral dynasticism have given way to complex political systems. Modern polities are a balancing act between hierarchical privilege, economic power, ideological standpoints and democratic mandates. But, whatever their colour or composition, we expect political calculation to form the basis of policy choices.

We are more used to, and the professoriate at least is more comfortable with, the idea that authoritative knowledge about society is propagated within the groves of academe. So whilst everyone can lay claim to a capacity for self-reflection and mutual understanding, it is only certain branches of social science that profess to operate such processes formally and with any certainty. The main pay-off from the intellectual impulse to understand the human condition, however, has been to cram library shelves, to populate university corridors and to create disciplines, perspectives, paradigms and methodologies by the day, and by the dozen. Because social science is a science like no other, it delivers a curious knowledge base beset with inconsistency and rivalry, which operates with due and proper caution about its lack of predictive power.

So how is it, as we move into the twenty-first century, that there are serious aspirations to unite these seemingly wayward ways of thinking? Why in the UK, for instance, was the following ambition prominent in the very new New Labour government's agenda for modernization?

> This government expects more of policy makers. More new ideas, more willingness to question inherited ways of doing things, *better use of evidence and research in policy making* and better focus on policies that will deliver long term goals. (Cabinet Office, 1999: ch. 2, paragraph 6; my emphasis)

And why was it that a European Commission White Paper on governance, of about the same vintage, intoned much the same message?

> ... scientific and other experts play an increasingly significant role in preparing and monitoring decisions. From human and animal health to social legislation, the institutions rely on specialist expertise to anticipate and identify the nature of problems and uncertainties that the Union faces, to take decisions and to ensure risks can be explained clearly and simply to the public. (European Commission, 2001: 19)

The immediate point to remember in accounting for this leap of faith in evidence-based policy is to refrain from exaggerating about millennial movements at millennium moments. The coming together of social knowing and political doing has actually been a long process, following the time-honoured route of two steps forwards followed by one step backwards. In 1969, Donald T. Campbell penned the following statement on the evidence-based policy of the time, namely his vision of the 'experimenting society':

> The United States and other modern nations should be ready for an experimental approach to social reform, an approach in which we try out new programs designed to cure specific problems, in which we learn whether or not these programs are effective, and in which we retain, imitate, modify or discard them on the basis of their apparent effectiveness on the multiple imperfect criteria available. Our readiness for this stage is indicated by the inclusion of specific provisions for program evaluation in the first wave of the 'Great Society' legislation and by the current congressional proposals for establishing 'social indicators' and 'data banks'. (Campbell, 1969: 409)

The next point to grasp in understanding the rise (or resurgence) of evidence-based policy is that it is premised on a partnership, and we need to clarify the basis on which the match is being made. There are several suitors and numerous nubiles within the modern-day ranks of evidence providers and evidence users, and it is worth taking a brief tour of their respective positions as an initial gauge of their relationship.

Solesbury (2001) has identified a range of institutional conditions that signal the polity's new readiness to heed evidence. In the UK, the 'new' evidence-based policy is strongly associated with the so-called pragmatic, anti-ideological turn in modern politics. I have my doubts about whether this transformation ever took a grip around the Cabinet table, but it is clear that a crop of government agencies has shot up, whose job it is to marshal and monitor the evidence base to better inform government decisions. Examples include the National Institute for Health and Clinical Excellence and the Social Care Institute for Excellence. Another factor in the rise of evidence is the 'retreat from the priesthood' in professional practice and power. Corporations, charities, patients, parents, clients, customers of all kinds, argues Solesbury, are less and less inclined to take professional views on trust and demand to be shown the supporting evidence. The third welcoming embrace for evidence-based policy is provided by the growth of 'knowledge management systems'. We live in the information age and inhabit complex social systems. In these circumstances it is knowledge that provides competitive advantage, and information systems and data-banks, once again, are called for to provide the vital currency.

The other side of the partnership, evidence provision, is equally complex. In my introductory remarks I based 'the evidence' in academe, as a symbol of the expertise and impartiality required to produce such a precious commodity. However, evidence can also be an article of trade, with the livelihoods of research institutes dependent on their capacity to manufacture evidence to meet the needs of inquisitive customers. On a bad day, the ivory tower can look awfully like a shopping mall. In the UK, much if not most, policy inquiry is conducted by units and centres that perch on the edge of mainstream university departments, and whose existence depends on winning the *next* contract. Oftentimes, this means that the policy-research relationship is financially circular, with one arm of government providing the funds for another to supply the evidence base. Sometimes, the loop is much tighter, with many central and local government departments having their own 'analytic' divisions and 'research and intelligence' units.

In addition, there is considerable involvement by charities and foundations in the construction of an evidence base. This source may operate generically in the interest of social betterment or specifically in trying to bring a considered, evidential approach to a special concern such as child welfare. Whether these activities sit well with the traditional lobby function is a moot point. Finally, the increasing role of the private sector in the evidence 'industry' should be noted, as both recipients and providers of information. Unhappily, one also observes that this new function for auditors coincided with the outbreak of corporate scandals about their traditional role as independent regulators.

One observes, in short, an assortment of information recipients and providers who engage in intricate and potentially fragile relationships. No one will need reminding that Great Society free thinking was followed by Watergate-style cynicism. No one in the UK will need reminding that New Labour's introductory nod to the evidence supplier was mixed with an enthusiastic embrace of the spin-doctor and, perhaps, with some envy of steely Thatcherite certainty. And at a global level, no one will need reminding of the shifting sands of evidence and the malleable dossiers of intelligence that formed the basis for the Iraq War.

It is hardly surprising, therefore, that alongside the literature arguing for a more evidential approach to policy and practice one finds a powerful counterpoint, arguing that evidence is cynically exploited in the interests of retaining rather than refining the exercise of power (Majone, 1989). And even more bizarrely, amidst the plain-speaking world of research on burglar alarms, school breakfast clubs and pension benefits, one hears the voice of 'post-modern evaluators'. From them comes a denial of the very notion of evidence, based on a critique of scientific 'logocentrism' and a wish to gather the people around the banner of 'transgressive action' under conditions of 'polyvocality' (Stronach, 1997; Fox, 2003).

Evidence-based policy: runners and riders

From the outset, then, it should be recognized that there are competing affiliations and strategies that aspire to offer better use of evidence and research in policy-making, or oppose the very idea of evidence-based anything. I cannot do justice to all such standpoints in one volume and the purpose of this section is to isolate my chosen specimen from six other approaches that are sometimes designated as evidence-based policy. Although these undoubtedly deserve a more considered treatment, my purpose here is to apply quick cuffs around assorted ears in order to inform the reader where the argument is and is not heading. So, in my book, the following half-dozen phenomena do *not* constitute evidence-based policy-making.

Positioning

There has always been a degree of personal cross-fertilization of the polity and the academy in the form of gamekeepers turned poachers (judgements on which I leave to the reader). Socrates, doyen of the original Academy and the inventor of dialectical reasoning, is said to have had a steady personal influence on Athenian public affairs until scandal broke and the Assembly ushered him away to a final dialogue with the hemlock. In the present day, former politicians are considered to make fine college presidents and university vice-chancellors. Whether this stems from the wisdom and equanimity gained in electoral defeat, or from the remnants of political clout, is a matter on which I also remain silent. The tide flows the other way, of course, one notable example being the creator of the 'double hermeneutic' (Giddens, 1984) turning up as an author of the UK government's 'third way' (Giddens, 2000). Perhaps even more significant was the German philosopher-historian, arguably the best-known social scientist of all, who came up with the maxim about the priority being to change the world rather than understand it. Arguments still rage on whether Marx preferred the theorist's armchair or the political soap-box, although one can hardly gainsay the real political action taken in his name. Today's evidence-based policy has, without doubt, hastened the interchange between the common room and the corridors of power, but we must not confuse the agents with the process and demand occupational mobility as a defining characteristic.

Portals

Another, and altogether different, entry to the world of evidence-based policy is through the digital gateway of knowledge management (KM). All modern enterprises (private or public) depend on knowledge as the key resource; information sources are multiplying exponentially, and harnessing them requires a completely new set of 'e-tools' from automated document search and retrieval systems to content management software. KM is often conducted in its own secret language; for instance: 'the latest platform encompasses a set of basic knowledge management functionalities, along with the ability to rapidly develop collaborative knowledge, portal and e-learning solutions within a pull-communications culture'. Although I will cover some of the tools of the information scientist who brings together the raw materials of the evidence base, this activity does not constitute the defining feature of evidence-based policy within this study. No doubt most readers will be grateful to peer no further into the geeky world of the 'knowledge data capability manager' or the 'knowledge tool trainer', and I accept their thanks.

Polling

Evidence-based policy is preceded by an altogether more mundane mechanism for connecting political action and social wisdom. No doubt, in their heart of hearts, plenty of politicians still think 'I've asked my constituents, laddie, and that's evidence enough for me.' The weekly surgery and the local agent's briefings may have given way to the opinion poll and the focus group, but this particular information flow still remains as a counterweight to the unfettered application of politics to decision-making. It may never quite constitute a reality check, however, for public opinion is fidgety and elusive, and attitudinal information is always one vital step removed from the actuality of social conditions. So whilst the research methods for penetrating the mood of the public have become more firmly grounded, and the significance of their findings more pronounced, the pollsters remain an adjunct to evidence-based policy rather than its embodiment.

Partnership

Another strategy driven by the commitment to social betterment through research is the 'co-participatory' approach, which in bygone days was known as action research. This shares with the evidence-based approach the basic aim of blending research and practice but does so in a rather distinctive way, namely by embodying the two pursuits in one and the same person. Researcher-practitioners operate by sharing all of their technical skills with those being researched. The result, so the argument goes, is that such research imposes neither hypotheses nor solutions, all findings being automatically grounded in mutual, agreed forms of practice. There seems little problem with such a strategy when the policy concern is local and immediate, and the vested interests are narrow. Practitioner research is ideal for assisting the parent–teacher association to thrash out an agreement on the homework requirements of a new curriculum, or helping the works committee to figure out the pay implications of a new shift system. In such circumstances, a quiet look at the evidence can help all parties reach accommodation. However, this is not evidence-based policy, but rather evidence-based local practice. It is eliminated from further discussion simply on the grounds of scope. Co-participatory research is utilization-focused. It neither attempts nor makes claims for the transferability of its findings. Evidence-based policy, as defined here, is all about public policy where vested interests sprawl, and the central issue is the compass and generalizability of research findings.

Partisanship

This is the scaled up version of the participatory approach, sometimes called emancipatory research. The idea is that policy research should recognize the special wisdom belonging to those who are oppressed by the prevailing system. For instance, it is argued that the problems of people with disabilities are created by a social system that treats impairment within the medical model. Emancipatory research thus pursues the social model and seeks to prioritize policy solutions that challenge the material forces acting to limit the potential of people with impairments. The difficulty with this approach is that every policy and every intervention creates disagreement, dispute and rivalry amongst the groups of stakeholders that gather around it. Programmes work for some and to the detriment of others, they create benefits for some and poverty traps for others, what seems sound in California may not apply in New Jersey, what is good for geese rarely satisfies ganders. When examined closely, the 'oppressed' includes people left suicidal and without hope, people rendered optionless, people made angry, people desperate to escape their lot, people who can put up with anything, people who show gratitude for small mercies, and people who malinger. Accordingly, it is difficult to avoid the conclusion that working from one standpoint involves making claims for entire peoples whilst speaking selectively. A more comprehensive and dispassionate approach is needed in order to understand the always multiple, sometimes contradictory and occasionally perverse impacts of policy reform. To me, being both partisan and researcher is a bit like having one's cake and eating it. I've often put this to colleagues who operate from within these perspectives. They reply with puzzlement, asking what else one should do with one's cake. Needless to say, this is not the version of evidence-based policy pursued here.

Punditry

Finally, there are the pundits, special advisers, policy analysts, 'wise men', think-tanks and so on. Politicians have always surrounded themselves with such people and in the past their function was unambiguous, if somewhat disguised by these job titles. Their task was to summon up helpful information, sympathetic data, subsidiary arguments and fetching modes of presentation in support of politically favoured and pre-established policy lines. Quite unashamedly, such 'research' travels straight from ideology to policy recommendations via the cherry-picking of evidence; in reality, it is policy-based evidence. The interesting thing about modern day think-tanks is that many have secured a degree of independence from their political masters. Some of them claim to 'think the unthinkable', and most have adopted the paraphernalia of social science research. They go about the business of economic modelling, evaluation research, cost–benefit analysis and the kind of evidential review that takes us near to the key concerns of this book. Yet, they remain content to define themselves minutely in terms of political complexion, being 'left of centre', offering 'clear blue water', and so on. Accordingly, ambiguity abounds about the nature of the evidence they, and other pundits, offer. Evidence-based policy, in contrast, is based on the brave assumption that the truth will out, and that it is possible to provide dispassionate, independent and objective evidence to evaluate policy options. Whilst these are horrendously difficult objectives to achieve, they remain a defining feature – perhaps *the* defining feature – of the research strategies to be addressed in this book.

Systematic review: rationale and challenge

So much for what evidence-based policy is not. Let me now pull back the curtains to reveal the real subject matter of the book. Present day hopes for evidence-based policy are pinned increasingly on the *systematic review* of all the existing research on particular interventions. From whence do those hopes spring? In a word, it is disappointment. Applied social research is by now quite long in the tooth, and all manner of programmes have been tried and tried again, and researched and researched again. Yet there is little sign that this evaluative activity operates according to Campbell's vision of the experimenting society. There are precious few examples of it leading to actual decisions to 'retain, imitate, modify or discard' programmes. Evaluation research, in short, has reached industrial proportions but remains feudal in its capacity to create change.

The current solution to the problem is to confederate and co-ordinate this multifarious and fragmented body of empirical work by pooling and assessing the weight of evidence in relation to whole families of interventions. The quest is on to launch comprehensive syntheses of existing research in order to produce objective overviews of 'what works', policy sector by policy sector (Davies et al., 2000). There can be no doubting the size and significance of this endeavour. The apparatus of systematic review is now considerable, and its arrival constitutes one of the major innovations in the machinery of applied social research in recent years. I will not attempt to list all the various collaborations, initiatives and agencies involved, but for the newcomer in search of an overview I can recommend the admirable website of one such organization (http://www.evidencenetwork.org).

I have already sketched, via Solesbury (2001), some of the reasons for the recent embrace of evidence-based policy. I now want to complete the curtain-raising by considering the specific rationale for systematic review as its method of choice. The key to understanding the paradigm change is to appreciate why evaluation research is no longer the preferred methodological partner of policy development. Recall that it is not the first time that hopes have been raised. This is the second coming of evidence-based policy, following the Great Society and its high hopes for an evaluation culture. Somewhat paradoxically, therefore, I begin with the observation that evaluation research has been one of the great successes of modern applied social research. Not an initiative gets designed, not a programme gets implemented without the attachment of an evaluator to discover whether it 'works'. And yet, it seems few expect evaluation to direct policy development. Why? The reasoning is illustrated in Figure 1.1 and can be spelled out in two simple propositions about the positioning and cumulation of evidence.

The failure of evaluation research to feed significantly and successfully into the policy process may be explained via a stunningly obvious point about the timing of research *vis-à-vis* policy – namely, that in order to inform policy, the research must come before the policy. To appreciate this does not require high quality methodological training, a chair in public policy, or years of experience in government. Yet, curiously, this proposition does not correspond to the sequence employed in the procurement of most evaluation research, which occurs *after* programme design and implementation. Systematic reviews are thus proposed as a solution. The expectation is that policy-makers on the threshold of a decision will summon reviewers to have a close look at the evidence *before* the leap into policy and practice.

The other sense of disappointment about evaluation research stems from the fact that, though widespread, it remains a cottage industry. It is demand-driven and for hire, with each evaluation encapsulated in its own contractual bubble. Apart from the intrinsic limitation of having to tailor evidence to each individual client's requirements, this arrangement cuts off the cross-fertilization on which scientific advance depends. The evidence base is composed of fragments, with no one responsible for mortaring the mosaic together. Systematic reviews are thus proposed as a solution. The aim is to capture and pool the burgeoning mass of primary research activity, under the simple principle that two (and more) heads are better than one. The aim is to approximate to 'big science', with systematic review, according to one enthusiast, being the method through which 'science takes stock' (Hunt, 1997).

Figure 1.1 illustrates these ideas, beginning at the top with the most significant manifestation of public policy in the modern era, namely the programme, the intervention or the initiative. The gestation of such schemes follows the familiar sequence of design → implementation → impact, with each phase associated with a different group of stakeholders, namely programme architects, practitioners and participants. As a rule of thumb, evaluators are invited on-site in the early phases of programme implementation, after the contractors have been hired and the foundations laid. Another iron law of research timing is that evaluators are usually required to report on programme impact before the intervention has run its course.

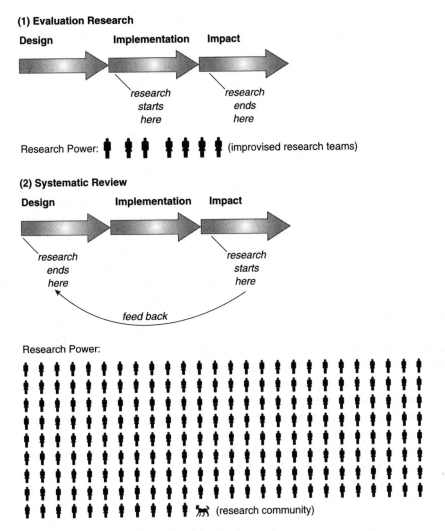

FIGURE 1.1   *The potential benefits of systematic review*

Every evaluator will be familiar with the demand to get the report finished, or at least the preliminary findings established, before the next 'spending review' or other political milestone. Evaluations, in short, operate within a rather narrow bandwidth, and the standard 'letting and reporting' interval is depicted in the figure.

   Much ink has flowed in response to the frustrations engendered by this sequencing. There is no need for me to repeat all the criticisms of 'breathless', 'brownie point' and 'quick and dirty' evaluations. The key point to underscore is that, even if a programme evaluation manages to be painstaking and clean under present conditions, programme design is frequently a research-free zone. Of course, there are good reasons for a division of labour between design and evaluation; we are rarely inclined to be harsh on our own brain-children. Nevertheless, it is clear that valuing the evaluator's independence has the effect of keeping evaluation's wisdom well away from policy-making's inception.

At the end of the research sequence, there is another set of impediments that make it difficult to translate evaluation results into subsequent policy action. Significant social and individual change often takes a while to accomplish and, when noteworthy intervention outcomes are discovered, they are usually accompanied by doubts about their staying power. Programme practitioners and subjects may procrastinate and change their minds at the very time that evaluators have to begin churning out the findings. Whilst these may be accompanied with right and proper cautions about mixed outcomes, perverse effects, decay, displacement, showcasing and all the rest, tracking down and articulating such caveats undoubtedly slows down the reporting process.

In the meantime, the surrounding realpolitik crowds in. During an evaluation the direction of the political wind often changes, displacing the fundamental programme philosophy and deeming it unworthy of investigation. And given the turnover in, and the career ambitions of, policy-makers and practitioners, there is always a burgeoning new wave of programme ideas waiting their turn for development and evaluation. Research conclusions are thus often dispatched into very different policy climates from whence they sprang. My own experiences will again be familiar. I evaluated one programme that was pronounced dead by one arm of government in the very same month as funding for its evaluation had been raised from another. In at least two others, a major redirection of programmes and services was announced whilst evaluators were still in the field. And in yet another, the research team had to report to four different managers as the client became involved in restructuring. Under these all too familiar circumstances, it is not surprising that the most familiar destination of the evaluation report is the shelf.

Figure 1.1 also depicts a key concern about the staffing of evaluation by way of the stick figures illustrating 'research power'. Evaluation is an applied science and depth of application often works against breadth of vision. This type of research operates with a unique division of labour. It tends to be commissioned by, or on behalf of, organizations charged with putting specific policies and programmes into action. It tends to be in-house research, funded by either private sector organizations interested in gaining an outside view of their own activities or, in the case of public sector programmes, by the state itself or, for smaller interventions, by charitable foundations. It tends to be conducted by specialist research units and institutes, which are usually detached or semi-detached from the somewhat 'purer' research environment of the university, and are highly dependent on the flow of commissions. It tends to look for technical and methodological development to the academy, where sit specialists in evaluation theory (like me), who are more likely to be bookish and tenured. It also tends to trade heavily on the goodwill of practitioners who are likely to regard the provision of assistance and data to evaluators as an extra burden on top of already difficult schedules.

So where's the rub? The key point is that these complex arrangements are assembled from scratch in each and every evaluation, with the result that there is a degree of improvisation about the team assembled, the approach chosen, the evidence gathered and the advice proffered. There are all sorts of interesting alliances between the parties but none of them is really responsible for the cumulation of evaluation findings; there is no job on the list whose function is to feed the evidence steadily back into policy-making and then on to the design of further inquiries. Evaluations thus continue to be generated *ab ovo* but without inspection of previous broken eggs. The result is a mass of evaluation activity, with endless trials and plenty of error but little cumulation of effort or results.

Such is the case for the prosecution against evaluation research and its contribution to evidence-based policy. Note that the argument is not that evaluation research is flawed, or any more flawed than the rest of social research. The line of reasoning is that evaluation results are not being properly marshalled, organized and utilized. This imperfection may, of course, be seen as an opportunity and I now turn to the key methodological manoeuvre in the defence of the new evidence-based policy. The remedy suggested for all this misplaced, misspent effort is to put research in its appropriate station (at the end of the line) and to push rather more scholars back to where they belong (in the library).

This strategy is illustrated in the lower portion of Figure 1.1, which draws out the basic logic of systematic review. It takes as its starting point the idea that there is nothing entirely new in the world of policy-making and programme architecture. In the era of global social policy, international programmes and cross-continental evaluation societies, one can find few policy initiatives that have not been trialled and trialled again. Hence, the argument goes, if we renew inquiry at the point where many similar programmes have run their course and the ink has well and truly dried on their evaluation reports, we may then be in a better position to offer evidence-based wisdom on what works and what does not.

On this model, the key driver of research implementation is the feedback loop from past to present programming. If a method can be devised to synthesize the findings of previous attempts at reform, we then have the capacity to draw sound lessons for future practice. This bygone evidence might not quite correspond to any current intervention but since policy initiatives are by nature mutable and bend according to the local circumstances of implementation, even real-time research has trouble keeping pace. No one believes that the feedback from systematic review occurs in one big jump and does so with perfect predictive power. The idea is that periodic reviews, regularly refreshed, can bring a measure of rationality to the planning process.

Like all of the best ideas, the big idea here is a simple one – that research should pass on *collective* wisdom about the successes and failures of previous initiatives in particular policy domains. Note the emphasis on collective, for, as illustrated in the figure, the act of synthesis is intended to harness together the partial and haphazard efforts of discrete and dispersed research groups. The tempting prize is an antidote to policy-making's frequent lapses into crowd-pleasing, political-pandering, window-dressing and god-acting.

This is the basic reasoning through which systematic review has grabbed the methodological mantle of evidence-based policy. Systematic review is not intended to displace evaluation research, for the former provides most of the evidence base for the latter. Systematic review is intended to act as the conduit from the evidence to the policy – no more and no less.

The synthesizing society?

The hopes for systematic review lie engraved in this simple proposition, which accounts for its rise to methodological prominence. This is not the entire story, of course. There is also the little matter of prudence. Systematic review involves no battles with gatekeepers, no cosying up to stakeholders, no idle control groups, no observation of subjects, no long-term follow-up, and no programmes to run and maintain (and is thus remarkably cheap!).

On many a score then, systematic review makes perfect sense. Once again, there is a clear attachment of evidence-based policy to a particular research strategy, and the key players of old have given way to a new breed of information scientists, meta-analysts and research synthesists. In the rest of the book I will examine the challenges confronting them. Although the basic rationale described above seems to me to be irrefutable, this is not to say that turning stimulating first principles into sound prac- tice is ever straightforward. Nor is it to say that all policy-makers and researchers have gathered joyfully around this vision. We have to temper ambition with caution, lest the 'synthesizing society' turns out to be the latest false dawn of rationality. To illustrate the hurdles, I leave the reader with two little vignettes illustrating the dilemmas to come.

Carts and horses

The most sensible of the many sensible claims for systematic review is that it gets the evidence cart before the policy horse. To synthesize is to gather together and, timed properly, this can amount to a foregathering of evidence before fresh policy decisions are made. What is more, the idea of systematic review providing a refreshable feed- back loop of findings begins to get away from the simplistic 'find the panacea' ambi- tions that bedevilled first-wave evidence-based policy.

However, in the real world policy formation takes place in an unregulated chariot race of carts and horses. Nothing happens from scratch. Policy interventions are always policy changes, added to a beam balance already loaded with existing pro- vision. In such circumstances, it is not easy to identify a clean point of incision in which to inject evidence. Consider, for instance, the residents of the UK's 'sink estates'. These citizens may have been on the receiving end of a succession of area- based initiatives such as Single Regeneration Budgets (SRB), City Challenges (CC), European Social Funds–Community Empowerment Fund (ESF–CEF) and, more recently, the New Deal for Communities (NDC) and the Neighbourhood Renewal Strategy (NRS). Social problems cluster in such localities and there may also have been a Health Action Zone (HAZ), an Education Action Zone (EAZ) or a Sure Start initiative (SS). The young people in the area may have had the benefit of a

Connexions (CXS) office in which youth and careers advice workers operate in tandem. The areas are deprived and so too are the individual residents, who may also come under the purview of the other New Deals for lone parents, the unemployed, disabled people and so forth (NDLP, NDU, NDDP). As well as salvation by acronym, remember that community members are also beneficiaries of the mainstream provisions of the welfare state, as well as many local government initiatives.

Some time ago I was involved in a scoping study for the evaluation of the NDC and it is interesting how little the client's expectations turned on the issue of the collective impact of these successive endeavours. If anything, the requirement was the other way around, one obsession being to design the evaluation for the nigh-on impossible task of separating out the effects of the NDC from those of other past and present initiatives. It is important that this mistake is not duplicated when it comes to absorbing the lessons of systematic review. We may be destined for disappointment if research synthesis is envisaged as a way of producing concentrated nuggets of information about isolated policy interventions.

The moral of this little tale is that the new enthusiasts for systematic review need to be mindful of the policy context and the practitioner climate into which the evidence is emitted. Not only is it hard to envision the precise point of entry where the evidence will carry most weight, the synthetic recommendations can never match the complexity of the policy systems that will host them. Indeed, the process of continual policy renewal and endless evaluation can inoculate practitioners against listening to evidence. I end this tale of woe with a disheartening little story. As part of the aforementioned scoping exercise I visited one of the communities in question and got talking to a veteran of many past projects. The conversation went as follows:

Practitioner:　What does 'NDC' stand for?
Pawson:　'New Deal for Communities', of course.
Practitioner:　No, it means 'No Discernible Change'.

Great minds think

Another pearl of wisdom about systematic review is the notion that many heads are better than one and that rather than relying on single evaluations, it is better to draw a cumulative picture based on the findings of many such studies. This stout insight begs an important question about the nature of cumulation, and there are very different views abroad about how the evidence will combine (Hammersley, 2001). The foundational, meta-analytic models of systematic review use arithmetic methods to pool outcome evidence. However, as soon as one widens the scope of the primary studies beyond impact assessments, then the additive model makes no sense at all. No one seriously suggests that we 'add' quantitative to qualitative evidence, and that the synthesis is what emerges after the equals sign.

Accordingly, the development of a new model of cumulation of evidence will be the central task of this book (in Chapter 4). As a taster here, I pose the overall challenge – what chance cumulation? Let us go back a phase to see how evaluation research has risen to this test. Arguably, evaluation is a success story on this score because it has evolved an ever-increasing toolkit of research strategies. No longer are inquiries aimed at the simple issue of charting the success or failure of specific interventions. Evaluation questions now rove over the topics of when, where, why, for whom and in what respects programmes work, as well as how, in what manner and at what cost they may be improved. As a result, we no longer have simple 'evaluation research' but a collection of many and varied approaches, including randomized controlled trials, audit, action research, formative evaluation, dialogic evaluation, developmental evaluation, realist evaluation, theories-of-change evaluation and so on.

What is more, a modest peace has broken out in the 'paradigm wars', with the realization that different admixtures of these strategies are required to tackle the evaluation of different types of programmes in their different stages of development (Stern, 1995; Oakley, 2000). But before we get too dewy-eyed about the prospects, it must also be recognized that this state of affairs is a truce and not yet a coalition. Although there are now many examples of multi-method evaluations, the designs are always piecemeal. The objective in such studies is the perfectly reasonable one of assembling different parts of the overall picture but, as yet, there is no agreed formula on how many parts should be inspected, which parts should be prioritized or, crucially, how to dovetail the parts during analysis. Welcome as it is, I would characterize the present tendency towards more comprehensive evaluations as just that, the agglomeration of piles of information. Systematic review will have the opportunity to stockpile even more evidence ever higher, and it is important that it strives for more than this. In the electronic age, it is all too easy to be compendious but data-banks are depositories and not in themselves branches of learning. The *sine qua non* of evidence-based policy is a cumulative and progressive body of knowledge.

This then is the task that faces systematic review and research synthesis. It is a daunting challenge because there seems little chance of producing a progressive evidence base unless the disciplines that furnish the evidence are themselves cumulative. Again, I am prompted to put the question, 'what are the prospects?' and, once again, my initial thoughts tend to the pessimistic. Take my own discipline of sociology. The vignette offered in this instance is the curriculum at a certain university in the North of England, as it is 'now' and was 'then'. Table 1.1 lists the turnover in optional courses (or modules as they became). The example is trivial in itself, but what it illustrates is a discipline fidgeting to establish its place in an environment characterized by a huge appetite for novelty. None of the substantive topics in the left-hand column can be said to have been mastered; attention was merely drawn away. If sociology were human, she would be a bored teenager, forever in search of the 'neglected topic'. It is much the same picture when it comes to the grand narratives; these too have come and gone. In the beginning scholars thought in either Marxian, Weberian or Durkheimian terms. A generation ago we dropped to small case and became functionalists, positivists, phenomenologists or, indeed, realists. More recently still we returned to doffing caps to mainland Europe and became

TABLE 1.1 *Sociology then and now*

Then	Now
Sociology of education	Theorizing the body
Sociology of work	Sex trade and the diaspora
Sociology of the family	Sociology of homicide
Sociology of organizations	Mind, self and society
Sociology of science	Sociology of Hollywood cinema
Sociology of development	Sociology of the environment
Sociology of deviance	Men and masculinity
Race relations and society	Globalization and society
Gender and society	Disability and society
Sociology of Great Britain	Sociology of the WWWeb

Habermasians, Althusserians and Foucauldians. And finally, we have ended up in the arms of post-modernism – the grand narrative that despises grand narratives. Fatigue and fashion rather than rational argument have led to this succession. Any conceptual framework can colour any substantive investigation, with the result that sociologists just follow the rainbow.

In its defence sociology is sometimes said to be a 'multiple paradigm' science (Ritzer, 1975). This is usually claimed in homage to Kuhn (1970) and it is thought to provide a legitimation, of sorts, for heterogeneity and change. Did not this great historian and philosopher of science point out that physics itself goes through revolutionary paradigm changes? Indeed he did, but he also characterized social science quite unambiguously as pre-paradigmatic. His understanding was that social science has yet to make it to first base because it has existed without any prolonged period of 'normal science' in which bodies of theories mature and refine. This seems as reasonable a portrayal of the present state of play as it was of the situation 35 years ago.

So where does this leave us? Think back to Figure 1.1 and the rationale about the intensification of research power, and remember I have not even begun to consider the rivalries that beset other contributory disciplines that might provide an evidence base for policy formation. Rather than having all of those researchers lined up to attention, perhaps the diagram should be all of a-squabble, with everyone name-calling and hair-pulling.

These two vignettes are meant to be thought-provoking rather than fatal. Although they signal troubles ahead, I do not think the prospects for systematic review are quite that bleak. After decades of evaluative and policy research, we are on the threshold of a huge opportunity to marshal the evidence together and, since programmes and services are complex and many-sided, we should expect to draw in evidence from a range of research methods and strategies. However, pulling these together necessitates much more than a technical fix; it requires a model of how evidence accumulates and of how scientific knowledge grows, and we have yet to fully understand what these aspirations mean. What we have at present is:

1 A rather narrow experimental trial-based model of valid knowledge and a statistical model of accumulation, which risk ignoring vital evidence that might be gained from other means and sources.
2 An ambition, perhaps no more than wishful thinking, about synthesizing a plurality of data, which risks glossing over the considerable epistemological divides on which different knowledge perspectives are founded.

What is clear is that we cannot just cut and paste and expect evidence-based policy to emerge. We cannot admit everything, because the more one takes on all-comers the more the end result will look like Babel. We have to find room for more evidence, but not all evidence, and a new model for piecing it together. The next chapter begins that quest, and I warn that this will not be a chronicle in which everyone lives happily ever after.

2

Realist Methodology: The Building Blocks of Evidence

This chapter introduces the platform on which I wish to build. The basic argument is that, of the rival perspectives claiming to act as the foundation stone of social science, 'realism' provides the most comprehensive account of principles and practice, theory and method, promise and limitations. Given this pedigree, realism is solidly placed to supply a durable understanding of the process of cumulation of social scientific knowledge. Evidence-based policy seeks to stockpile the collective wisdom of thousands of pieces of applied research and can do no better than to look to realism for a methodology of synthesizing the available evidence.

Terminological prologue

Realist social science has a long and complex lineage and, with advancing age, has evolved significant family differences of its own. Before I embark on the task of identifying the key realist principles that should inform evidence-based policy, it is appropriate to locate my own interpretation within the wider spectrum of realist thought. This preamble offers a very brief glimpse of the family tree and points the reader to the precise bloodline.

Realism now figures strongly in the litany of competing perspectives and paradigms in modern social science, and examples of realist inquiry can be found in almost every sub-discipline, for example: law (Norrie, 1993), psychology (Greenwood, 1994), economics (Lawson, 1997), sociology (Layder, 1998), management studies (Ackroyd and Fleetwood, 2000), geography (Sayer, 2000), nursing (McEvoy and Richards, 2003), comparative historical studies (Steinmetz, 1998) and evaluative inquiry (Pawson and Tilley, 1997; Henry et al., 1998; Mark et al., 2000).

Realism is a methodological orientation, or a broad logic of inquiry that is grounded in the philosophy of science and social science (Bhaskar, 1978, 1979; Harré, 1978; Putnam and Conant, 1990; Collier, 1994). In these circles, realism is regarded as the principal post-positivist perspective, whose place is at the centre of things where it steers a path between empiricist and constructivist accounts of scientific explanation.

It perceives social change to be neither linear nor haphazard but transformational (Archer, 1995). In terms of the practice of research, it favours neither the qualitative nor the quantitative (Sayer, 1992). It is 'neither nomothetic (that is law-seeking) nor ideographic (concerned with documenting the unique)' (Sayer, 2000). And some say that because it engages in neither abstracted empiricism nor grand theory, it is Mertonian in its preference for the middle range (Pawson, 2000).

At the core of all this far flung scholarship lies agreement on the basic apparatus of social scientific explanation. What makes this body of work realist is a common understanding of some very basic building blocks of social science, such as the nature of causation, the constitution of the social world, the stratification of social reality, the emergent nature of social change, and so on. All of these features will be explained in due course. It is sufficient here to emphasize that it is this explanatory apparatus I want to celebrate and hone for the purpose of conducting research synthesis.

There is, however, one schism on which realism itself divides, namely on the 'open system' nature of social explanation. Put simply, this says that social systems are the product of literally endless components and forces. When social science tries to focus on what seems a uniform pattern of behaviour it soon discovers that it is shaped by historical forces, with the result that it may occur in one culture but not the next. Secondly, institutional forces also play an inevitable part. These render behavioural patterns susceptible to change under different organizational arrangements and political structures. Thirdly, behavioural regularities are, of course, also influenced by the volition and choices of the people who act them out. A key aspect of these decisions is the human capacity to modify the uniformities in which behaviour is channelled. Collectively, our actions are always prone to change the conditions that prompt them. On top of all this, even the research act itself is transformative; social research always has the tendency to disturb what it is trying to describe. A ceaselessly changing complexity is the norm in social life, and this is the open system predicament.

Grim news apparently follows. Such a complex and messy social reality appears to render extremely unlikely the opportunity for experimentally isolating and manipulating all the contributory explanatory elements. However one looks at it, the implication is that we can never exercise control over all the historical and contemporaneous, macro- and micro-conditions that have influenced the situation we wish to explain. All roads appear to lead away from 'closed systems' science and its key ability to isolate systems physically (as in laboratory experiments and machines).

The open systems dilemma has produced a variety of responses in social science. One has been to ignore it and attempt to approximate to experimental manipulation using randomized controlled trials as the lead investigatory strategy. Findings from artificially closed comparisons are then used to proffer advice on how to organize the incessantly shifting complexity of policy systems. I will return to the futility of this approach in the next chapter.

The consequence I wish to pursue here is that social science's struggle to imitate closed system investigation has created a dividing of the ways in realism itself, on the matter of whether social science should primarily be a critical exercise or an empirical science. On the one hand, there is the push towards 'critical realism'. The guiding assumptions here are that there will always be an overabundance of explanatory possibilities, that some of these will be mistaken, and that the primary task of social science is to be critical of the lay thought and actions that lie behind the false explanations (Archer et al., 1998; Bhaskar, 2002). This requires the social scientist to find a privileged standpoint from which to commence investigation, and ultimately draws realism into finding some moral high ground from which to sustain the critical edge (Edgley, 1998; Bhaskar, 2000). Much more could be said about the political and religious vantage points that have been chosen. All I am able do here is shake my head about how, in this normative turn, the exacting understanding of the mechanics of scientific explanation produced by the pioneers of realism has evaporated into doctrinaire idealism.

Fortunately, there is another realist pathway in social science. This is the route taken by a somewhat looser amalgam of researchers who have tried to develop realism as an empirical method (Pawson, 1989; Hedström and Swedberg, 1998; Williams, 2000; Carter and New, 2004). To date, this second sect lacks a distinctive nomenclature, although labels like scientific realism, empirical realism, emergent realism, analytic realism, 'realismo pane e burro' and middle-range realism have been suggested (and found wanting). The guiding impulse is that it is still worth trying to adjudicate between alternative explanations even in the knowledge that further explanatory possibilities remain untapped in the unrelentingly open systems in which we live. What is more, it is assumed that much of the classic apparatus of empirical science – such as clear conceptualization and hypothesis-making, the usage of critical comparisons, the discovery of empirical patterns and the monitoring of their scope and extent – are of considerable use in this explanatory quest.

Remember that I am tracing genealogy here and so make only scant attempt to justify this preference at this point, although I will return to the practical ramifications of the open systems problem in Chapters 4 and 8. The background information on the two tribes of realism is proffered for two reasons. For newcomers it might lessen confusion, should they attempt to read across from one clan to the other. The second and crucial motive, however, is to assert that critical realism is not one jot of use to us here because its leap into the arms of the normative (Sayer, 2000) is precisely the political embrace from which evidence-based policy is trying to escape. Accordingly, the realism pursued here is the other sort, the one without the adjective. Fortunately, the lack of label presents no problem because this movement has had its clearest impact in the field of evaluation methodology in social policy (Pawson and Tilley, 1997; Henry et al., 1998; Mark et al., 2000). It is from this literature that the signature arguments of this book are drawn, which form the basis of its reformulation of systematic review and evidence-based policy.

Before leaving the matter of realist terminology, here is a final, delicious twist. It may already be clear that I shall be casting some doubt on the approach to research synthesis of the Campbell Collaboration. This assemblage of scholars constitutes the orthodox paradigm in systematic review and meta-analysis and is named in honour of Donald T. Campbell, whose work was a blend of empirical inquiry, methodology of policy research and philosophy of science. And the name he gave to the principles that underlie this admixture? It was 'post-positivist critical realism' (Campbell, 1984).

To explain this fully would require a festschrift but, to summarize, Campbell's thinking was as follows. The 'post-positivist' element is not a problem. Campbell's adherence to realism was prompted by his recognition of the failure of logical positivist accounts of scientific discovery. He appreciated that scientific explanation went far beyond the painstaking measurement of facts and the steady accumulation of empirical generalizations. In particular, he emphasized the importance of theory, both in manufacturing the data and in explaining the observed regularities. Campbell thus sits between positivism (and the assumption that facts speak for themselves) and relativism (and the belief that we see what we want to see). He was a realist in that he accepted the existence of a reality which is independent of our senses, but which we can only discover through our senses.

It is the 'critical' element that causes the confusion. Fittingly, it turns out that Campbell is a critical realist in a quite, quite different sense from Bhaskar and his emancipatory colleagues. For Bhaskarians criticism is warranted on the basis of the analyst's privileged understanding of the oppressive aspects of the social condition and those responsible for it. For Campbell, criticism is something that scientists apply to each other, and this 'competitive cross-validation' is the means by which they get closer to the truth. His vision was of the community of scientists in constant, focused disputation, attending to each other's arguments and illustrations, mutually monitoring and 'keeping each other honest' until some working consensus emerged. The contrast in critical intent with the Bhaskarians could not be starker. It is, in short, that between righteous indignation and organized scepticism.

Hopefully, these brief remarks have begun to locate the present work in the wider realist context. In a nutshell, it is realist in exploiting the principles laid down in early realist philosophy of science, and the working tools established in the application of that philosophy to evaluation methodology. It is critical realist only in its understanding of the quarrelsome process through which scientists approach objectivity and, just maybe, in the hope of stirring into action a disputatious community of truth-seekers in the world of evidence-based policy.

The signature argument

Evidence-based policy is dominated by one question. Attend a conference, read a textbook, peruse a proposal, buy a tee-shirt on the said topic and somewhere in headline font appears the phrase – 'what works?'. This is a causal question. It is a challenge to bring together all the research on the effects that follow social interventions. The very purpose of interventions is to produce change and the mission of systematic review is to find out whether they do so. However, before diving headlong into the data it is worth pausing a moment to consider precisely what 'what works?' means. How do social programmes bring about their effects? How do interventions intervene? What is the nature of causality in the world of policies and programmes?

Realists have a ready-made answer to these questions. Indeed it is the signature argument. From its youthful first steps as a philosophy of science, through all the assorted disciplinary applications, and despite the bouts of infighting, realism stands foursquare behind the *generative model of causation*.

Its distinctive feature is to look for causal powers within the objects or agents or structures under investigation. If one asks why gunpowder has the capacity to explode, one would seek the causal explanation in terms of its chemical composition. If one asked why I have the power to examine PhD theses, one would look (hopefully) to my experience, qualifications and stock of knowledge. If one asked why a huge number of organizations took a bureaucratic turn in the mid-twentieth century, one would look to the advantages that flow from a division of labour, hierarchical structures, written rules, powers of surveillance and so on.

In each case there is a regularity involved (ignite powder and stand clear, expect viva with old timer, traditional authority gives way to bureaucratic regulation), but it is not the empirical uniformity that convinces us of the causal link. Indeed, our understanding of the causal linkage will survive even in the face of some irregularity. So, for instance, gunpowder does not always ignite in the presence of a flame. The powder barrel may have become damp or the powder trail may be insufficiently compacted. Since PhDs have become ten-a-penny and the pay rate for examining them rather similar, you may now see a fresh-faced youngster conducting the oral. Bureaucracies are also known for their tendency to stifle innovation and to over-complicate transactions, and so the iron cage turns out to have plastic bars as new organizational structures are sought to gain the competitive edge.

Although I have put the case in a rather merry way, a profound conclusion lies within the examples, namely this:

> Consequently, for realists, causation is *not* understood on the model of the regular success of events, and hence does not depend on finding them or searching for putative social laws. The conventional impulse to prove causation by gathering data on regularities, repeated occurrences, is therefore misguided: at best these might suggest where to look for candidates for causal mechanisms. What causes something to happen has nothing to do with the number of times we observe it happening. (Sayer, 2000: 14)

Here, note well, is a preliminary shot across the bows of those who have sought to discover 'what works' on the basis of pooling observations in search of programmes with consistently powerful net effects. This remark is left as a censorious aside here because the immediate task is to complete the model of generative causal explanation. The basic trio of components is depicted in Figure 2.1 (Pawson, 1989; Pawson and Tilley, 1997).

Outcome patterns

Let us begin with O, the outcome pattern. Whilst it is not a sufficient base for establishing causality, there is little doubt that the sighting of regularities, uniformities and constants is what makes science perk up and take notice. Indeed, when it comes to the applied sciences like engineering the ultimate objective is to achieve control

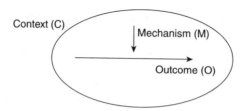

FIGURE 2.1   *Basic components of realist causal explanation*

over such regularities. As applied social science, evidence-based policy's mission is to choose an intervention on the basis that it has a reasonable chance of repeating successful outcomes achieved elsewhere. However, this is not achieved by the simple repetition of a winning formula. We know that there are no universal panaceas and no magic bullets in the world of social and public programmes. Everyone understands that what works in Dulwich might not go down so well in Darlington, still less in Detroit. The consequence is quite simple; in order to identify causal connections, we need to understand outcome *patterns* rather than seek outcome *regularities*. It is the totality of outcomes – successful, unsuccessful, bit of both – that may act as an initial empirical guide for future optimal locations.

Lawson (1997) provides a useful realist tag to describe these badly behaved uniformities, namely 'demi-regularities' (or demi-regs for short), which feature prominently in natural science explanation and subsequent innovation. Let us return to our plot about gunpowder for an example. The firing of early flintlock pistols was so haphazard it might be considered a demi-semi-reg. Reliability (regularity) was achieved only after considerable theoretical and empirical effort involving the idea of better encasing the powder to make it more stable, and controlling the spark to focus the ignition.

Even the so-called laws of physics are demi-regs in raw empirical investigation. If we take the gas law, it is certainly not the case that there is a linear increase in pressure every time the temperature of a gas is increased. Try introducing hot air in a seminar room. Will its atmospheric pressure increase? Metaphorically maybe but not necessarily in a physical sense, because the room is not sealed and the law demands that it applies only to a fixed mass. Even under experimental conditions the law is not perfect. For instance, gases near liquefaction point do not obey the linear law. Natural science, however, is content to go along with the approximation, even to refer to it as a law, because it has a beautiful explanation awaiting (to be described in a moment) of why increasing temperature should cause pressure to rise.

The moral of the tale for evidence-based policy is that we should not be discouraged by demi-regs. On the contrary, the empirical evidence that welfare-to-work regimes work better for young men than young women, the data showing that many criminal justice interventions work well at first before their effects tail off, the huge disparity between the results of pay-for-performance schemes in the public and private sectors are all manna from heaven. They show that interventions work selectively. They are the beginnings of causal explanation.

Generative mechanisms

Mechanisms (M) are the engines of explanation in realist analysis. We can make rough sense of the world through its demi-regularities. The rhythms and associations of natural and even social systems are constant enough that we can navigate our way through them, although, as just argued, we are never particularly surprised when things don't work out as expected. We rely on mechanisms to tell us why interconnections should occur. A sequence of events or a pattern of behaviour are explained as being part of a system and the mechanism tells us what it is about that system that generates the uniformity. Mechanisms explain causal relations by describing the 'powers' inherent in a system, be those systems substances (like gases and gunpowder) or agents (like examiners or policy-makers) or structures (like bureaucracies or social programmes). In all cases it is something about the 'propensity' of the system that explains the causal regularities. The mechanism explains what it is about the system that makes things happen.

   In order to reinforce the point that this is a general model of explanation, let us continue with the same examples. Bureaucracies make things happen because of what they are. Because the workforce is organized in a hierarchy and because agreements are struck on responsibilities, work gets done in routinized ways. The structure generates the work pattern. Gunpowder has the tendency to go off with a bang because of what it is. Chemicals react and combine in different ways. Some combinations give off a large amount of energy under the application of heat (exothermic reactions) and it is this capacity that makes the mix of potassium nitrate, charcoal and sulphur so excitable. The chemical composition generates the capacity to explode.

   Scientific knowledge begins to accumulate when the same generative mechanisms are used generically. The generic, generative mechanism that is used to explain the behaviour of gases is kinetic theory. From Bernoulli's time physicists have come to understand the properties of gases 'internally', as part of a system governed by the motion of a mass of microscopic particles in a confined space. Pressure is understood as the molecular force created on the walls of the container, and temperature is related to the extent of molecular motion (or kinetic energy). Using this mechanical model it is possible to calculate the precise linear relationship between temperature and pressure for a fixed mass and volume of gas. The maths are omitted here, but even the lay person can appreciate that if the application of heat makes the molecules go faster, the greater is the bombardment and thus the pressure on the container. It is this theory that has made the gas laws persuasive. The explanation has become even more compelling as those irritating demi-regularities have been brought into the fold. Near liquefaction, gas molecules are more tightly packed. Accordingly, kinetic theory makes an adjustment for a greater degree of intermolecular collisions and a lessening of impact on the container, and thus accounts for the observed departure from the linear law at low temperatures. Gases behave as they do because of what they are.

Moving to the example that concerns us here, we arrive at the premise that social programmes make things happen because of what they are. But what are they? What is it about them that makes a difference? What goes on within them to influence people to change? What are the underlying generative mechanisms? The precise causal levers will be explained in detail throughout the book, but in abstract terms one can say that programmes work only if people choose to make them work. At the broadest level of generality, one can say that programmes offer resources and whether they work depends on the reasoning of the subjects. The nature of the carrot of inducement may be different (material, social, cognitive) and the offer may include resource withdrawal (the stick). But whatever the intervention, it can only work as intended if the subjects go along with the programme theory and choose to use the resources as intended.

For the realist, then, causal explanation cannot begin without the identification of generative mechanisms. As far as evidence-based policy goes it means breaking with the lazy linguistic habit of supposing that it is programmes that work, and resting content with counting how often they work. The prerequisite is to look beneath the surface in order to inspect how they work. The development of cumulative knowledge about 'what works' requires sustained investigation of the generic mechanism, namely the operation of choices under the inducement of programme resources.

Contextual conditions

Context (C) is mechanism's partner concept in the realist understanding of causality. Causal relationships only occur when a generative mechanism comes into operation. Discovering the explanatory mechanism in action, however, is only half the battle because the association between its operation and the occurrence of the expected outcome is not fixed. Rather, outcome patterns are also contingent on context.

To take our trio of examples, gunpowder has the chemical composition to create exothermic reactions under an initial application of heat, but whether it does so depends on other conditions such as the absence of damp and the presence of oxygen. Gas molecules have kinetic energy so that their movement creates uniform relations between properties such as pressure, volume and temperature. Irregularities and non-linearities begin to occur if the mass of gas is not fixed or the molecules are sufficiently compressed so that intermolecular forces become significant. I have the academic capacity to do a reasonable amount of external examining but this is not turned into a regularity in the absence of an adequate system of rewards, norms of collegiality, a supply of candidates with appealing topics and so on. Bureaucracies organize work routines in certain ways and provide tightly specified employment functions for their workforces, but whether any of this happens depends on the availability of work and, ultimately, on the overall economic health of a nation. The efficacy of bureaucratic management is also contingent on the type of work carried out. In sectors that thrive on innovation and entrepreneurial activity, the application of fixed duties to fixed roles is likely to flop.

The success of social programmes is, likewise, limited by contextual constraints. Interventions, by definition, are always inserted into pre-existing conditions.

A mass of different contextual constraints lurks in wait for every programme and the interrelationships, institutions and structures in which it is embedded all shape its fortune. Despite the differences in such circumstances, it is possible to provide a general picture of how context works. It operates by constraining the choices of stakeholders in a programme. Programme subjects are always faced with a choice, but it is both a limited and a loaded one. They have different pre-given characteristics that leave some well disposed, and some badly disposed, to the programme theory. They enjoy different pre-existing relationships that leave some well placed and some ill placed to take up the opportunities provided by the intervention. They come to programmes with power, or a lack of it, which enables some to resist and some to embrace the ideas of the programme. There is always choice but it is never a matter of free will. Programmes are met with constrained choices, located in pre-existing conditions, and these, as well as the processes internal to the intervention, determine the balance of winners and losers. Thanks to context, there will always be a footprint of programme success and failure, and this brings us back full circle to 'demi-regs'.

What this little realist tutorial on causality is designed to show is that understanding causal powers is an explanatory quest. Knowing how social programmes work involves tracing the limits on when and where they work, and this in turn conditions how, when and where to look for evidence. Interventions offer resources which trigger choice mechanisms (M), which are taken up selectively according to the characteristics and circumstances of subjects (C), resulting in a varied pattern of impact (O). These three locations are the key sources of evidence. In realist jargon the causal connections are established via 'context, mechanism, outcome configurations' (CMOCs). Although this is a clumsy term it does present a stark contrast with the successionist view, which prioritizes the search for outcome regularities. In the realist view, all three elements must be considered in order to address the master question, 'what works?' Put rather more concretely, it introduces a new bottom line. Evaluative research only really begins if it tackles the question of 'what works for whom in what circumstances?'.

Systematic review widens the evidential canvas in considering the impact of whole families of programmes in many applications, but it does not change the causal question. The crucial evidence is still to be found in terms of outcomes *and* mechanisms *and* contexts. This maxim provides the broad agenda for building a model of realist synthesis.

The basic agenda for research synthesis　The nature of causality in social programmes is such that any synthesis of evidence on whether they work will need to investigate how they work. This requires unearthing information on mechanisms, contexts and outcomes. The central quest is to understand the conditions of programme efficacy and this will involve the synthesist in investigating for whom, in what circumstances, and in what respects a family of programmes works.

The basic anatomy of a social programme

This section of the chapter takes a much closer look at the workings of social programmes and interventions, following an obvious but profound working principle of good science, namely, that it should utilize methods that are suitable for and compatible with the subject matter under investigation. This simple rule applies with just as much force to secondary analysis and research synthesis as it does to undertaking primary inquiries. Having established an overall framework for understanding the causal powers of programmes, it is necessary to examine much more minutely how they are implemented, for this too will teach us where to look for evidence.

The explanation, once again, is that insufficient attention has been paid to the way that social programmes roll out before the evidence on them has been obliged to roll in to the machinery of a review. If there is a culprit, it may perhaps be careless thinking about the word 'intervention'. This is a useful catch-all term in that it captures a totality of activities subsumed across social and public policy but, in doing so, it conflates initiatives that are, ontologically speaking, quite separate. Take, for instance, health interventions. It is as clear as day that a clinical 'treatment' is not the same thing as a health care 'programme', which is not to be confused with health 'service delivery', which is a different animal from health 'policy'. There are also endless subdivisions within these categories, as when the focus of attention on, say, service delivery switches from 'innovation' to 'management' to 'regulation'. If the focus is broadened to include interventions in education, welfare, criminal justice and all the rest, one sees that the nature of intercession, the very subject matter of inquiry, is constantly and subtly in transformation.

The key methodological point is that the conventional techniques of systematic review and meta-analysis are much better developed for pooling research results from the clinical treatment end of this spectrum, and there is grave danger in assuming that they will have utility elsewhere. I delay pursuit of this critique until the next chapter in order to capture some of the essential features of interventions that fall outside the clinical treatment category. Seven elements are identified, which arguably figure in most 'mainstream' social and public programmes.

Interventions are theories

This is the most fundamental realist claim about interventions. A more conventional perspective sees interventions in more tangible terms such as collections of resources, equipment and personnel but, for the realist, such resources are theories incarnate. Interventions are always based on a hypothesis that postulates 'If we deliver a programme in this way or we manage services like so, then it will bring about some improved outcome'. Such conjectures are grounded on assumptions about what gives rise to poor performance, inappropriate behaviour and so on, and then move to speculate how changes may be made to these patterns. Interventions are always inserted into existing social systems that are thought to underpin and account for present problems. Improvements in patterns of behaviour, events or conditions are then generated, it is supposed, by bringing fresh inputs to that system in the hope of changing and re-balancing it.

Let us begin with a particularly entertaining example of an intervention hypothesis. Some health education theories explain the unhealthy life styles of adolescents by the undue influence of popular culture and the poor examples created by film, soap and rock stars. This has led to the programme theory of trying to insinuate equally attractive but decidedly healthy role models (for example, sports stars) into the pages and onto the airwaves of the teen media. Such a conjecture, known amongst UK denizens of health education as the 'Dishy David Beckham theory', runs risks in both diagnosis and remedy. Suffice to say that the evidence confirms the popularity of poring over pictures of Beckham and friends in the teen magazines, but shows that as an activity it continues to exercise girls' minds rather than their bodies (Mitchell, 1997).

Agenda item 1　Broadly speaking, we should expect as a core task that reviews pick up, track and evaluate the theories that underlie families of interventions.

Interventions are active

This proposition considers how interventions bring about change. The triggers of change in most interventions are ultimately located in the reasoning of those touched by the initiative, so that effects are generally produced by, and require the active engagement of, individuals. Take two dental health programmes: the fluoridation of water and publicity on the wisdom of brushing twice a day. The former is an example of a passive programme. It works whenever water is swallowed and happens to whole populations who are not required actively to engage with it. In the second example, however, the message is the medium and that message may not be so readily swallowed. The advice on the importance of dental hygiene may indeed be welcome, heeded and thus acted upon. Equally, it may be missed, ignored, forgotten, found boring and thus overlooked; or it may be challenged on scientific grounds, regarded as paternalistic and thus disputed; or it may simply be overridden by the lure of sugar.

And so it is with the vast majority of programme incentives, management strategies, service delivery changes and so on. The inescapable fact that policy is delivered through active interventions to active subjects has profound implications for research methodology. In clinical trials, human volition is seen as a contaminator. The experimental propositions under test are about whether the treatment (and the treatment alone) is effective, and researchers will go to considerable lengths to protect this causal inference, including random allocation of subjects, the use of placebos and double-blinding. The aim is to remove any shred of human intentionality from the investigation of whether treatment brings about cure. Active programmes, by contrast, only work through the stakeholders' reasoning, and knowledge of that reasoning is integral to understanding their outcomes.

> *Agenda item 2*   Broadly speaking, we should expect that, in tracking the successes and failures of interventions, reviews will find elements of the explanation in the reasoning and reactions of different stakeholders.

Intervention chains are long and thickly populated

Intervention theories have a long journey. They begin in the heads of policy architects, pass into the hands of practitioners and, sometimes, into the hearts and minds of subjects. According to the make-up of the initiative, different groups will be crucial to implementation. Sometimes the flow from management to staff (and through its different levels) will be the vital link; sometimes the participation of the general public will be the key interchange; almost always the reception of the theory by programme subjects will be of the essence. The critical upshot is that interventions carry not one, but several, theories. The success of an intervention thus depends on the cumulative success of the entire sequence of theories.

An example is the chain of reasoning that supports the registration and community notification programme for released sex offenders in the USA (Megan's Law). Decisions have to be made on who are the high risk cases, what information should be registered on them and over what periods, how and to whom their identities should be released, how to monitor and regulate their movement, how to control community reactions and encourage surveillance, and so on.

In each of these instances those responsible for the programme have ideas about what is likely to be best practice. So, for instance, there has to be a programme theory about the boundary of the community within which notification should occur. On the release of the offender, some authorities deposit posters according to a standard measure of the number of blocks or a yardage radius from the offender's dwelling. Some authorities prefer to 'eyeball' a map and make decisions ad hoc. Some use a piece of software called Megan's Mapper to make the decision for them (as well as printing address labels). One official even reports that his county draws the line on the basis of 'looking at how far the offender has to travel to buy cigarettes'. I hope that a rather jovial observation on the weakness of this hypothesis for non-smoking offenders will not obliterate the crucial point that some of these hunches are probably more helpful than others, and that the effectiveness of programmes as a whole will depend on the combined efficacy of such theories.

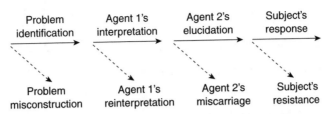

FIGURE 2.2   *Theory chains (with intended and unintended outcomes)*

All such theories are potentially fallible. The initial identification of the problem may be on the button or wide of the mark. As successive groups of stakeholders are summoned to forward the programme, they may sustain or undermine earlier implementation decisions, and their own decisions will induce support or opposition down the line. And, as we have seen, the final recipients (programme subjects) always have a measure of choice over whether to accept the concoction finally served up. In short, the intended sequence may misfire at any point, leading to unintended outcomes, as depicted in Figure 2.2.

> *Agenda Item 3*   Broadly speaking, we should expect reviews to inspect the integrity of the implementation chain, examining which intermediate outputs need to be in place for successful outcomes to occur, as well as noting flows and blockages and points of contention.

Intervention chains are non-linear and sometimes go into reverse

So far, I have presented interventions as a series of decision points or programme theories being passed down an intervention chain, and Agenda Item 2 reminds us that each of these stages is active in that it depends for its effect on the recipients' response. This places a further onus on the evaluator or reviewer, namely to appreciate that such responses themselves have the power to shape and reshape the intervention, meaning that most intervention chains are non-linear.

There are several modes whereby a top-down intervention becomes, in some respects, bottom-up. The most obvious is the negotiation between stakeholders at every transaction within a scheme. Consider the application of performance measurement regimes such as school 'league tables' or hospital 'star ratings'. Quite customarily, one sees a struggle between professional associations and management authorities about the fairness of the indicators (on the need for risk-adjusted and value-added indicators, and so on). The indicators that finally come to be used take shape according to the punching power of the respective parties. This is depicted in

FIGURE 2.3   *Negotiation and feedback in interventions*

Figure 2.3 by applying dotted, double heads to some of the arrows in a typical implementation chain.

A more marked inversion of an implementation scheme occurs if there is commitment to 'user involvement'. This is a popular notion in, for instance, urban regeneration initiatives in which much of the wisdom about renewal is considered to lie in the hands of members of the community (Stewart and Taylor, 1995). Many 'independent living' programmes in social care trade on a similar philosophy (Kestenbaum, 1996). What this produces is a feedback loop in implementation. Members of a community are consulted on the optimal shape of the intervention. These theories are then thrust back up the chain of stakeholders so that they can amass the appropriate resources to put them into place. Once again, the actuality and viability of such adjustments depend on the respective powers of the agents and agencies involved. The feedback notion is also depicted in the dashed reverse arrow in Figure 2.3. Note that in reality there will probably be multiple stakeholder groups vying for influence at more than one point in the implementation chain.

Agenda Item 4   Broadly speaking, we should expect the review to be able to take into consideration how the relative positioning and influence of different decision-makers are able to direct and redirect programme implementation.

Interventions are embedded in multiple social systems

Thus far, interventions have been depicted as if they were populated only by individuals, and activated only through individual reasoning and behaviour. However, a critical feature of all programmes is that, as they are delivered, they are embedded in social systems. It is through the workings of entire systems of social relationships that any changes in behaviours, events and social conditions are effected. Interventions are fragile creatures. Rarely, if ever, is the 'same' programme equally effective in all circumstances. The standard requirement of realist inquiry, therefore, is to take heed of context and in the case of social programmes this means unravelling the different layers of social reality that make up and surround them.

Take, for example, a prisoner education programme, introduced with the Herculean goal of reducing reoffending. Such a proposal will carry a theory about how the intervention is assumed to work; for example, that adult education provides a second chance to regain a place in the job market, or that the cognitive skills acquired may allow for second thoughts in the face of opportunities for crime. Of course, these theories about education and recidivism may be fundamentally flawed, as illustrated in the previous sections, but even if they are not the success of the educational policy will also depend critically on the setting in which it is introduced. The 'same' prisoner education package will unfold very differently in a young offenders' institute, maximum security penitentiary, local jail, vulnerable offenders' wing, open prison, day release scheme in a local further education college, and so on. And these variants, moreover, just begin to scratch the surface of contextual variation.

In general, realist analysis admits to the shaping influence of at least four contextual layers (the four Is):

- The *individual* capacities of the key actors: In the above example, do the educators have the appropriate motivations, capabilities and credibility to take the intervention forward? Do the prisoners have the corresponding characteristics and motives?
- The *interpersonal* relationships supporting the intervention: How intensively can a learning environment be created? Are the lines of communication between prison management, administration and custody staff supportive or damaging to the delivery of education by the teaching staff?
- The *institutional* setting: Does the culture, character and ethos of the prison support a rehabilitative thrust or is this overwhelmed by concerns with punishment, containment, warehousing, control, safety?
- The wider *infra-structural* system: Does the intervention have the political backing to drive it into the heart of the prison service? Are there welfare resources to underpin it? Is there public support for offering such opportunities and a second chance to released offenders? Will the criminal community override second thoughts?

All interventions are conditioned by the action of layer upon layer of contextual influences, and this state of play is depicted in Figure 2.4. Such contingencies represent the greatest challenge to evidence-based policy. Generating transferable lessons about interventions will always be difficult because they are never embedded in the same structures and contexts.

Agenda Item 5 Broadly speaking, we should expect the 'same' intervention to meet with both success and failure (and all points in between), when applied in different contexts and settings. Whilst it is impossible to cover every angle (the open system predicament), a review presents a crucial opportunity to analyze the contextual differences operating across the primary systems investigated.

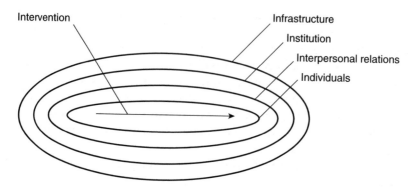

FIGURE 2.4   *The intervention as the product of its context*

Interventions are leaky and prone to be borrowed

One of the greatest bugbears of evaluation occurs when researchers perceive that the programme under inspection is changing within the grasp of their inquiry. The account thus far has stressed that interventions are sequences of theories, and that viewpoint makes plain why interventions always evolve in the course of research. A programme or service delivery reform might begin with something like an 'official' intervention theory and an 'expected' implementation chain. It will be put into practice in many different locations and by many different hands, and in the course of implementation further programme theories will enter from outside the officially sanctioned process.

The reason for this is all too obvious. Practitioners and managers implement change and in the process of doing so they talk to each other. When a multi-site scheme is put in place there is always cross-fertilization and borrowing of ideas from other participants. When it comes to putting flesh on the bones of an intervention mission statement, practitioners will consult with colleagues. Especially when it comes to ironing out snags, there will be a considerable amount of rubbernecking from scheme to scheme as stakeholders compare notes on solutions. I have already given a rather dramatic account of some unfortunate consequences of practitioner information exchange in the first chapter with my New Deal for Communities practitioner suffering extreme cynicism brought on by a terrible case of 'interventionitis'.

In general, such a diffusion of ideas may be perfectly benign, with most programmes possessing a rummage bin of ideas that are drawn upon and adapted by a range of stakeholders. Such sideways chains of communication are actively encouraged in all programme-producing bureaucracies. In modern health services, for instance, large-scale innovations will generally be supported in national progress meetings, which encourage the sharing of tricks-of-the-trade as, for example, in quality improvement collaboratives, learning sets and quality circles (Øvretveit et al., 2002). The hallmark of professionalism is always said to be induction into secret knowledge (Eraut, 1994), and the professionalization of the public services quickens this circulation of tacit knowledge.

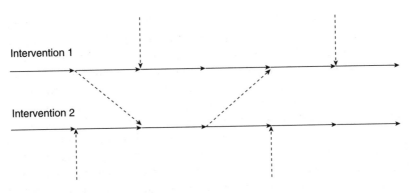

Intervention 1

Intervention 2

FIGURE 2.5   *Intervention facsimile and overlay*

The continual makeover of schemes under borrowing and imitation from others is illustrated by in Figure 2.5. The horizontal arrows show the intended unfolding of an intervention in two settings. The shaping, and sometimes distorting, forces of other schemes and services are illustrated by the vertical arrows (in the case of distant, external programmes) and by the diagonal arrows (in the case of cross-fertilization between local, companion sites). The result is that the overlay of formal and informal programme theories can become massively convoluted, especially if the service change in question is itself about promoting communication and collaboration!

The key point here is that tacit knowledge about a scheme may sometimes standardize it and may sometimes fragment it, but will always change it. The result is that reviewers must always beware what Øvretveit and Gustafson (2002) call 'label naiveté'. The intervention to be reviewed will carry a title and that title will speak to a general and abstract programme theory, but that conjecture will not be quite the one evaluators have encountered, or that reviewers will disinter.

Agenda Item 6   Broadly speaking, we should expect the implementation of programmes to be enwrapped in established expectations about how to deliver such schemes. Interventions always have a history and a place within a wider range of policy decisions, and another potential agenda for a review is to consider how their success is shaped by previous/co-existing service delivery.

Interventions are open systems and change the conditions that make them work in the first place

As we have seen, interventions are active and absorptive, permeable and plastic. The result is that they are never implemented in quite the same way and never interpreted in quite the same way. Realism, however, goes a step further in understanding the changing nature of programmes. That is to say, they are regarded as self-transformational (Archer, 1995). Successful interventions may well change the conditions that made them work in the first place. Such 'morphogenesis' may be self-defeating or self-affirming.

The so-called arms race in crime reduction programmes is a prime example. Having suffered a setback from the introduction of a crime reduction scheme, lawbreakers are often able to figure out the intervention's *modus operandi* and adapt their own criminal *modus operandi* accordingly. A rather vivid example is provided by the changing impact of town centre CCTV cameras. On installation, these were regarded with some foreboding by marauding youth. However, once their positioning and range was understood, and when it was grasped that their impact depended on the deciphering of hazy images by a distant operator, and as soon as it was figured out that the police response could not be instant, a different set of options opened up. Norris et al. (1998: Part 4) noted the bizarre chicanery that followed. Familiarity bred contempt and, after the initial honeymoon period, the authors observed youths staging mock fights in front of city centre cameras. The combatants were plausible enough to prompt operator action and smart enough to become solid citizens at the sound of the sirens. The result here and across the crime prevention field is that schemes often become self-defeating, and a constant stream of fresh initiatives is required to keep pace.

Rarely are programme theories decoded and resisted to such dramatic effect. There is, however, a more modest self-defeating effect in many interventions. On their first introduction, performance targets and progress reviews may lead to a significant period of self-reflection on the activities in question. If such monitoring becomes routinized, various short-cuts and tricks-of-the-trade may also follow, and the desired introspection can become perfunctory (see Evans, 2003 on this theme in relation to the National Health Service appraisal scheme for senior clinicians).

There are other conditions that lead interventions to become self-fulfilling, at least in the short and medium term. Familiarity may breed contempt *or* content. Management innovations tend to work if they curry favour with existing staff, and can be greatly assisted if recruitment and promotion of programme-friendly staff are also part of the package. Such a condition remains self-affirming only in so far as staff restructuring can keep pace with innovation in ideas. Otherwise, managers are faced with the self-defeating task of teaching new tricks to old dogs.

The post-conditioning of initial outputs by subsequent decisions is illustrated in Figure 2.6. The line of solid arrows represents the initial reception of a programme theory. The dashed arrows represent subsequent reinterpretation of the primary programme measure, with the untoward consequence pushing the intervention off course.

Agenda Item 7   Broadly speaking, in reviewing the collective impact of programmes, a further task is to chart the significance of familiarization and habituation, including the self-defeating and self-affirming effects that appear as programmes mature.

FIGURE 2.6   *Self-affirming and self-defeating change*

From the agenda and into action

The case for systematic review has been put most famously in Lipsey's compelling metaphor, 'what can you build with thousands of bricks?' (Lipsey, 1997). His answer was that it is high time to put aside solitary evaluations, which tend to come up with answers that range from the quick and dirty to the overdue and ambivalent. These can and should be replaced, he goes on to say, with the considered appraisal of the collective findings of dozens, hundreds and, just occasionally, thousands of primary studies to construct a solid citadel of evidence.

This chapter has attempted to give a sketch of the building blocks. What I have tried to show is that in order to be true to the nature of causal explanation and to be faithful to the character of social interventions, the evidence base must attempt to get to grips with social processes of extraordinary complexity. Thanks to the creativity of language (or put more unkindly, management-speak), innovations can seemingly be captured in a few words and may appear quite singular. In the realist view, social interventions are always *complex systems thrust amidst complex systems*.

This message about the intricacy and convolution of programme delivery will come as no surprise to key stakeholders. I am confident that there will be a sense of recognition on the part of policy-makers, managers and practitioners that the processes and structures described above are routine features of most interventions. If anything, those on the streets and in the hospital wards and classrooms are likely to perceive an even more messy and animated process. Negotiation, leakage, borrowing, resistance, mismatch, adjustment, bloom and fade and so on are part and parcel of everyday programme implementation. This core condition of programmes is summarized in Figure 2.7, which brings together all the propositions and diagrams in this chapter. It depicts the passage of four interventions, which are nominally the same, but as a result of variation in contextual locations and policy-maker, practitioner and subject interpretations they begin to bend. Thanks to user feedback and negotiation, the exchange of know-how, familiarization and over-familiarization with due process, they begin to twist over time, generating further shifts and unconsidered effects.

This make-up of programmes places profound limitations on what can be expected from evidence synthesis. The reviewer will always be confronted by an array of programme theories played out in varying contexts and implemented in different ways. It goes without saying that reviewing the effectiveness of such systems-within-systems will be a battle with complexity, and this chapter concludes by laying out the broad parameters of that challenge. One thing that is evident from the start of the endeavour is that the evidential bricks will not be uniform. Data on all

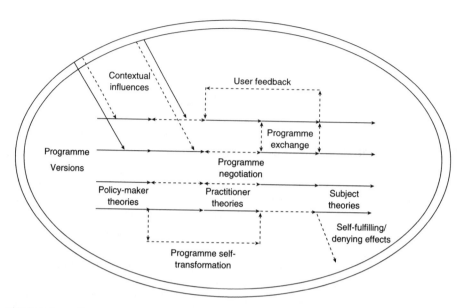

FIGURE 2.7   *Programme complexity*

the constituent mechanisms, contexts and outcomes will not come in standardized slabs, reducible to a net effect score. Potentially, the entire apparatus of social science will be needed to examine processes at the individual, interpersonal, institutional and infrastructural levels. Three significant limitations can thus be anticipated from the outset.

First, there is a limit on what a review can cover. The realist approach shifts the unit of analysis from programmes to programme theories. Quite properly, this gets us away from the vision of social programmes as treatments or dosages, which themselves have effects that can be pooled and averaged. Recognizing programme theories as the engine of change, however, does have a drawback because these working ideas are endless. At the limit, there will be mundane links in a particular implementation chain about 'employing Eric to do the IT because he's a reliable sort'. Although the programme may well suffer if this conjecture is wrong, the moral of the story is that realist synthesis will need to prioritize the investigation of particular processes and theories.

Secondly, there is a limit on what information can be retrieved. Primary research studies will probably have focused on formal documentation (such as policies, guidance, minutes of meetings), tangible processes (such as the activities of steering groups), and easily measured outcomes (such as attendance figures or reported opinions). Information about the informal (and sometimes overtly off the record) exchange of knowledge, the interpersonal relationships and power struggles, and the subtle contextual conditions that can make interventions float or sink in an organization will be much harder to come by, and is often frustratingly absent from reports. Even if the review is committed to tracking some back-stage mechanism or unintended process, it may not always be possible to do so.

Thirdly, there is a limit on what a review can deliver. The reviewer can never grasp the totality of the constraints on the effectiveness of interventions, and certainly cannot anticipate the circumstances in which subsequent schemes might be implemented. This places ineluctable limitations on the recommendations that follow a review and the certainty with which they can be put forward. A necessarily selective and prioritized review will generate qualified and provisional findings, and thus modest and cautious recommendations. Realist reviewers eschew the goal of discovering best buys and delivering verdicts. Rather, they attempt to place on the table an account of the workings of complex interventions and a hopefully better understanding of how theory may be improved.

As an overall conclusion I return to my pet irritation about the use of the term 'intervention' to describe the lumbering pachyderms of modern social and public policy. Policy masterplans always end up as elephantine in their complexity. In response, I have argued that research synthesis needs to work with a more powerful understanding of causality and an appreciation of at least seven different ways in which programmes may be said to 'work'. Already, it is clear that it will not be possible to review them all, and since selection and prioritization will be part of the analysis, there must always be caution and diffidence in deriving any conclusions and policy recommendations. If evidence-based policy were human, he would be a modest soul with much to be modest about.

3

Systematic Obfuscation: A Critical Analysis of the Meta-analytic Approach

This chapter contains the critical element of the book, confronting some of the orthodox and, to my mind, misleading ideas that have made the running in evidence-based policy. Evidence-based policy is, of course, a kissing cousin of evidence-based medicine, and many principles and practices have been inherited from the hearth and home of clinical treatments and trials. The essential argument, as should be clear by now, is that it would have been better to start from scratch and to produce a strategy for systematic review that befits our subject matter – the labyrinthine, mutating entanglement that is social and public policy.

There is no intention to produce a critique of evidence-based medicine here, although some of the arguments raised are beginning to travel back up through the family tree as the complexity of many 'treatments' is beginning to be unravelled. Nor does this chapter include a full critical exposition of the technical apparatus of systematic review. Research synthesis has to handle primary components by the thousands and an assembly line of some description will always be needed to shift, sort and synthesize information. Nor, finally, is this critical assessment of systematic review fully comprehensive. Evidence-based policy is a rapidly expanding field and, happily, the green shoots of diversity are beginning to show, even in the mainstream. Unhappily, this means that I will not be able to extend coverage to the many novel forms of research synthesis, such as meta-ethnography, Bayesian analysis, 'EPPI reviews' and hybrid qualitative-and-quantitative methods, or to old timers like the literature review and narrative review (for a useful overview of the widening portfolio, see Dixon-Woods et al., 2004).

The aim here is to deliver a short, sharp shock to the basic logic of the 'conventional approach' and in particular its notion of how knowledge cumulates. My interest is in what Davies et al. (2000) have called the 'rigorous paradigm'. Such an enterprise can, perhaps, be captured best of all in the ambition 'to do for evidence-based policy what Cochrane has done for evidence-based medicine' (Smith, 1996; Petrosino et al., 2001). What the Cochrane Collaboration is perceived to have done is 'to provide the best source of evidence on the effectiveness of health care and medical treatments' (Weisburd et al., 2003), and what the new movement seeks to do is create the same kind of evidential backbone for other areas of policy-making that are perceived as blighted by rhetoric and woolly thinking:

> Anecdotal evidence, program favorites of the month, and political ideology seemingly drive much of the crime policy agenda. As a result, we are left with a patchwork of programs that are of unknown potential in preventing crime. Crime prevention programs may or may not work or worse may provide harmful or iatrogenic results. We are not suggesting that the public is being intentionally misled by law makers and policy makers who are funding programs with no scientific evidence but rather law makers and policy makers are shirking their responsibility to the taxpaying public by not funding only those programs with evidence of effectiveness in crime prevention. (Welsh and Farrington, 2001: 159)

This hardboiled ambition involves setting up reviews that focus on the 'does it work?' question about a particular class of interventions, collecting data only from reputable primary studies on their effects, and then reaching a statistical verdict on whether, on balance, they indeed do work. The core assumption is that, properly formalized and rigorously executed, such an approach establishes conclusions that are more accurate and credible than those presented in any one of the primary studies. Following the recommended procedures will guarantee the scientific status of ensuing evidence, which can then 'be rationally integrated into decisions about interventions by policymakers and practitioners alike' (Petrosino, 2000).

How shall I term this classic review strategy? As already described, it becomes increasingly difficult to use the label 'systematic review' because this is a territory in methodological flux (and, besides, I want to dispute copyright over the adjective systematic). The title of the chapter refers to the 'meta-analytic approach' but this is a rather clumsy designation and, with some trepidation, I have settled on 'meta-analysis' as a snappier term for use in the discussion. This is done in the full knowledge that I do violence to the precise definition of a term that correctly refers just to the statistical apparatus used to aggregate findings. Let me make it clear that what follows is a challenge to the overall logic of the 'traditional' or 'conventional' approach that uses meta-analytic techniques, and I indict the more specific term – meta-analysis – in this wider sense.

The chapter begins with a brief exposition of the basic logic and the practical steps in conducting a meta-analytic review, before putting them to critical scrutiny.

In what way is it 'meta'-analysis?

Why is it 'meta'-analysis? The thinking is that the approach represents the sum total of analysis; an analysis of all previous analyses. Hunt (1997) was persuaded that meta-analysis was the technique through which 'science takes stock' because he considered it the supreme act of cumulation. Researchers and research teams lap the track of science but the reviewer goes the whole distance, harnessing and reproducing previous efforts in one great marathon. The Olympian imagery may be a trifle gushing,

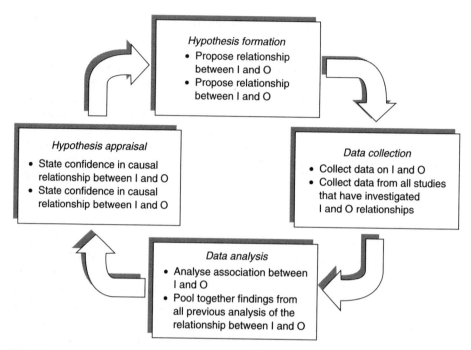

FIGURE 3.1   *The research cycle as primary analysis and meta-analysis*

but it contains a useful evocation of the core logic of meta-analysis, namely a belief that the successful replication of scientific experiments is the source of enduring knowledge. There are many accounts of the logic of scientific discovery or the 'wheel of science', which depict scientific discovery as a journey around the cycle of hypothesis formation, data collection, data analysis and hypothesis appraisal depicted in Figure 3.1.

Any single (primary) evaluation will commence with a hypothesis about the causal relationship between an intervention (I) and its outcome (O). It will then mount an experiment, introducing the intervention and collecting before-and-after measures on the outcome of interest. It will then perform a rigorous analysis of pre/post-intervention shifts in order to test whether the relationship is significant. The original hypothesis can then be appraised to determine whether the causal inference is warranted. A strong design that delivers results with great statistical power is considered the basis of a powerful causal claim. If no such evidence is found, hypotheses are revised and the wheel of science takes another turn. Although it trades on secondary analysis, meta-analysis is seen as reproducing all of the standard steps of rigorous primary analysis. It begins with the same hypotheses about the relationship between (I) and (O); it goes in search of apposite, high quality data to interrogate that hypothesis; it uses statistical methods to test and to come to some judgement on the original hypothesis; and it utilizes the findings to prompt further questions.

Figure 3.1 follows the cycles for primary experiments and meta-analysis (upper and lower bullets respectively) and shows that the starting point and terminus are the same, but with the scouring of data in the middle being much more comprehensive in the case of meta-analysis. Here is the key to its logic. It sees itself as an overlay of one inquiry upon another. Primary science, in the guise of evaluation research, is seen as performing roughly the same inquiry over and again, but with each experiment having a limited scope and being carried out with varying degrees of methodological imperfection. Replication, as noted, is judged to be the source of scientific certitude. Its exponents, therefore, regard meta-analysis as providing a kind of post hoc replication of similar inquiries, searching out the best and pooling their findings together. When the cycle of replication is considered well travelled and secure enough, natural science goes on to generate engineering applications. The same aspiration pervades meta-analysis, with robust net effect calculations being seen as the platform for social engineering.

Procedural uniformity

The other principal claim of meta-analysis resides in the notion of procedural uniformity. It is secondary analysis and gains its clout from treating each primary study in exactly the same, even-handed way. A set of steps, known as a protocol, is established through which all reviews have to pass, and in the passing they are deemed to produce a cumulative and objective body of knowledge.

A template of the typical review sequence is reproduced in Box 3.1. There are any number of such operational diagrams and flowcharts in the literature. Some specify six stages, some seven and more. Some include an initial decision-making stage on the need for and feasibility of conducting a review. Some include a planning stage. Some make room for periodic updating as new primary studies trickle in. Readers new to the approach might like to consult the pandect of review manuals, that produced by the Centre for Reviews and Dissemination (CRD) at the University of York (2001). It outlines a three-stage, nine-phase approach, each spelled out in practical detail and annotated with examples. The box below is intended to capture the essentials:

BOX 3.1   THE BASIC SYSTEMATIC REVIEW/ META-ANALYSIS TEMPLATE

1   *Formulating the review question.* Identifying the problem and the purported solution. Formalizing the exact hypothesis to be tested about the particular outcomes of a particular class of interventions.

2   *Identifying and collecting the evidence.* Searching for and retrieving the published results of all evaluations of the intervention in question. Comprehensive probing of databases, bibliographies and websites to amass all the relevant primary studies.

3   *Appraising the quality of the evidence.* Deciding which of the foregathered studies are valid and serviceable for further analysis by distinguishing rigorous from flawed primary studies.

(Continued)

BOX 3.1　(CONTINUED)

4　*Extracting and processing the data.* Presenting the raw evidence on a grid, gathering the same points of information from all primary inquiries. The features assembled are those deemed relevant for addressing the review hypothesis, so will include details of the intervention, population, significant outcomes etc.

5　*Synthesizing the data.* Collating and summarizing the evidence in order to address the review hypothesis. Using statistical methods to estimate the efficacy and, sometimes, the efficiency of programmes. Expressing the causal powers of programmes in terms of their mean effects, heterogeneity, homogeneity and so on.

6　*Disseminating the findings.* Reporting the results to the wider policy community in order to influence new programming decisions. Identifying best practice and eliminating dangerous interventions by examining the net outcomes from the whole body of evidence.

Box 3.1 encapsulates the basic strategy of meta-analysis. It describes in more detail the journey that the review takes around the wheel of science. A good review will work through this sequence precisely, and a faithful honouring of the protocol is considered to give reviews their scientific edge. Not only does following this exact recipe make the review systematic, having all the ingredients specified up-front guarantees that reviews are reliable and reproducible. With the template in mind, the reviewer is required to document each stage and decision point along the way. This renders the whole exercise transparent, allowing others to retrace the steps and scrutinize the reasoning, so adding to public confidence in the results.

Meta-analysis, therefore, stands for replication, procedural uniformity and transparency. The good news is that, with this movement, a demand for rigour and clear thinking has been brought to the heart of evidence-based policy. These procedures put existing social research to unparalleled inspection and scrutiny, and make the speculative, normative forays that pass elsewhere for social science look like amateur gossip.

The critique: simplification and obfuscation

The bad news, however, is that the recipe does not really work. It has yet to provide us with a stockpile of solutions to the ills and inequities confronting modern society and, if the following critique is correct, it is incapable of doing so.

At every stage of the meta-analytic review, simplifications are made. Hypotheses are abridged, studies are dropped, programme details are filtered out, contextual information is eliminated, selected findings are utilized, averages are taken, estimates are made. This is all done in the attempt to wash out 'bias' and reduce the evidence base to a common body of information from a reliable set of replica studies, on the basis of which a decision is made on the overall efficacy of a particular intervention. However, in this purgative process the very features that explain how interventions work are eliminated from the reckoning. Complex programmes are cast as simple treatments. The way in which stakeholders think and change their thinking under an intervention is expunged. The context, which does so much to shape the efficacy of a programme, is ignored. The effort to ensure that evidence is assessed and compared to a common yardstick renders dynamic open systems as closed systems. Because it works at high levels of aggregation, because there is so little inspection of what goes on beneath the surface, and because programmes always contain wayward, contradictory, self-transformatory processes, meta-analysis usually ends with the detection of rather minor intervention effects. The typical product is in fact metaequivocation. Alternatively, so much is winnowed away that meta-analysis is left with only a few studies that pass methodological muster. In this case, it may produce a result with magnitude and an ostensible degree of certitude, but the chances are that it is artificial and misleading.

This is a summary of the case for the prosecution and, at paragraph length, it makes a bold (some will say brash) methodological judgement. The rest of this chapter argues the case in detail by following how the policy questions under investigation are framed as they pass through the review stepping stones of Box 3.1. Rigorous and painstaking as it is, this review chain is not benign. Certain erroneous causal assumptions are pushed to the foreground and crucial explanatory issues are jettisoned as the evidence passes through the sequence. What is lost is much of the aetiology of social programmes described in the previous chapter and summarized in Figure 2.7. The critique is mounted against all six stages of the classic review sequence, although it gathers pace (and space) as we come to the analysis and policy recommendations. As each stage is navigated, a set of key presuppositions of meta-analysis, labelled (a) to (k), is identified and criticized. Each one is met by a 'counterpoint', suggesting a more fruitful pathway for research synthesis.

Stage one: formulating the review question

Setting up the review question is no perfunctory preliminary. It governs where the review will tread and the policy advice that will follow. As a rule, meta-analysis settles for relatively simple cause and effect questions, linking an intervention to its outcome, within a relevant population.

> When framing precise questions, the important facets to be considered are the population, the intervention and the outcomes relevant to the objectives of the review. (CRD, 2001: para. 1.2.2)

This expresses the classic way review hypotheses are formulated and articulates what might be thought of as the PIO (population, intervention, outcome) view of causality. Although this propositional structure is supposed to cover all manner of interventions, the stamp of the medical model is clear to see. The population (P) to which an intervention is applied is expected to condition its effectiveness. The examples given by CRD are age of patients, severity of the illness, presence of other conditions and so on, each of which is likely to moderate the efficacy of a medical treatment. The intervention itself (I) may vary. A particular treatment may be prescribed but its dosage, intensity, adherence, care setting, administering agent and so on may all differ, and are expected to have a marked influence on efficacy. Outcomes (O) may also be understood and measured in a variety of ways. Sometimes the test of a treatment is assessed through changes in mortality or morbidity rates; sometimes improvements in health and well-being, including subjective assessments, might be more pertinent.

From the outset, there is always a penumbra of uncertainty about what exactly a review should tackle, and within the family of meta-analysis there are two ways of dealing with potential ambiguities. In 'first-level' meta-analysis the rule is to reduce contrariety by pre-specifying the precise meaning of the Ps, Is and Os that will be covered in the review. In the 'second-level' variant, primary studies are inspected with the aim of unearthing data that will cover some of the most significant variations in the way the programme is delivered, to whom it is delivered and with what effect it is delivered. This overview begins by looking at the first-level approach, moving to the second-level later in the chapter with a consideration of 'mediator and moderator' analysis.

The guiding impulse in classic, first-level meta-analysis is to reduce conceptual ambiguity by focusing upon precise variables via closer specifications and operational definitions of the key terms. The CRD manual gives the example of a review examining whether patients undergoing hip replacement (P) experience a lowering of post-operative infection (O) as the result of a specific regime of antimicrobial prophylaxis (I). This is considered to be a relatively clean-cut review exercise, given that it carries a definite hypothesis with defined terms and a restricted scope. Once established, this terminological fix guides the search for evidence, ensuring that only interventions and investigations bearing these pre-specified characteristics are inspected. These conceptual preliminaries are considered essential, ensuring that only studies of truly comparable interventions are included in the subsequent processing of evidence.

A similar approach is taken by the meta-analysts when moving from medical potions to social programmes. Let me stay within the medical setting for a trio of illustrations. Instead of inquiring if prescriptions of non-steroidal anti-inflammatory drugs (I) work to relieve arthritis (O) in adults (P), the question might be whether informal social support networks (I) work to encourage more first-time mothers (P) to breastfeed (O), or whether managers and medics (P) work more efficiently (O) under the preparation called performance-related pay (I).

This little ironic play on a common propositional structure is used to emphasize that quite different programmes can, seemingly, be scrutinized under the same propositional structure. There are, however, considerable differences in the nature of the three interventions on offer in our hospital. The latter two are indubitably the kind of social interventions that are the concern of this book. They are constituted in a different way. They work in a different way. And to review whether they work requires a different body of evidence. What is misunderstood, what is omitted as a result of framing the question in this way (I causes O, limited by P)? Three features are selected for critical scrutiny because they jar completely with the analysis of programmes presented in the previous chapter.

a. Meta-analysis assumes that the 'intervention' has causal powers

The primary intention of the meta-analytic approach is to measure the effectiveness of an intervention, which is considered to be a causal agent in its own right. It is interventions that do the changing. They are the independent variable, coming first in all statistical analysis. This possession of causal powers is an unspoken assumption in evidence-based medicine because that, after all, is what medicines are there to do; the ointment reduces the rash, the vapour unblocks the airways, the antibiotics act on the micro-organisms, the radiotherapy kills the cancerous cells. Medics tend to describe their deeds using terms like treatments, therapies, remedies, correctives, cures, painkillers, restoratives and so forth. All of these terms indicate that the active agent resides in the intervention.

Social interventions are termed programmes, initiatives, schemes, projects, compacts, innovations and so forth. There is a huge linguistic clue here that they operate in a quite different way. Social programmes, as discussed in detail in Chapter 2, offer resources (material, social, cognitive) to subjects, and whether they work depends on the reasoning of these individuals. Subjects may seek out programmes (or not), volunteer for them (or not), find meaning in them (or not), develop positive feelings about them (or not), learn lessons from them (or not), apply the lessons (or not), talk to others about them (or not). It is within this interpretative process – or mechanism – that the causal powers of programmes reside. Any method of systematic review that omits such a vital agent from its core hypotheses automatically sets up a depleted inquiry. It imperils the mission by sending out the search parties for an incomplete set of evidential bricks.

> **Counterpoint (a)**   Fixing the review question by operational definitions of the intervention directs attention away from the vital causal agents. A better meta-question would be to investigate the different ways in which they work by unearthing evidence on the resources offered by programmes and the choices made by their subjects.

b. Meta-analysis assumes that interventions are highly reproducible

The framing of tight operational hypotheses in evidence-based medicine is made possible by the fact that medical treatments tend to be highly reproducible.

Performing a trial with precision depends on achieving high levels of control over the application of the treatment, and this depends on its integrity and portability. In the case of medications, getting the active chemical ingredients into a capsule in the right proportion and to reliable quality standards is hardly an impediment to the replication of medical trials. It is also a relatively straightforward matter to isolate the treatment as an entity, manage and control its application, and arrange for a trial of its effectiveness by comparing its presence and absence. Further controls may need to be applied to ensure adherence to dosage, the elimination of placebo effects and so on, but the point about reproducibility still holds good. There is always a sound chance that one medical trial can duplicate another, and so the idea of phrasing the review question about a common intervention has some mileage.

Social programmes are quite different. They are reproduced by word of mouth and realism assumes, accordingly, that they always transform. Managers and practitioners implement them and it is not their job to manufacture and apply uniform treatments. They are there to nurse, cajole and bully the programme into active life, and to fine-tune, head-bang or arm-twist if it is not working to scratch. They make their livelihoods from interventions and thus may also be there to prolong them at all costs, to steer them into calmer waters, keep them out of the evaluative spotlight and so on. Replication is not foremost in their minds.

Counterpoint (b)   It is not wise to inquire whether some unadulterated, unalloyed, perfectly formed, correctly configured programme has worked in its various properly implemented incarnations. Learning and adaptation is a condition of being for social programmes. Rather than being a conceptual fixture in the review hypothesis, a useful meta-question involves probing the life-course and dynamics of programmes.

c. Meta-analysis assumes that the intervention theory is not an issue

Perhaps the most decisive aspect of question-setting in the traditional models of systematic review is the use of formulations from the 'what works' family. The interest is in whether, or to what extent, an intervention works, whether it is safe, whether it is cost effective and so on. Very rarely is meta-analysis sent on an explanatory quest in order to explain 'why' an intervention works.

Again, the rationale has its roots in evidence-based medicine. Treatments, for the most part, have a pre-established clinical basis. They are developed in the light of well-established knowledge of their underlying microbiological, genetic and chemical characteristics, and of the pathology of diseases to which they might be applied. They are often developments of pre-existing treatments but, even so, must successfully negotiate a complex obstacle course of laboratory testing, animal studies and other pre-clinical trials before they reach the stage at which they enter the reviewer's consciousness – the large-scale randomized controlled trial (RCT) involving human subjects. Medical treatments, in short, are the embodiment of years of theory-testing. They are already scientific inquiry incarnate before the first Phase III RCT is even designed. By this stage, medical science knows pretty well how a treatment works and it entrusts to the RCT a slightly different question about how well it works in a particular manifestation. Whole episodes of pure science are played out, and their lessons digested, before the applied science kicks in.

This contrasts starkly with the situation in evidence-based policy. Social programmes are also based on theories – as was discussed at length in the previous chapter – but theories of a very different kind. They take the form of hunches, bright ideas and policy fashions, which are then flung untested into programmes and hurled untried into their evaluations. There is a world of difference between encouraging healthy life styles using the Dishy David Beckham theory of teenage infatuation, and developing a treatment for high blood pressure using theories about the role of angiotensin-converting enzyme inhibitors in widening blood vessels.

> *Counterpoint (c)*   Tightly fixed review hypotheses work best with, and stem from, a pre-established understanding of how interventions work. The theoretical base of a social programme is inevitably fragile and limited in scope, so that theory-testing remains essential in each evaluation and each review. We need to persist in asking how an intervention works in order to figure out how well it works. The better meta-question is an explanatory one.

In summary, this argument on hypothesis-setting states that the conventional protocols of systematic review lay down restricted, artificial and prematurely closed questions, and this sets meta-analysis on the road to producing restricted, artificial and prematurely closed answers.

Stage two: identifying and collecting the evidence

The second stage in meta-analysis calls forth the mining metaphors. The idea is to unearth, dig out and dust down the relevant primary studies that should assist in answering the review question. The skills and strategies required here belong to the domain of the information scientist. The craft and talents required are necessary to any mode of systematic review, and there are many good accounts of methods employed in trying to make a search exhaustive (e.g. Armstrong and Large, 2001). These range from the ancient (hand searches of the library stacks, reference tracking and personal advice on relevant sources) to the modern (electronic database selection, search strategy formulation, search execution using more-or-less complex variants of Boolean logic, citation searching and so on). The Internet has added an extra dimension, offering the prospect of tracking down much more of that elusive 'grey literature', but lacking the kind of sophisticated search facilities provided by the major bibliographic databases.

d. Meta-analysis assumes that there is a limited, accessible
universe of relevant primary materials

There is, however, one assumption of a meta-analytic search that is worthy of censure and that is the attempt to create and gather a 'census' of relevant primary studies. The goal, quite literally, is to tap into *all* pertinent primary studies. This ambition stems from the tightly defined focus of the typical review question and we return, for an example, to the question about the efficacy of a particular non-steroidal anti-inflammatory drug in relieving pain in arthritis sufferers. Most clinical trials are set up to answer precisely such a question, most will be written up under such a rubric and so the appropriate family of cases almost defines itself. Ambiguity is low because the trials deal with highly evolved treatments aimed at much-studied ailments seeking standard outcomes. The literature is equally well behaved: 'The clinical medical literature is well organized and easily accessible through large-scale, sophisticated databases such as Medline and EMBASE. It is dominated by the peer review journal format, and has a relatively well controlled and stable technical terminology that facilitates the retrieval of information on very specific questions' (Grayson and Gomersall, 2003).

Note the word 'relatively'. Even in the medical field, the retrieval of relevant information is rarely trouble-free. However, as soon as one moves away from one-question-one-answer meta-analysis and crosses over to the multiple aims, contexts, stakeholders and delivery mechanisms of a social programme, life gets even harder for the information scientist (although, to repeat, the *modus operandi* remains the same). Programmes are made up of dozens of components played out in scores of situations and each of these elements will have a primary literature and an evidence base of its own. Rather than using the specialized terminology characteristic of the natural sciences, much of this literature employs everyday language, which is often imprecise and always in flux. Constructing effective search strategies in these circumstances is difficult. As a result, one can never accumulate *all* the evidence, and search procedures are always tortured with uncertainty on where to draw the line.

> *Counterpoint (d)*   The notion that one can be truly comprehensive in identifying relevant evidence is quite disingenuous. A better meta-search strategy would presume that social programmes are always complex systems thrust amidst complex systems. Many, many different sets and subsets of studies need to be consulted and there is always an element of judgement to be made in selecting primary sources. Purposive and iterative sampling strategies are required to locate them.

Stage three: appraising the quality of evidence

Moving further down the spine of systematic review, we come to the critical appraisal or 'quality threshold' stage at which the primary studies are lined up and inspected for their rigour and trustworthiness. The implication is that evidence comes in all sorts of shapes and sizes, and that some of it is distinctly sloppy and untrustworthy. The origin of this sentiment is, once again, rooted in evidence-based medicine and is fixed upon its bête noire, namely the 'expert opinions' of doctors and clinicians.

> The publication of Archie Cochrane's radical critique, *Efficiency and Effectiveness*, 25 years ago stimulated a penetrating examination of the degree to which medical practice is based on robust demonstrations of clinical effectiveness. The finding that even the most commonly used procedures and therapies are not necessarily those shown by research studies to be the most efficacious, and that a non-substantial amount of practice has not been particularly well evaluated has led to pressures for medicine to become 'evidence-based'. Instead of practice being dominated by opinion (possibly ill-informed) and by consensus formed in poorly understood ways by 'experts', the idea is to shift the centre of gravity of health care decision making towards an explicit consideration and incorporation of research evidence. (Sheldon, 1997: vii)

e. Meta-analysis assumes that only high quality primary research can beget high quality secondary analysis, and there is thus a 'hierarchy of evidence'

This call for a methodological tribunal at the centre of systematic reviews aims to exclude entirely from further analysis any research that falls short of acceptable scientific standards. There are a number of such hierarchies of evidence designed for evidence-based policy, which use a variety of rankings and sub-groupings. Box 3.2 serves as a rough amalgam, illustrating the standing of different strategies according to the rigorous paradigm. Note the fairly seamless adoption from health into other policy domains, with the Campbell Collaboration's affirmation (Shepherd, 2003) of a partner gold standard for the randomized controlled trial, namely the randomized field trial.

BOX 3.2   TYPICAL STRUCTURE OF A HIERARCHY OF EVIDENCE IN META-ANALYSIS

Level 1 Randomized controlled trials (with concealed allocation)
Level 2 Quasi-experimental studies (using matching)
Level 3 Before-and-after comparisons
Level 4 Cross-sectional, random sample studies
Level 5 Process evaluation, formative studies and action research
Level 6 Qualitative case study and ethnographic research
Level 7 Descriptive guides and examples of good practice
Level 8 Professional and expert opinion
Level 9 User opinion

The invocation of gold standards and methodological tribunals has inevitably caused a great stir in the paradigm vortex that is social research. The stock criticism is that such a hierarchy undervalues the contribution made by many research perspectives and should be replaced by a horses-for-courses approach, which recognizes the value of particular approaches in particular circumstances. Let me quote an example of this sentiment, with no further embellishment other than to nudge the reader into noting the name of its author:

> Qualitative knowledge is absolutely essential as a prerequisite foundation for quantification in any science. Without competence at the qualitative level, one's computer printout is misleading or meaningless. We failed in our thinking about programme evaluation methods to emphasize the need for a qualitative context that could be depended upon ... To rule out plausible hypotheses we need situation specific wisdom. The lack of this knowledge (whether it be called ethnography or program history or gossip) makes us incompetent estimators of programme impacts, turning out conclusions that are not only wrong, but often wrong in socially destructive ways. (Campbell, 1984: 36)

Good research of any stripe must be included in a good synthesis. In this respect it is worth noting the fine print of Campbell's argument, for it is not only qualitative evidence that is undervalued in the standard hierarchies. His call is to embrace any method that delivers 'situation specific wisdom'. In order to be truly systematic, the evidence base should include data procured by comparative research, historical research, discourse analysis, legislative inquiry, action research, emancipatory research, and so on.

> *Counterpoint (e)*   Given the complex operation of social programmes, there is a clear need for systematic review to abandon the notion of a single hierarchy of evidence. A better meta-toolkit would call upon a range of primary studies employing the entire range of research strategies, and quality standards would respond accordingly.

The horses-for-courses argument is always a good methodological wager. Calls for methodological pluralism in the appraisal of evidence have become widespread and some, repeat some, within the mainstream of systematic review have taken this censure on the chin. Attempts to establish a more comprehensive set of quality controls are under way and, in particular, huge strides have been taken in formulating appraisal criteria for qualitative research (Spencer et al., 2003). However, as will become clear, I do not believe that merely bolting on further appraisal tools solves the question of research quality in systematic review.

> 📖 **Supplementary reading** Readers interested in this line of thought should consult R. Pawson *Assessing the quality of evidence in evidence-based policy: why, how and when?*, which is included in the web page support materials.⍟

f. Meta-analysis assumes that the supreme body of evidence for establishing causal relations lies in the randomized controlled trial and its derivatives

My main and radical charge against the hierarchy of evidence is that it fails to provide the gold standard for the job it purports to do: RCTs are not the best basis upon which to make causal inferences in the world of social programmes. The presumed supremacy of experimental trials has been questioned on many occasions (Pawson and Tilley, 1997), and it is unlikely that the argument will be fully resolved here. The abbreviated account that follows concentrates on how vital evidence gets jettisoned in systematic reviews that use an appraisal formula based on the supremacy of randomized designs.

Let us re-examine the familiar rationale. If the task of research synthesis is to examine whether an intervention (I) brings about a specific outcome (O), then the key method of generating evidence lies in switching the intervention on and off, and comparing effects. If one can arrange for a trial comprising two identical situations and introduce the intervention into only one of them, then it can be assumed that any subsequent difference in outcome must be the result of the application of the programme – the one thing that has changed. This forms the rationale for the celebration of randomized trials as the highest form of evidence within systematic review.

However, compelling though the logic seems, it runs counter to what we know about the genesis of social programmes in which it is never possible to achieve a clean policy-on/policy-off comparison. Figure 2.7 in the previous chapter shows that there is no singular 'application of the programme'. Instead, the programme *is* the negotiated product of the transfer of ideas down and back up an implementation chain. The programme *is* a self-monitoring and adaptive system responding continually to immediate perceptions of its success. The programme *is* the upshot of all previous and concurrent attempts to alleviate the problem under assault. And the programme *is* the contextual influences stemming from the individuals, interactions, institutions and infrastructures involved – all of which in their different combinations shape and change the way the programme is delivered.

And what of the control? This is not a piece of apparatus at idle. This is not the world in repose. This is no vacuum, because there is no such thing as a policy vacuum. Control groups or control areas are in fact kept very busy. All things already going on in a locality and everything happening simultaneously to an individual, constitute 'the control'. So it too will be crammed with other, concurrent policies and programmes, pounded by previous policies and programmes, stuffed with stakeholder interests, and surrounded by a full repertoire of contextual constraints.

All is on the move, but under a different and unknown combination of forces in a different and unknown state of development.

It is, of course, possible to contrive surrogate experimental contrasts, examining for differences between a situation designated to run a programme, 'matched' with one not so nominated. One can sometimes locate a group of candidates and send some through the intervention whilst holding others back. However, if researchers ignore the labyrinthine processes whereby an intervention has been introduced in the field, or the equally labyrinthine processes that occur in its absence, they will remain in the dark about the precise combination of mechanisms and contexts that generate any subsequent differences. It is *always* necessary to know what goes on within the black box of an intervention to understand its outcomes.

Before developing this counterpoint, it is worth appreciating the potency of the RCT headlock. Even in the world of experimental trials it is recognized that the random allocation of subjects to treatment and control conditions does not rule out every conceivable extraneous influence. Those hierarchies influenced by medical trials methodology thus give an alpha-plus rating to studies that incorporate additional layers of control. Let us start with the great predicament of health research. Pills are often swallowed in high anticipation or grave desperation that they will improve the patient's condition, and we know that hope alone may have healing properties. Accordingly, pure gold trials are blinded, with the patient not knowing whether she is in the experimental or control group, so that the placebo effect can be stripped away from calculations of treatment effectiveness. The positive expectations of practitioners and researchers for their newly developed therapies may also be passed, subtly or otherwise, onto their subjects (Rosenthal, 1991; Fergusson et al., 2004), and so double-blinding is put in place to wipe out the distortions of another swathe of high hopes.

Further inexactitudes are introduced because treatments and trials have duration. During these days, weeks and months, trial subjects may change their minds, move away, catch new diseases, have accidents or, most inconsiderately, die of other causes. Hospital procedures are imperfect, and treatment and non-treatment designations may be loosened by administrative failure. Membership of experimental and control groups may thus become somewhat rough and ragged. Once again, such human influences are wiped clean using another methodological eraser known as intention-to-treat analysis.

The point of rehearsing these methodological remedies to the various threats to the internal validity of the exemplary trial is to emphasize that the good clinical experimentalist deals with such threats by attempting to expel them from the scene. In line with the fundamental assumption that the intervention itself is the causal agent, every attempt is made to neutralize the effects of human volition. This is the standard to which the meta-analysis of social programmes aspires. However, to repeat once more, social programmes are active and not passive. They generate choice after choice, and the admiration of meta-analysis for a method that obliterates human volition is more than a touch ironic. Human intentionality is not a confounding influence but the very medium through which such interventions work.

Lurking in these critiques is the alternative vision that a true gold standard needs to operate within the black box – unseen in experimentalism – and reinforces the previous counterpoint on the need for multiple standards tailored to a multiplicity of research techniques. However, there is something else missing from the hierarchy. Using the traditional appraisal tools, research quality is defined by technical criteria (is it a double-blinded RCT?) and demonstrated in the choice of research designs. There is no room at the quality inn for what I consider to be the main purpose of research – namely, explanation-building. The previous chapter argued that causal explanations are configurational; they attempt to explain why programmes work, and this involves bringing together (and adjudicating between) different bodies of evidence to build, test and refine theories. The whole quality issue is thus downgraded if the notion of theory-building is excluded.

Counterpoint (f)   Causal inferences are secured by theory-building, and this is a feature of inquiry that cannot be detected by simply inspecting research designs. A better meta-synthesis strategy would include appraisal of the explanatory purchase of primary research. Understanding the capacity of individual inquiries on this score allows the reviewer to assemble even more powerful and nuanced explanations.

Stage four: extracting and processing the data

The next stage in systematic review is one of its more mechanical phases and thus, arguably, less contentious in terms of methodological principles. One must never forget the huge process of compression involved in research synthesis. Reviews begin with hundreds or, sometimes, thousands of papers and, perhaps, millions of words, which eventually are crushed into a small set of policy recommendations. True to form, the hallmark of the meta-analytic review is to conduct the extraction of information to a standard, pre-determined formula.

The procedure is to treat primary research as a set of cases and to identify and extract the same pieces of information from each study, as in Figure 3.2. The logic is identical to that of survey research in which each respondent is asked the same question, so producing a data matrix with the same range of information on each subject. In meta-analysis, the variables are chosen to embody the review hypothesis and facilitate the subsequent analytic process. Thus, some combination of measures describing the intervention ($I_{1...n}$), its outcomes ($O_{1...n}$) and the population to which it is applied ($P_{1...n}$) is extracted. First-level meta-analysis requires only an elementary set of input and output information, while the second-level variant can include dozens of intervening variables.

Explanatory variables

Studies	I_1	I_2	P_1	P_2	O_1	O_2	O_3
Case 1							
Case 2							
... ...							
Case N							

FIGURE 3.2   *The systematic review information matrix*

The exact content of the information matrix is decided at this stage and each study is then combed for information on the selected variables. Coding the details of dozens upon dozens of primary studies is a difficult, laborious business and the efforts of research assistants assigned the task are subjected to reliability checks. Again, the commitment is to orderliness and transparency, exemplified in this phase by a requirement for high levels of inter-coding agreement on the classification of each item.

g. Meta-analysis assumes that all relevant materials to assist in drawing causal inferences are included in the data matrix

The content of the data matrix is the stick that I use to beat meta-analysis. However lengthy, the rows and columns of variables will always omit the crucial explanatory apparatus needed to understand how programmes work. Anything that cannot be expressed as a variable – any information on process, reasoning, negotiation, choice, programme history and so on – is excluded from this standard information warehouse, abruptly killing off all explanatory options. It is possible, of course, to parse primary studies for qualitative information, and fill the matrix with text. This is a familiar enough process in some forms of data extraction in narrative review and I will deal with the limitations of this idea presently. The crucial point, for present purposes, is that this does not occur in meta-analysis; data extraction is numerical, explanation resides in the variables, and the analysis is statistical.

Counterpoint (g)   All manner of qualitative, historical and comparative data are lost in standard extraction techniques and, equally, so is all the inference-making and theory-building that resides in primary studies.
A much more rounded way of drawing information from primary research is required, and a better meta-strategy must include the extraction of descriptive narratives and explanatory propositions.

*h. The meta-analysis extraction matrix assumes that primary studies
are organized as a series of parallel replications*

Implicit in the plan of producing a standardized data matrix is the idea that each primary study is an investigation of basically the same hypothesis. Each inquiry is treated as a replication of other members of a set, with the expectation that they will all produce more or less the same package of information. Meta-analysis then takes on the task of measuring and estimating the same interrelationships across all studies. This overlaying of studies is axiomatic to meta-analytic reviews.

In reality, what one generally confronts in evaluations of the 'same' social programme are highly discontinuous studies of subtly different implementation plans, seeking different outcomes and played out in quite different contexts within different policy regimes. Look again at Figure 2.7 for illustration. Social programmes are monstrously complex and it is little wonder that the typical analysis leaves many evidential stones unturned. No study can investigate all stages of policy formation, and all issues involved in implementation and staffing, and all constraints provided by previous and companion programmes, and all learning and internal correction in the course of delivery, and all short-term and intermediate outputs, and all long-term outcomes, and so on and so forth.

If no study can be completely comprehensive, the obvious result is that individual studies choose to prioritize and, therefore, differ. Given the massive canvas of contingencies, the natural tendency for all research is to innovate rather than replicate. Studies driven academically tend to be on the look out for new conceptual angles and methodological twists. Studies driven administratively tend to focus on the latest delivery arrangements and on the people and places responsible for their provision.

This omnifariety of primary materials calls into question both the overlay model and the rationale behind collecting the same body of information from each study. It suggests the need for an alternative vision of what it means for studies to cumulate. This is the topic for the next chapter, but the simple metaphor of assembling the pieces of a jigsaw can be raised as an initial contrast. The puzzler knows that no two pieces will be alike, but that out of component-level asymmetry can be built a composite picture that fits together and draws into proper relief each mismatched piece. Faced with an array of explanatory components, the reviewer is faced with a similar need to assemble a composite of ingredients from the range of studies.

> *Counterpoint (h)* Different elements of different primary studies are needed to account for the efficacy of a class of programmes. A better meta-strategy for extracting data from primary studies is to be purposive, pulling together explanatory ingredients rather than piling them high.

Stage five: synthesizing the data

By this stage, the primary studies have been ransacked for information and the purpose of the synthesis is to reveal what the data have to say on the efficacy of the intervention. Here it is important to note that meta-analysis has had a change of heart on the best approach to fusing the findings of individual studies. In first-level meta-analysis the idea is to aggregate the findings in order to deliver a net effect calculation, a statistic summarizing the overall impact of a particular type of intervention. The imagery here is of pooling or smelting the data to reveal a general verdict on a family of programmes. In second-level meta-analysis, it is conceded that social programmes work through more complex causal chains and the aim is to produce a statistical model that describes some of the intermediate linkages and contexts that condition successful outcomes.

Readers who find the argument so far to be a plausible one might feel that the second-level meta-analysts have stolen the realists' thunder. The first point to note is that there seems to be no wholesale shift to the second-level approach. Meta-analysis, especially in promotional materials, is presented very much as the supreme court for ruling on 'what works' and I want to pursue vigorously my doubts on that score, arguing that the search for blanket (net) verdicts is meaningless and futile. This brings us to second-level analysis, which is partly an extension of first-level analysis but also an auto-critique. There are members of the second generation who accept that 'one-answer' meta-analysis is too simplistic to capture the workings of social programmes (Lau et al., 1998), but this admission does not protect them from further censure. The second-level strategy is basically about adding more variables into the reckoning on the assumption that aggregative, multivariate, statistical models represent an explanation of how programmes work. For the realist, these models amount only to more complicated descriptions of programme regularities for which it is still necessary to seek, hunt down, apply and appraise explanations.

i. Level-one meta-analysis aims to reach definitive and universal estimates of the effectiveness of whole classes of social interventions

This approach pursues a version of the original tenet of evidence-based medicine, namely that we should have more confidence in treatments that have withstood a number of trials successfully. The principle of replication is the cornerstone of the method. Rather than relying on a one-off study, whose results may contain an element of chance, there needs to be a way of pooling the results from a series of trials, which provide a better representation of the real spectrum of outcomes.

Because medical treatments are highly evolved and aimed at well-recognized pathologies, replication is commonplace enough. However, because medical trials occur in the midst of hospital regimes it is assumed that real-world conditions always generate small variations in who is treated, how the treatment is applied and by what measure it is appraised. Accordingly, the purpose of the analysis is to discover the mean impact of the treatment and to mop up any circumstantial (random) variations that arise from field application to field application.

Let us follow the idea through in terms of the variation in the population undergoing the treatment. The clinical trial begins with the assumption that the intervention is aimed at the class of subjects suffering from a specific disease. However, diseases come in different strains, levels of severity and stages of advancement, and any single clinical trial will inevitably be set down in a particular constellation of those conditions. In addition, any one-off trial will pull in a sub-population of subjects with different susceptibilities to a disease and its cure, who also vary by age, sex, weight, profession, region, class, diet, exercise regime, mental health, genetic make-up, cigarette and alcohol intake and so on and so forth. All of these factors may shape the likelihood of cure and, for that matter, the probability of seeking a cure.

Any individual trial will still be considered unbiased in the sense that, through randomization, it will have assigned to the treatment and to the control a good balance of individuals with these different characteristics. Patients, however, turn up for treatment by dint of health service procedures. As one roves across place and time, each trial will be rooted in a slightly different set of practical arrangements and thus populated by a somewhat different profile of patients. Accordingly, it is acknowledged that whilst all patients will have met a broad eligibility requirement to enter a trial, any single investigation may well fetch up a sub-population that could favour or hinder the treatment. One hospital may, for instance, take on a somewhat riskier or more elderly set of patients than another by dint of admissions priorities or demography. An element of *between*-trial variation is always anticipated.

However, the gaze of evidence-based medicine is still fixed on the general population of sufferers, precisely because it is expecting to license treatments to the general population of sufferers. The whole exercise is thus geared up to look for the net effect, to seek out results that are generally true. The inevitable population, treatment and measurement variations are regarded as the random play of chance, and the key function of meta-analysis is to make Lady Luck vanish. Local contingencies are scrubbed out by aggregation and, by pooling the rigorous findings, the strategy gradually establishes a result that is true of the population as a whole. Meta-analysis is perceived as lapping the track of inquiry, so producing the equivalent of one massive trial touching all corners of the relevant population.

The original meta-analysis method, now rarely practised, was known as vote-counting. Each trial will produce a finding revealing on balance that the treatment works or that it does not, and vote-counting shows whether the ayes or the nays are in the ascendancy. This crudest of all methods of aggregation was soon superseded on the grounds that effects are not merely positive or negative but come in a range of sizes, that effects are not uniform for every member of a trial but have a distribution, and that one-trial-one-vote aggregation undervalues the significance of bigger, more powerful trials.

Accordingly, different statistical techniques were devised to produce a more effective way of pooling the trial results. The method is best understood through

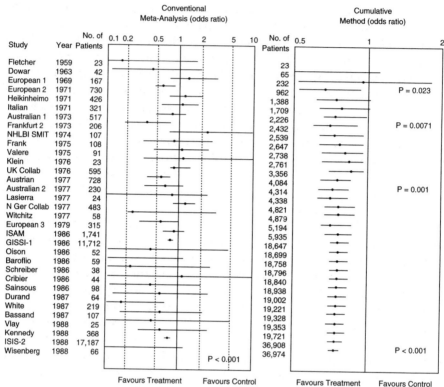

Note: The odds ratios and 95 per cent confidence intervals for an effect of treatment on mortality are shown on a logarithmic scale.

FIGURE 3.3 *Conventional and cumulative meta-analyses of 33 trials of intravenous streptokinase for acute myocardial infarction* (*Source*: Lau et al., 1992)

the favoured graphical presentation – the 'forest plot' – an example of which is reproduced as Figure 3.3

These are the results from 33 placebo-controlled trials of intravenous streptokinese for acute myocardial infarction. Each trial is displayed in terms of its mean effect (dot) and confidence interval (line spread). The left-hand side of the figure shows some inconsistency from trial to trial, with some showing higher rates of survival in the control sample. On the right the studies, and thus the patients, are pooled together to make up one 'expanding' trial. It can be seen at a glance that the method of cumulation gives more weight to bigger studies and those that show less variance in results, so that in the end a positive effect is established in which it is possible to have great confidence.

Is this a model for social programmes? For the realist it is a grave mistake to consider programme variation as happenstance, as the random vagaries of implementation. Social interventions are active; they work through the interpretations of their providers and subjects. These responses take the programme along different courses;

the active ingredient differs in the minds of different subjects. These interpretations are not irritating contingencies; the subjects' reactions are the programme lever. It would be an absurdity in most medical trials to imagine that the patient transforms the treatment but this is precisely what happens in social programmes. Lady Luck is not the problem; the variation lies in the mind of Joe Soap, the typical subject.

Likewise, it is wrongheaded to regard contextual differences as the random play of space and time, as assorted sub-populations that have happened to turn up for a trial. Context is far more than an indiscriminate blend of passive receptors of treatment; it shapes how the intervention is delivered and received. It would be an absurdity in most medical trials to imagine that the social context transforms the treatment but this is precisely what happens in social programmes. The efficacy of a social intervention depends on how well its ideas are received, and gain weight, not only in the minds of individual subjects but also in inter-relationships, institutions and the wider society.

In short, variation is not happenstance; variation is intrinsic. People involved in programmes differentiate between and discriminate within them; they chop and change them. Accordingly, it makes no sense to blend these actions into a common outcome via the statistical average. Programmes do not work in the general flux of circumstances; they work because they are in the right conditions. Programmes happen in the here and now and it makes no sense to imagine that one can aggregate their findings to arrive at a meaningful net effect calculation that applies to some amorphous blend of all people, all interrelationships, all institutions, all localities, and all societies that embody an intervention.

What is the result if aggregation is tried? What transpires when net effect meta-analysis is performed on complex social programmes? I have two answers, the first provided by Rossi (1987: 5):

> The expected value of any net impact assessment of any social program is zero. This means that our best a priori estimate of a net impact assessment of a program is that it will have no effect. It also means that the average of net impact assessments of a large set of social programmes will crawl asymptotically toward zero.

This wonderfully iconoclastic remark is offered amidst a rather tongue-in-cheek set of propositions describing the iron cage of restrictions limiting the policy leverage provided by evaluative research. Commentators have wondered whether it is whimsy or wisdom. Undoubtedly it is the latter. Rossi is describing why social problems are so intractable by reflecting on the fact that applying the same programme in different contexts can reverse its impact. This insight, no doubt, arose from his most famous evaluation, namely of a scheme offering transitional financial aid to prisoners on their release (Rossi et al., 1980).

The effectiveness of this – like all – social interventions depended on how it was interpreted. The cash handouts could, potentially, contribute to the ex-cons finding their feet or finding work or supporting families or laying prone or buying booze or planning heists and so on. This variability would enter the scene no matter how uniformly the 'treatment' was delivered. If the payments were the same down to the last dime, timed to last three months and not a day more, and delivered only on Wednesday afternoons, they would still provoke a range of reasoning and usage. The particular combination of effects that gains the ascendancy depends on whom and in what circumstances the aid is bestowed. Rossi's research followed a sadly familiar trail of a promising pilot (in a restricted and conducive setting) and a disappointing main programme (involving a wider set of offenders in a broader setting).

His iron law, quoted above, is an extension of this tale. The more a programme is carried out in different terrains and the more it is pushed to its useful limits, the more its meaning multiplies and the more it will harvest a full range of both helpful and obstructive contexts. A likely cumulative result of increasing an intervention's scope is thus to cancel out its effects, and the best a priori estimate of its net impact is zero.

It is hardly surprising, therefore, that first-level meta-analysis often generates remarkably modest net effects for social programmes. However, this is not to say that all such studies are inconclusive. Consider, for instance, the bullish finale to HORS (Home Office Research Study) 251. This synthesis of studies on 13 (five British, eight US) street lighting schemes claims the following impact on crime levels:

> A meta-analysis found that these five [UK] studies showed that improved street lighting reduced crime by 30 per cent. The weighted effect size in all thirteen studies was substantial: a 20 per cent decrease in experimental areas compared with control areas. (Farrington and Welsh, 2002: 39)

A Home Secretary would give a right arm for crime reductions of this magnitude. However, before the present incumbent shakes on a deal with the ACME Lighting Company, a closer look at the data is warranted, much of which I owe to Marchant (2004).

The problem is the high level of aggregation in meta-analysis. In order to register a clean mean effect size, meta-analysis needs a pure and simple effect size calculation from each primary study. It does not need doubts, equivocation, conditions, complications or even explanations; it just needs a number. Providing that the primary study has some before-and-after data and a comparison group, it is always possible to crank out that number. However, complex programmes always generate complex outcome patterns, and a good evaluation will always deliver conditional truths, uncovering the underlying contexts and mechanisms that generate different outcomes. All this is ignored in level-one meta-analysis. It just top-slices a study for its net effect and pools it together with the top slices from other studies. As a result, the end product can be quite arbitrary.

Marchant's (2004) paper goes back to the primary studies in the Farrington and Welsh study, putting the microscope to their distinctly equivocal findings and comparing these to the seeming solidity of the meta-analysis. Recall that meta-analysis produces a weighted average and so sets great store by studies examining large

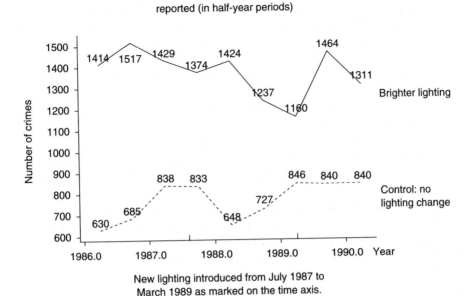

FIGURE 3.4   *Outcome complexity: results from a street lighting evaluation* (*Source*: Shaffoe, 1994)

populations. Let us examine some data from the big hitter of the street lighting study in Figure 3.4.

The lighting scheme was introduced from July 1987 to March 1989, as indicated on the time axis, and the upper and lower lines chart the fluctuating levels of crime in, respectively, the experimental area and the control area. The simple question, on which so much depends is, at what point should one take the before-and-after measures in order to calculate the changes produced by the scheme? There is no heaven-sent yardstick for this. Brighter lighting cannot physically prevent crime; it merely changes the choices open to residents and potential criminals. There is nothing to say that the effect will be felt the moment the first switch is thrown or at a point when people have become settled in the new environment. And making such a call is, of course, that much more difficult if installation takes place over the best part of two years. Judgement has to be applied.

So what are the options? Just by observing the fluctuations in the experimental area, one sees instability in crime levels before the scheme, then a slight rise immediately after work commenced, followed by a sharp mid-construction fall, followed by a steep rise immediately after completion, followed by another substantial fall as the calendar turns again. What is going on? Quite typically, the outcome graph wavers, and it does so as an outward reflection of some complex action, reaction and re-reaction to the lighting changes.

As ever in social programmes there are competing theories about why street lighting might affect crime and Farrington and Welsh, to their credit, list some of these (increased visibility increases the risk that potential offenders might be recognized or interrupted, increased flows of pedestrians, the 'feel-good factor', improved community confidence, and so on). Each of these potential mechanisms will bite at different times and, in addition, there is a whole range of potential side-effects that are nothing at all to do with the increased wattage *per se*, but which may have an impact (anticipation and publicity surrounding the scheme, disruption and surveillance by cable layers, intensified monitoring of crime levels, researcher effects, Hawthorne effects, and so on). Each one of these may chime in at different times. What is more, and by dint of being a high crime area, the experimental group is likely to be on the receiving end of changes in police activity, as well as other educational, welfare and work interventions, which may also affect crime levels through the 'feel-good factor'. Each one of these will also have its own tempo.

What all of this means is that there is no single, unequivocal measure to be had of the effect of the intervention on crime. The graph jitterbugs because this *is* the way that communities react to such schemes. An accompanying process analysis might help to rule in or rule out some of the outcome levers noted above by encouraging subjects to explain their reactions to the scheme. However, meta-analysis is not interested in situation-specific analysis; it wants its number. And where do Farrington and Welsh find it?

They compare crime rates in the year before and in the year after installation (the first pair and last pair on the graph) and this shows a helpful decrease in the experimental area of 5.3 per cent. They term this a 'conservative choice' of time intervals on the grounds, presumably, that they have not claimed that invitingly low 1160, recorded towards the end of, but not after, the installation. However, look closely at what their calculation has dragged in. This is a quasi-experimental comparison and so the net effect calculation examines the respective changes in experimental and non-experimental areas – a statistic known as the odds-ratio. What has happened in the control? Crime has jumped by 27.8 per cent. There is no clue about why this should have happened, although constancy of that neighbourhood's lighting does not seem to be an obvious explanation.

The key methodological point is that a whopping net effect estimate is pitched into the mean intervention effect calculation, despite the vast majority of it being composed of an unexplained change in the control community, which has nothing to do with street lighting. Recall that this is the largest of the studies in the meta-analysis and so has substantial influence on the 30 per cent reduction in crime claimed for the UK by the authors.

In short, a close look at this primary study provides nothing more than a mixed and changing picture of the outcomes of an intervention. Indeed, there is enough ambiguity for the original author to refrain from making any claim that the lighting scheme has been effective (Shaftoe, 1994). However, because of the arbitrary way that it has been top-sliced, it becomes decisive in the meta-analysis.

I should make it clear that this critique is not just about the injection of a freak result into an otherwise competent analysis. One notes further that Farrington and Welsh rely on only five UK studies in their analysis, and that most of these display the high background variability that bedevils the clear interpretation of crime data. One notes, despite the claim that the primary studies are of 'the highest methodological quality', that the main strategy in use is the matched area, quasi-experimental comparison. It is something of a puzzle, therefore, in the above example and others, that areas with vastly different initial crime rates could be chosen as a match. One notes that although the synthesis is supposedly on the effects of street lighting, two of the highly positive results come from lighting schemes in a car park entrance and an indoor market. One notes that the crime data are taken from different sources across the studies, and that victim survey and police records are notorious for manufacturing discrepancies.

Consider finally, the vintage of the primary studies. One notes that the Bristol data relate to the 1980s. Other inquiries in the review reach back into the 1970s and, as with much evaluation, this evidence tends to relate to pioneering studies in which the showcasing effect itself can have a positive effect. So, on temporal grounds alone, can the review be said to have tapped into an appropriate range of investigations? In pondering whether this meta-analysis is a useful guide to present day policy, have a walk tonight around your residential area. You may well find yourself so illuminated by the glow of high intensity domestic security lighting that the street lighting all but disappears. People have this nasty habit of changing the odds and the odds-ratios.

The picture here is typical of what one might regard as lucky-dip meta-analysis, in which a small number of studies put together in quite different conditions are filleted and the top slices are combined. A forest plot can be manufactured, an overall effect can always be calculated, but there is plenty of room for abnormal variability in each contribution stemming from the capricious decisions embodied in its making. A host of explanatory factors remain unknown, and are ignored, in coming to the mean of means. HORS 251 feels, and is, a makeshift summary, rather than the enduring product of a scrupulous census of an entire universe of studies.

Is this example typical of first-level meta-analysis? Have I merely selected a bad apple for further bruising? I think not, for the root of the problem is that meta-analysis simply cannot absorb all of the structures and processes that account for the observed changes in the life of a programme. What is carried into the net calculations will always depend on blanket technical decisions, which will always be insensitive to the particulars of any individual scheme.

📖 **Supplementary reading** For another example of the high-aggregation, top-slicing approach, see the critique of the meta-analysis of mental health programmes in R. Pawson *Evidence-based policy: in search of a method*, which is included in the web page support materials. ✰

> *Counterpoint (i)*   Net effect calculations for complex social programme are
> either disappointing or misleading. They are far too simplistic to act as a
> guide to future policy-making. All interventions, even those with zero net
> effects, have successful and unsuccessful applications. This prompts a more
> promising idea that comparison rather than aggregation should be at the
> core of research synthesis. A better meta-mission for social programmes is to
> perform analysis with the goal of assisting in their targeting.

j. Level-two meta-analysis assumes that variation in programme outcomes can be explained by incorporating 'mediator' and 'moderator' variables

Sophisticated exponents of meta-analysis will have waited, brows furrowed, for the critique to reach this point. All the previous criticism, they would chide, is the retailing of old news. They would acknowledge the weakness of one-answer, net effect synthesis and point out that such a mode of analysis has been long surpassed by forms of meta-analysis that employ mediating and moderating variables in the analysis of programme efficacy. This is the revised mission statement:

> The proper agenda for the next generation of treatment effectiveness research ... is investigation of which treatments are most effective, the mediating causal process through which they work, and the characteristics of recipients, providers and settings that most influence the results. (Lipsey and Wilson, 1993: 1201)

A mediator is an intermediate variable. Many programmes are reckoned to work in terms of one causal change begetting another, and the standard black box analysis ($X \rightarrow Y$) is replaced by one seeking the intermediate correlates of change ($X \rightarrow Y \rightarrow Z$). For instance, a mentoring programme (X) for disadvantaged youth may induce better parental relationships (Y) and gains in this respect might be the trigger for improvements in behavioural and scholastic goals (Z), which are the intended aim of the programme (Rhodes et al., 2000). In general, any number of such intermediate factors may feature in programme implementation and, in the new mission, the efficacious causal pathways must be discovered if knowledge is to be reliably transferred.

A moderator describes a context in which the causal efficacy of an intervention changes. They describe sub-population effects, which are commonplace in programme evaluation and lead to the intervention having a different effect in one subgroup ($G_1: X \rightarrow Y_1$) than another ($G_2: X \rightarrow Y_2$). For instance, a welfare-to-work programme involving financial incentives to move off assistance, as well as help in finding a job, may be discovered to be more successful for male than female subjects. In general, a programme's effectiveness may vary across any number of subgroups, differentiated by any number of individual characteristics and societal locations, and – according to the revised mission – transferable knowledge requires such contextual specification.

These contingencies are indeed a feature of all programmes and the new meta-analysis tackles such conditional causation as follows. The initial question posed in the review becomes more complex. It is not only a hypothesis about whether a treatment works, but must also pre-specify the potential mediators and moderators in order to test whether they influence the efficacy of the intervention. Accordingly, the basket of approved primary studies becomes particularly choice. The need for random allocation in order to get an unbiased measure of effect is set in stone, but there is an added requirement. The original research must also have had the foresight to measure a comprehensive set of potential mediator and moderator variables. Each of these primary studies must yield a data matrix capable of detecting intermediate and sub-group influences of the type described above. Second-level meta-analysis, then, has the task of discovering which of the hypothesized mediator and moderator effects applies across the entire family of such studies. Just as it is possible to sum up an overall net effect using a forest plot, meta-regression identifies the net influence of any potential mediator and moderator by holding constant all other explanatory variables in the regression model.

Such an approach is incomparably more insightful than standard meta-analysis, but it still cannot provide a solution to the basic problems identified throughout this chapter. It further reduces the amount of evidence available for review, and is still unable to address the fundamentals of social causation.

The statistical requirements of meta-regression limit, rather than widen, the pool of usable primary studies. The prize of bias avoidance still captivates the new school and so randomized field trials remain the gold standard design. In addition, a much more comprehensive set of PIO measures is now *de rigueur*. The task is to locate key differences in the people and places where the intervention might take a better hold, to identify differences in the way the intervention is delivered and to track not only final but intermediate outputs. The overlay rule also still applies. Every study in the meta-regression should have the same capacity to fill every column of the much extended data extraction matrix.

This requires replication with a vengeance. Recall, in the street lighting example, that even the standard outcome indicators were not performed with common instruments. This raises two obvious questions: whether such multivariate controlled trials are thick on the ground, and whether they use identical sets of mediators and moderators. The answers to both are not encouraging. Bibliometric research by Petrosino (2000) on the use of intermediate and contextual causal analysis in a wide swathe of primary research on 'programs for children' concludes that, 'The use of mediators and moderators is sporadic and vague at best.' This conclusion represents double-trouble for meta-analysis because randomized controlled trials are themselves a rarity, and mediator and moderator variants rarer still.

> I completed a meta-analysis of 150 randomized trials in juvenile and crime prevention ... only 5 per cent included at least one mediating variable and only 35 per cent included an analysis of at least one moderator. (Petrosino, 2000: 55)

Indeed there is treble-trouble, for it is unlikely that primary researchers think alike on which are key confounding variables. Petrosino's estimates are important to the argument here because of his acknowledged support for meta-regression techniques and his prominent role in the Campbell Collaboration. He uses the 'disturbing picture' to call for the upgrading of standards in future primary research. However, what it signifies for the present is that meta-regression can only be performed on families of studies funded and managed by the large US agencies and often investigated by their associated laboratories. Ashworth et al.'s (2004) meta-evaluation of welfare-to-work programmes provides a typical example, stretching to just 24 mandatory programmes, more than half using the same evaluator (MDRC). The questionable wisdom of creating universal policy recommendations solely on the back of high-profile US programmes is one obvious response to this state of affairs. Another is that it leaves the vast majority of interventions inaccessible to the method and in need of an alternative means of delivering a synthesis.

The real issue, however, is not one of bemoaning the lack of primary studies or waiting for them to come up to scratch. For the realist, meta-analysis in the form of the new meta-regression is, even now, deficient in its understanding of the causal powers of interventions. Causation, according to the signature argument of the previous chapter, is not established by observing the regular succession of events, and putative social laws cannot be established by searching for uniformities.

The significance of this proposition can be clearly observed in respect of mediator and moderator analysis, using one of the examples above. Ashworth et al.'s study reproduces a well-known pattern in welfare-to-work programmes, namely that they are more successful with male than female subjects. Is the fact that this partial correlation shows up clearly and repeatedly across a couple of dozen primary studies sufficient evidence that some causal relation is in operation? The answer is no. Gender does not cause the programme to operate one way and then another. The variable measured by the sex of the programme recipient does not cause anything. What is going on and what is causing the outcome difference is that a substantial number of women are making different choices than do men when confronted by programme resources. To understand what causes these differential choices requires some situation-specific wisdom.

Edin and Lein (1997) provide some useful clues on the mechanisms and contexts involved. The intervention offers a package of carrots and sticks to influence subjects to move from welfare to work. Whether women do so depends, partly, on their decision about the overall change in household budget that would result from losing some benefits and taking up low-paid work. Edin and Lein quantified the typical weekly spend and discovered that most women welfare recipients have a family budget which is not wholly covered by welfare income. Accordingly, many of them operate 'on the side' to make ends meet. Supplemental income comes from unreported work in the moonlight economy, illegal work in the drugs and sex trade and informal work for the family and neighbours, as well as donations from charities, friends and kin. Which of these opportunities presents itself varies, in turn, according to the circumstances in which they live, with some local economies offering substantial opportunities for side work, some casework regimes allowing more latitude for working unnoticed and so on. In short, the introduction of the welfare-to-work regime is met by an extremely subtle calculation about which of the above activities will have to be jettisoned and which can be maintained once inside the workforce, and, on balance, whether needs will be met any more comfortably.

These little fragments of evidence begin to supply the real causal analysis of why men and women might differ in their response to the programme. Broadly speaking, women seem to have less good prospects in the formal economy and more obligations that can be met informally. The key methodological point, however, is about causation. It is only when primary research begins to supply an explanation of the constrained choices involved that the moderator pattern begins to make sense. Research like Edin and Lein's, employing surveys, in-depth interviews, city-on-city comparisons and so on, is necessary to understand the observed partial correlations.

Note, incidentally, that exactly the same point can be made about mediator analysis. The fact that in mentoring programmes an intermediary improvement in relations with parents usually intercedes before progress is made at school is not itself a causal explanation. It is something that still needs to be explained. One needs to know what is going on between the three parties, and more will be revealed on this score when the example is treated in full in Chapter 6.

Everyone knows that correlation does not equal causation and this venerable truth holds for partial correlations. The real explanation of causation comes from additional process and contextual information, and by way of other types of primary studies. Process knowledge is always needed to make sense of causal outcomes, and meta-regression gets nowhere near such a balanced explanatory portfolio. Dozens of mediators and moderators can be introduced (replica primary research permitting), and the statistical model will always cough up an inventory of variables that happen to be significant. It is this that is seen as the prize, as the end of the analytic journey. To be precise, what one usually gets for each concomitant variable is a paragraph or two rendering a plausible account of why the difference or inter-connection comes about. However, this operates at the level of 'common sense' (Ashworth et al., 2004) about the subjects involved rather than a proper investigation of all the qualitative, administrative, comparative, action and discourse analysis, which has been discarded from the synthesis.

Although they are vested with the status of enduring empirical generalizations, mediator and moderator models are no more than snapshot descriptions of uniformities that happen to crop up within the slim ration of data that happens to be retrievable. Causal influences, in meta-regression, are detected whenever a main effect connecting two variables is altered by the consideration of inter-correlation with a third. Everything is reduced to the relationships between variables and, in the absence of a method to explain the causal pattern, the approach proceeds into an infinite regress. The inter-relationships will change with the introduction of further studies and further variables. Moderators will always be further moderated, and mediators will be mediated again and again (Lipsey, 2003).

In this respect, consider again the welfare-to-work example. I have indicated some basic evidence to show that, broadly speaking, women might reason differently from men in relation to the deal offered by the programme. Because these constrained choices are the vital mechanism in programme operation, one would expect the sophisticated calculations of budget balances to generate a whole patchwork of programme successes and failures. The equation of formal opportunities opened versus the risk to informal income streams will not just differentiate male and female subjects. For instance, the same programme compact will, probably, play in a different way to women with and without children, women with and without parental support, big city and small town women, women with social security cards and with false IDs, and so on and so on. This is, of course, just the beginning of moderation and mediation. Responses to the deal offered by the programme can also be expected to differ by dint of each respondent's sex, age, race, ability, disability, locality and so forth, and according to the myriad differences in existing welfare regimes within which it is introduced.

The upshot is that mediator and moderator analysis will, of its own accord, go on forever. The list of nooks and crannies revealing for whom and in what circumstances and in what respects a programme will work is potentially infinite. The only limitation on discovering them in meta-regression is the practical one of needing blanket coverage of variables across primary studies to generate sufficient sample sizes to spot the behavioural differences between sub-sub-sub-groups. Mediator and moderator models are very useful records of complex input, output and outcome patterns associated with social programmes, but they are nothing more than that.

Two further steps are required before they become causal explanations. First, the review must supply the situation-specific wisdom that accounts for any intermediate step or sub-group behaviour. Second, there needs to be a way of muzzling the ever-growing list of potential contingencies. The factors influencing the response to a programme will reach right down into the individual biographical profiles of each subject. The factors influencing the attractiveness of the intervention will reach right down to the individual biographical characteristics of each practitioner. The factors influencing implementation success will reach back into the history of the institutions and communities involved. The natural consequence of teasing out all this variation is agglomeration and not accumulation. However, research synthesis cannot go on mapping every conceivable permutation, nor can programme architects plan for every eventuality.

What synthesis can do is begin to confederate the explanation of the pattern of success and failure. Underlying all the differences in programme outcomes in the welfare-to-work example, and indeed in all programmes, is the process of constrained choice for subjects of different status. So, whilst it is impossible to trace all the choices and all the constraints, this is not to say we cannot produce a middle-range theory of the risks and benefits involved in choice-making that begins to scoop some of them together. For example, social outsiders in one respect might have plenty in common with outsiders in a different demographic dimension. They are likely to share similar levels of economic deprivation, have similar hostilities and antagonisms to the current system, and have parallel difficulties in terms of 'coming on board'. Again, we come to the conclusion that abstraction – or theory – is the tool that begins to pull the cases together and provide the synthesis.

> *Counterpoint (j)*   Meta-regression represents an important step in allowing variation back into the conclusions of research synthesis, but it can only describe variation in terms of the interrelationships between variables. A better meta-explanation of the variation in programme outcomes can be developed from a full range of situational data although, even then, the contours of success and failure are likely to be never-ending and ever-changing. The sense of cumulation expected from a review needs to be acquired in another way, by explanatory synthesis.

Stage six: disseminating the findings

The ultimate purpose of research synthesis is to improve policy-making and programme effectiveness. Accordingly, most accounts of best practice in systematic review push one stage beyond analysis of the findings and have something to say about how to disseminate the results. There is a rare point of unanimity in the literature at this juncture, averring that simply to publish findings is insufficient and that dissemination involves the art of persuasive communication.

Systematic review involves a tortuous journey and convention has it that only the reviewer needs to suffer the pain, it being normal practice to encapsulate the trek in a concise and precise set of recommendations. The perils of simplification has been my theme throughout this critique and it is as evident at the end of meta-analysis as at the beginning. The whole exercise starts with a 'what works?' question and the natural terminus is a verdict on this score. There is an age-old quandary in evidence-based policy about the consequences of pandering to the inability of the powerful to read any more than seven bullet points on a side of A4. These 'best buy' recommendations constitute a giant pander.

k. Meta-analysis provides 'whole programme' counsel, and recommendations advise upon running or retaining or removing interventions

This section concentrates on the dissemination of, perhaps, the largest ever meta-analytic review, since it presents a wide-open window on the final layer of simplifications. Sherman et al. (1997) conducted a comprehensive review of the effectiveness of US criminal justice interventions and chose to disseminate their verdicts under the enticing banner of 'What works, What doesn't, What's promising'.

The point of interest is the auspices of these three statements. Where lie the cutting points? True to form, they are defined operationally:

> For a programme to be classified as working there must be a minimum of two level 3 studies with significance tests demonstrating effectiveness and the preponderance of evidence in support of the same conclusion. (Welsh and Farrington, 2001: 170)

The criterion for 'failure' is the obverse of the above, with the 'promising' verdict reserved for families of programmes with mixed results. 'Third-level' research support is defined as residing in before-and-after matched comparison (i.e. quasi-experimental) designs.

Yet again we see the willingness to engage in arbitrary simplification. These decision points are loaded with all the methodological preferences – misleading preferences, according to this critique – that are adopted in reaching the final phase of a review. Research that makes the methodological cut will refer to a only a small segment of the total family of programmes; complex outcome patterns will have been folded together to reach an overall verdict; all qualitative, historical and administrative studies will have been jettisoned from the judgement; matching will be flawed given the internal complexity of social programmes, and so on. In addition, in this case, the trio of verdicts are defined purely by fiat. Who is to say that 'two significant level 3 positives' plus a 'favourable balance' are sufficient to make the affirmative cut? The answer, of course, is that this is the opinion of Sherman and colleagues. Their standard would, however, cut no ice in the statistical bible-belt, which insists on unqualified randomization before any significance test of pro-gramme effects becomes reliable. It is equally anathema to the realist position, which insists on penetrating the black box before any call can be made on causal powers.

The fact that the gauge of effectiveness turns on a capricious simplification does not, however, foreclose opportunities for dissemination. Far from it, for what it provides are verdicts and verdicts, moreover, overlaid with a scientific veneer. The rush to per-suasive communication can be seen in some of the associated publicity material:

> … based on a review of more than 500 scientific evaluations … [and] building on a 565-page report submitted to Congress … the study presents the first summary list of what works, what doesn't and what's promising. The list of 'what works' includes:

- Nurses visiting high-risk infants at home
- Head Start programs with weekly visits by teachers to students' home
- Extra police patrols in high crime 'hot-spots'
- Anti-bullying programs in schools
- Drug treatment programs in prisons
- Special police units and prison for repeat offenders
- Rehabilitation programs focussed on offender risk factors

The list of programs that don't work includes:

- Gun buy backs
- Military-style correction boot camps
- Summer jobs for youth
- Home detention or electronic monitoring
- Neighborhood watch
- Drug Abuse Resistance Education (DARE) Classes taught to school children by police officers
  (www.inform.umd.edu/campusInfo/InstAdv/uniRel/outlook/199...)

The heart sinks. Yet again programmes and not people are invested with causal powers. One shudders at the idea that policy-makers are encouraged to skim through a few casual labels given to an array of crime reduction measures and simply tick or cross them off as fit or unfit for human consumption. In this policy arena, above all, we know that programmes have dramatic outcome swings, variable reach and a short shelf-life (Ekblom, 2002).

The one overriding lesson that should result from scouring the evidence base is a wariness of simple questions and over-simple answers. Whether programmes work depends on how they are implemented, to whom and in what circumstances they are applied, and on what precisely they are expected to achieve. This should be the first pronouncement of all reviews.

📖 **Supplementary reading** The alacrity with which all manner of reviewers, and not just meta-analysts, feel able to plunge into policy verdicts is the focus of A. Boaz and R. Pawson *The perilous journey from evidence to policy*, which is included in the web page support materials. 🏛

Counterpoint (k)   Better meta-advice is proffered by concentrating on what the evidence says about the shaping and targeting of programmes rather than on delivering verdicts and best buys. The real challenge of dissemination is how to convey the partial and conditional truths unravelled in systematic review (especially in seven bullet points on a side of A4!).

Conclusion

Moving from evidence (which is inexhaustible) to advice for policy-makers (who are easily exhausted) always involves a process of simplification. This chapter has traced the route that a meta-analytic review takes in making that journey. It is a rather complicated trek involving identifying and amassing potential sources, selecting and thinning them out, pin-pointing and standardizing the information extracted from each, aggregating and typifying crucial patterns in the remaining data, and highlighting policy verdicts and best buys. Evidence never speaks for itself and we have now witnessed at close range the manoeuvres involved before meta-analysis makes its utterances.

If one pulls away and looks at the voyage as a whole, a rather curious passage can be discerned. Humpty Dumpty is contemplated, pushed off the wall and put together again. The meta-analytic ideal is to begin with a grand assembly of all the evidence. Then there is a ferocious emphasis on screening and standardization; prospective review questions are abridged, potential primary studies are weeded out, selected contents are collapsed onto a common data matrix. Then, at the analytic stage, the emphasis reverts to the big picture and turns to generalization, to establishing the universal norms of intervention effectiveness. The overall pattern of outcomes is inspected for averages, uniformities and regularities. The end product is a purported 'state description' to the effect that the best N conducted studies of the impact of X and Y show a P per cent gain under conditions A, B and C.

I have argued that such a process of simplification, standardization and aggregation does not produce any such enduring truths. It produces a descriptive summary that is likely to be disappointing or misleading or in need of further clarification. Indeed, as we have seen, the overall result of selection and de-selection of information can be surprisingly sectarian. There is a dangerous flip-side to meta-analytic simplification. One needs to be clear about just what is omitted. With the main hypotheses truncated, with programme theories absent, with context untouched, with stakeholder choices ignored and with swathes of research by-passed, meta-analysis eliminates most of the evidence that is capable of telling us how interventions work and how we might account for their differential effectiveness. What is detritus for meta-analysis is, however, explanatory gold dust for the realist.

4

Realist Synthesis: New Protocols for Systematic Review

This chapter sets out the method of realist synthesis. It is the pivot of the book. In the first chapter I voiced the rationale for attempting to synthesize volumes of previous research and gave a glimpse of the daunting challenge involved in doing so. In the second, I introduced realism as a general logic of social science, as a tool for understanding how social programmes work, and as a framework for understanding their complexity. In the third, I followed the arduous route march of systematic review and found fault with the conventional way of making the journey from research evidence to policy recommendations. Now I want to apply the general principles of realist explanation and the lessons about programme complexity to the business of research synthesis.

The new model for systematic review is constructed in two ways. First, I pay attention to domain principles, establishing a totally revised model in which theory-building takes pride of place as the prime activity in research synthesis. Secondly, I provide a blueprint for realist synthesis in a way that captures the step-by-step process of searching, tracing, filtering, eviscerating and analysing all of the primary materials. All of the 'counterpoints' raised in the previous chapter are activated. Overall, this chapter aims to establish a new protocol for conducting a review in a manner that can be followed by anyone intent on conducting a realist synthesis. Much changes except, that is, for the hard slog.

First principles: synthesis as theory-building

Let us go back to square one. What are we actually doing in the protracted process of gathering together voluminous piles of primary research and rendering them down into policy advice? What is the essence of the activity? What does it mean to synthesize research? One can take a cue on this matter from other applications of the term synthesis, which in its various uses in chemistry, philosophy and linguistics suggests something rather more active and creative than combination or aggregation. In these formulations, the product emerging from synthesis is reckoned to be more than the sum of its parts. Some knowledge gain, some novel compound, some added value is produced in the process of synthesis. Such a notion is also vital to evidence-based policy. There is a need for systematic review to go beyond reportage and summary of an existing state of affairs. The point, after all, is to support fresh thinking to revise policy and launch it in new circumstances.

In the realist model, the primary ambition of research synthesis is explanation-building. The purpose is to articulate underlying programme theories and then to interrogate the existing evidence to find out whether and where these theories are pertinent and productive. Primary research is examined for its contribution to the developing theory. The overall intention is to create an abstract model of how and why programmes work, which then can be used to provide advice on the implementation and targeting of any novel incarnation of the intervention. The process is illustrated schematically in Figure 4.1.

Realist synthesis begins by identifying its subject matter – normally taken to be the class of programmes about to be reviewed – but the real work begins with the construction an embryonic theory of how they may work. This may be articulated in a variety of ways but (as illustrated in the top section of the figure) will contain some of the familiar features of realist explanation, namely conjectures on the generative mechanisms that change behaviour, ideas on the contexts that influence its operation, and hunches about the different outcome patterns that ensue. In other words, the preliminary hypotheses will raise speculative ideas about 'what works for whom in what circumstances and in what respects'.

The synthesis then moves on to the primary data. These are regarded as case studies, whose purpose is to test, revise and refine the preliminary theory. It is expected that they will reveal a mix of methods, a mix of information and, above all, mixed messages about the success of the intervention. The process is illustrated schematically in terms of the six primary inquiries in the middle section of the figure. The initial theory provides a lens through which to view the studies, and one anticipates a spectrum of different refractions. The research may offer direct support or outright contradiction to the preliminary theory, although a subtle modification in understanding is more likely. The evidence may improve or weaken or modify or ameliorate or revise or supplement or refocus the underlying programme ideas, and the purpose of synthesis is to make sense of these quite different challenges.

Let us now consider some of the different ways in which primary evidence might confront the review hypothesis, in order to see how the various empirical challenges might be taken on board. Some studies will be relatively revealing about underlying mechanisms, some will concentrate on outcomes, others may describe context in depth (illustrated by the presences and absences of these features in Cases 1 and 2). Here, the review is concerned with *juxtaposing* the evidence as, for instance, when one study provides the process data to make sense of the outcome pattern noted in another.

Contradiction between two primary studies – illustrated by the positive outcome in Case 3 and the failed (hence dashed) outcome in Case 4 – is also a common occurrence. In this case the analysis may attempt to *reconcile* them by unearthing contextual or implementation differences in the original programmes and showing

Initial programme theory

Primary studies

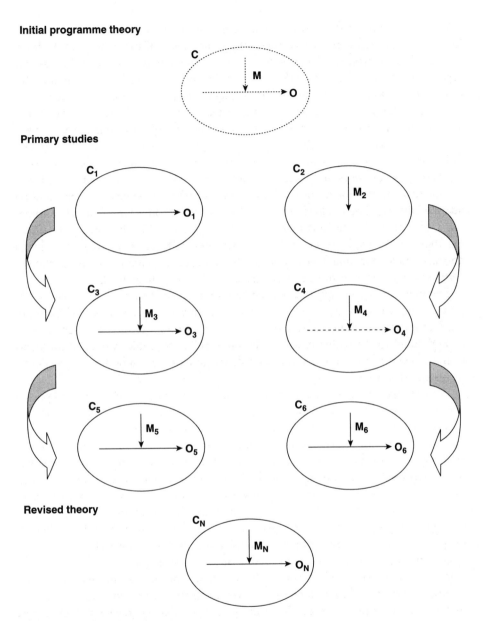

Revised theory

FIGURE 4.1   *The logic of realist synthesis*

how these led to opposing outcomes. An alternative in this situation is for the reviewer to *adjudicate* between the inquiries on the basis of a methodological excavation that reveals the relative virtues or shortcomings of the original conclusions.

In another familiar story, studies may arrive at different accounts of programme impact – illustrated here by two successful outcomes in Cases 5 and 6, which are explained as the product of different mechanisms and circumstances. In this case the reviewer might attempt to *consolidate* the results into a multifaceted explanation for programme success, and the synthesis might make the case for a combined approach. Alternatively, the reviewer may attempt to *situate* the rival explanations, arguing that the programme operates successfully through mechanism 5 in context 5 but that mechanism 6 might come into its own in contexts like 6. Both explanations survive as a result of understanding and reinterpreting their scope conditions.

The review continues in this way through many more primary inquiries, each one leading to an adaptation of the original review hypothesis (compare Layder, 1998 on adaptive theory). The finale is not an arithmetic verdict on a family of programmes but a refinement of its underlying theory. Figure 4.1 thus ends schematically by drawing together the exploration of the successes and failures of a programme in an abstract model explaining how efficacy (O_N) varies, depending on the particular *configuration* of its constituent mechanisms (M_N) and contexts (C_N).

The vital point to emphasize is that the analytic processes described above as juxtaposing, adjudicating, reconciling, consolidating and situating the evidence are none other than the elusive idea of synthesis. It is these reasoning processes that embody the logic of realist synthesis. It is this ability to think through studies and to make sense of their uniformities and discrepancies that embodies the real craft of systematic review.

The notion of synthesis as explanation-building has another key facet (and potential advantage), embodied in the role that *abstraction* plays in policy formation and evaluation. In devising and evaluating interventions, simple distinctions between a 'programme', its 'implementation', its 'outputs' and its 'outcomes' are made routinely. Similarly, the targets for intervention are often differentiated according to whether they are focused on the 'individual' or the 'area'. Likewise, interventions are described habitually in terms of the exchange between 'stakeholders', who comprise 'policy-makers', 'practitioners' and 'programme subjects'. These simple concepts can be applied to all programmes and not just the concrete one sitting before the evaluator, the point being that we perpetually carve up and define, navigate and make sense of interventions by thinking of them in terms of such abstractions.

In much systematic review, this basic vocabulary of intervention terms is taken for granted; the terms are treated as the given parameters of the investigation rather than as objects of investigation. It is simply assumed that the review will track this type of 'programme' aimed at this type of 'subject' seeking that type of 'outcome'. However, the precise coinage of such abstractions is of immense significance in determining the appropriate evidence base. Consider, for instance, the importance of defining the 'subjects' in a cognitive-skills programme designed to assist in offender rehabilitation. The term 'offender' is itself an abstraction and the perceived problem – a lack of thinking skills – might well, on deeper consideration, be thought to differ according to whether the inmate is in for criminal damage or embezzlement or aggravated vehicle taking or drug dealing or rape or fraud. The problem, to put it glibly, is that some of them might be just too damn clever to begin with. The programme theory (and thus the programme) will succeed or fail according to how accurately the notion of the 'cognitively deficient offender' is drawn. In general, policy wisdom depends on hitting the right level of abstraction and paying meticulous attention to the boundaries of explanation.

The overall importance of careful abstraction for realist enquiry is thus established:

> Social systems are always open and usually complex and messy. Unlike some of the natural sciences, we cannot isolate out these components and examine them under controlled conditions. We therefore have to rely on abstraction and careful conceptualisation, on attempting to abstract out the various components or influences in our heads, and only when we have done this and considered how they combine and interact can we expect to return to the concrete, many-sided object and make sense of it. (Sayer, 2000: 19)

Sense-making, our ultimate objective, relies heavily on vigilant conceptualization and watchful abstraction, and these tasks are a central objective of realist synthesis. Instead of assuming that the review is about a given programme X, acting on given subjects Y, with given objectives Z, the central intention is to question the reach and scope of each of these components. If one begins research synthesis from this standpoint, there are quite different opportunities to draw collective lessons about why programmes work. Let me pursue the most radical departure that can ensue by starting with programme concepts rather than programmes *per se*. A curious point about programme theories is their shared agenda, a feature noted decades ago by Salaman in urging the following change of emphasis:

> Rather than focusing on individual programs, as is now done, or even collections of programs grouped according to major 'purpose' as is frequently proposed, the suggestion here is that we should concentrate on the *generic tools of government action* that come to be used, in varying combinations in particular public programs. (1981: 256)

We tend to think of social and public policy as comprising a million different initiatives. We have welfare-to-work programmes and dietary improvement programmes and head start programmes and offender rehabilitation programmes and quit smoking programmes and peer mentoring programmes, and so on *ad infinitum*. Instead, Salaman argues that we should appreciate that these initiatives share common programme theories. Examined closely, it becomes apparent that interventions in quite different policy domains are expected to operate though the same or very similar programme mechanisms. The bravest rendition of this brave idea is the book by Bemelmans-Videc and colleagues (2003), which argues that, if one scrapes away programmes to their elemental bones, there are only three types of mechanism on offer, namely 'carrots, sticks and sermons'.

Take, for instance, 'carrot theory' or the idea of using incentives. These have a time-honoured place in public policy and come in a whole raft of different grants, bonuses, subsidies, payments, loans, give-aways, premiums and so forth. Subjects have been offered incentives by way of subsidized nicotine replacement patches to quit smoking; free distribution of smoke alarms to increase household safety; transitional payments to keep released prisoners from reoffending; cash payments to donate blood; bike loan schemes to reduce inner city congestion; price reductions to induce early payment of service charges; grants to improve insulation to save energy; subsidies for low-income families to reduce the cost of attending university; and so on. Since incentives are at the root of so many programmes, policy-makers on the point of introducing a fresh one may have much to learn about its chances by trawling through the evidence on these many and varied schemes.

📖 **Supplementary reading** Readers interested in further explorations of carrot theory should consult R. Pawson *Evidence-based policy: the promise of realist synthesis* and R. Pawson and N. Tilley *Realist evaluation bloodlines*, which are included in the web page support materials.🏯

The key methodological principle, however, lies beyond this specific example. The crucial point is that as soon as one begins to explore policy-making at different levels of abstraction, and as soon as one allows elements of programme theory to be the unit of analysis, then the cases and comparisons that are useful in the review change markedly. No longer is it a matter of chasing just the primary research that bears the title of a particular brand of intervention. Rather, the significant evidence is found by locating research that explores the precise set of assumptions held in the programme theory. Later in the chapter, we shall see how realist synthesis operates with a mixture of purposive samples of the primary data in order to pry open the evidence in relation to particular features of programme theory. For now, and for the purposes of establishing first principles, we arrive at the central claim of the book that:

> Research synthesis operates through processes of policy abstraction and theory-building rather than data extraction and number crunching.

Rethinking the standard template: practical steps in realist review

How can these markedly different principles be transformed into a work plan for conducting a review? This section develops the realist template by way of a step-by-step contrast with the standard review strategy that was criticized in the previous chapter. For easy reference, the standard review sequence laid out in Chapter 3 (Box 3.1) is reproduced again in miniature as Table 4.1. Realist synthesis also

TABLE 4.1 *The 'standard' sequence of systematic review*

1 Identifying the review question
2 Searching for primary studies
3 Quality appraisal
4 Extracting the data
5 Synthesizing the data
6 Disseminating the findings

moves from bygone evidence to present-day policy advice and thus has a comparable structure. However, there are many subtle differences in emphasis, in duration, in running order and, above all, in the methodological content of each stage. This section will absorb the critiques, develop the realist alternatives, and put an alternative prospectus in place. This is summarized in Figure 4.3. It might be useful for readers to locate this diagram at the very end of the chapter; a quick preview will reveal the calm that follows the storm.

Despite the differences, there is one area of methodological consensus between the traditional systematic review and the realist review, and that is the need for transparency or auditability in the review process. The purpose of the basic template is to set out a clear design for new reviews and novice reviewers to follow. But it also allows others – researchers, decision-makers and other stakeholders – to 'look behind' an existing review, to assure themselves of its rigour and of the validity, reliability and verifiability of its findings and conclusions. Realist synthesis involves different kinds of hypotheses and methodological decisions but it is equally important that the thread of explanation building is kept as visible as possible so that others can understand (and question) the roots of the policy recommendations. This perturbing principle is revisited through the following sequence and again in Chapter 8.

Stage one: identifying the review question

All reviews commence with an exercise in conceptual sharpening, attempting to refine and define precisely the question to be pursued in the forthcoming synthesis. In meta-analytic mode this involves paying close attention to defining the treatment under consideration, identifying the relevant population to which it is applied, and stipulating the outcome of interest. These decisions are enshrined in operational definitions within the review protocol, and used in the subsequent extraction of data from primary studies. The previous chapter showed how such operational closure leads to explanatory impoverishment, so a new approach to agenda-setting is needed.

The realist approach, too, must start with a sharpening of the question to be posed but this task goes well beyond the clarification of key terms. The divergence stems from the nature of the interventions studied (complex processes inserted into complex structures) and the very purpose of the review (explanatory rather than

TABLE 4.2   *An explanatory compendium for complex programmes*

- Programme theories – how is the programme supposed to work?
- Reasoning and reactions of stakeholders – are there differences in the understanding of the programme theory?
- Integrity of the implementation chain – is the programme theory applied consistently and cumulatively?
- Negotiation and feedback in implementation – does the programme theory tend to bend in actual usage?
- Contextual influences – does the programme theory fare better with particular individuals, interpersonal relations, institutions and infrastructures?
- History of the programme and relationships with other policies – does the policy apparatus surrounding the theory advance or impede it?
- Multiple, unintended, long-term effects – is the theory self-affirming or self-defeating or self-neutralizing?

summative). These differences bite enormously hard at stage one of a realist review, and effectively break it into several sub-stages. Both reviewers and commissioners should anticipate that 'focusing the question' will be a time-consuming and ongoing task, often continuing to the half-way mark and even beyond in a rapid review. One author (Greenhalgh et al., 2004) has referred to this stage of the synthesis of evidence on complex programmes as 'the swamp'. Anyone anticipating the quick fix of a watertight review question in an explanatory review should beware that they will very soon find themselves neck-deep in alternatives.

A realist review cannot comply with a commission to discover 'whether' an intervention works, but trades instead on its ability to discover 'why', 'when' and 'how' it might succeed. However, this explanatory orientation is not a single point of reference and will automatically generate a whole range of potential sub-questions. The best way to grasp this point is to refer back to the anatomy of programmes provided in Chapter 2 and summarized in Figure 2.7. There, in seven separate items, an agenda for understanding programmes was constructed and this also constitutes a potential explanatory landscape of realist synthesis, which is reconfigured as Table 4.2.

Even the standard realist shorthand for all this, namely 'what works for whom in what circumstances and in what respects', is itself an explanatory mire. But, in one way or another, diving into this explanatory swamp marks the first task in realist synthesis. The reviewer has to reconnoitre conceptually and decide on a chosen path, and this process can be usefully broken down into three steps, as follows.

Mapping the territory

First, the reviewer pitches in, using a checklist such as the one in Table 4.2, to surface the impending questions for review. The fate of an intervention depends on all of these processes and they must have at least the potential to surface in the review. The first task is thus to give them some substance in relation to the intervention under review: to establish which programme theories seem important; to get a feel for the circumstances in which they tend to get tried; to gather hunches on implementation difficulties; to tease out ways in which the programme might misfire; and so on. Experienced reviewers might well be able to anticipate some key issues, but the prospective explanatory agenda should be mapped in conjunction with an initial, exploratory reading of the primary materials.

Prioritizing review questions

The second task is to select the chosen questions for review from the preliminary set just identified. No review can ever be completely comprehensive and unless the reviewer has a year or two – or more – to spare, it is quite impossible to probe in depth all of the issues in Table 4.2. Prioritization has to be the rule but there is no golden rule for selecting the key explanatory issues. These may be settled pragmatically, on the basis of the prior interests of the commissioner, reviewer or practitioner. Somewhat more strategically, a particularly characteristic trait, a feature of palpable novelty, a point of potential fragility, or an area of dispute within a programme may be singled out as the burning issue for review.

By way of illustration, I introduce a couple of the syntheses pursued in later chapters. Chapter 5 reviews Megan's Law, the US scheme notifying neighbourhoods of the impending release of a former sex offender into their community. One of its distinguishing features is its particularly lengthy implementation chain, which runs back and forth from prison and police authorities to the public and probation services and, of course, to the released offender. Accordingly, the crucial issue determining whether a 'long sequence' intervention like Megan's Law works is the integrity of the implementation chain, and this was chosen as the focus of this review. The question for a second review on 'naming and shaming' (Chapter 7), was inspired by a quite different issue. The basic idea of taming underperformance by public disclosure of performance data through 'league tables', 'star ratings' and other such devices is used right across the policy waterfront. It might be thought of as a 'broad brush' scheme and so this review heads for the contextual boundaries, trying to find out the sectors in which shaming might be successful.

Formalizing the model

The third and final step in the first stage of a realist review is to formalize the model to be tested. These hypotheses are not in the form of yes/no, pass/fail questions about programme efficacy; they are explanatory and so exactly like the conjectures of substantive social science. They are also realist and so will speculate on configurations of mechanisms and contexts that give rise to varied programme outcomes. For example, the review of youth mentoring in Chapter 6 starts with a simple four-stage model of the requisite mechanisms. It postulates that in order to successfully re-engage disaffected youth, mentoring must work as befriending (making mentees feel differently about themselves), as confidence-building (offering a guiding hand though the difficult choices confronting the mentee), as coaching (coaxing mentees into practical gains, skills and qualifications) and as advocacy (sponsoring mentees by using contacts and networks). The model anticipates that this sequence will be difficult to achieve and sets the reviewer the task of finding the mentoring partnerships and circumstances that will trigger this sequence.

Note that I refer to the realist review hypothesis as a model. This is because, as in the mentoring example, it should refer to a *linked subset* of questions. Compared to a standard 'does X cause Y?' hypothesis, such a model will be policy and substantively rich. It locates the decisive aspects of the programme theory, allowing the reviewer to pass into the inner workings of a programme and establish programme re-engineering as the potential goal. So, when it comes to examining any particular youth mentoring programme, the review is primed to focus inquiry on whether it delivers on the four stages and why. I stress again the parallel with conventional empirical inquiry. The realist evaluator might ask that question of a particular scheme; the realist reviewer seeks the evidence across the totality of existing studies.

Note, again, that the process of abstraction is a key aspect of theory-specification. The explanatory terms in the mentoring hypotheses – befriending, confidence-building, coaching and advocacy – operate at a middle level of abstraction. They are concrete enough to be identified in particular primary studies and yet abstract enough that material on them can be uncovered across a medley of case studies. This intermediacy allows the reviewer to test and develop the theories under review and is the key to producing transferable policy lessons.

The first counterpoint to meta-analysis is thus sketched out within the first column of Figure 4.3 as a three-step process of mapping, prioritizing and formalizing a model to be explored in the review. This stage ends with a set of hypotheses that are explanatory, middle-range and interlinked.

Before moving on to the second stage of the realist review, an important aside is in order. I have emphasized the non-linearity of realist synthesis, and the connections with other stages can already be foreshadowed. First of all note that, with these initial decisions on the focus of the review, and with this initial analytic purchase, synthesis has already commenced. Note further, that it is only possible to carve out such a review question *after* a period of hard reading. One can only fix on a model with real potential for learning transferable lessons about policy if one already knows the territory quite well. Accordingly, a good deal of preliminary searching and extraction of materials will have already occurred in shaping up the preliminary model. Note finally, that commissioners have an important role to play here. Simply plumping for an 'explanatory review' is not a sensible alternative to meta-analysis. Rather than commissioners merely handing over an unspecified bundle of questions, and rather than reviewers picking up those sticks with which they feel most comfortable, both parties should work together on this pre-review stage to negotiate and clarify the focus.

Stage two: searching for primary studies

The second stage in a standard systematic review is to seek out studies that will throw light on the question established in stage one. Conventionally, this task has involved hunting down all the primary research examining the relationship between a tightly specified treatment and a narrowly defined outcome in a closely delineated population. As a result, searching is often seen as a relatively mechanical exercise whose sole purpose is to be meticulous and as comprehensive as possible in identifying every single research paper that corresponds to the given specification.

Realist review starts with a more complex question or, as just argued, with a series of interlinked hypotheses. Search procedures are correspondingly more intricate, and locating the apposite evidence is a prolonged task that stretches from spring (before the review question is fully framed) to autumn (when the synthesis is well underway). Put another way, realist synthesis, like any good empirical enquiry, feeds on fresh evidence as it unfolds. Accordingly, it is useful to think of the search strategy for realist review as having four separate components, although even this implies a neatness and linearity not achieved in the hurly-burly of a real paper chase.

A background search

This sizing up of the forthcoming task is no more than a preliminary range-finding exercise, and there are no specific technical tricks or procedural rules to be followed. Thus my profound existential advice is 'just do it'. Rather more helpfully, I might add that it is a good idea to get an information professional involved in order to pick the brains of someone who has knowledge of the spread of potentially useful databases and experience of the nuances of search terms and search techniques. The review of mentoring programmes in Chapter 6 was preceded by such a preliminary scout around in which I learned, to my surprise, that not only were mentoring programmes installed in every walk of life from accountancy to zookeeping but also that there was an industrial-sized literature on each. Hence came the abrupt lesson for the reviewer – draw in horns. There is no correct or incorrect procedure for making such discoveries. The measure of the success of such a scoping search is to enable the reviewer to make an initial judgement on whether the right volume of materials of the right substance is out there to answer the questions the review is likely to pose.

A search to track the programme theories

This search focuses on locating the sources of administrative thinking, policy history, legislative background and key points of contention that lie behind the intervention: to repeat for emphasis, it is *not* a search for evidence about the programmes *per se*. The purpose of such a reconnaissance is to initialize theory-building, to help surface the ideas and aspirations and plans and guidelines that underpin the intervention. In other words, it is a search whose purpose is to help formulate the review question, and thus occurs in parallel with stage one of the review.

As an example, let me return to the vexed question of publicizing league tables of the performance of public bodies such as hospitals and schools. The search for this review uncovered a variety of sources, making different claims about how the measure might work. Amongst other theories, there were those that saw league tables as a market measure (informed consumer choice drives up standards) and others that saw them as an internal regulator (ammunition to pressure poor performers into pulling up socks). Again, there is no formal method for searching out appropriate sources for key ideas, and what most characterizes this phase is the type of material under scrutiny. Programme theories are to be discovered in primary evaluative studies, especially in their 'summary' and 'discussion' phases, but they also feature in the 'no go' areas for traditional reviews – namely, the administrative, legislative and planning documents that accompany interventions and also in the 'think pieces' and critical work that surround them.

The goal is to find solid evidence about the main programme theories that guided the construction of an intervention, and to ensure that that they are 'in play' in accounts of its implementation. This is the rather pragmatic test of whether this phase of the search is adequate. Programme theories, of course, stretch right down into the minutiae of, say, a manager's capacity to lead project staff, but the aim here is to uncover core theories, the investigation of which may yield transferable lessons.

A search for empirical evidence to test the theories

This is in some senses the search proper, in which the reviewer moves on from browsing to shape up ideas, to delving in order to track down apposite evidence on the selected theories from a range of primary studies using a variety of research strategies. The methodological stakes are raised at this point, the goal being to scan the literature as thoroughly as possible.

The purpose of such a search is to find primary studies that will help interrogate the explanatory model about how the programme works. Take the Megan's Law example, which is described in detail in Chapter 5. I have characterized the intervention as having a long implementation chain, and the search thus needs to capture empirical material on each of the key linkages. The model in question (somewhat simplified) says that in order to work properly, the programme has to have: a secure means of identifying high-risk sex offenders; a method of producing and updating accurate registers; a clear channel to notify a community about the release of an offender; a scrupulous surveillance system mounted by the community; and stigmatized offenders with an awareness of heightened risk and decreased opportunities. Finding studies pertinent to each linkage requires subtle changes in conceptual focus and corresponding adjustments in keyword searches. The material sought here, however, is much more like the orthodox empirical evaluations that are the bread and butter of standard reviews.

A final search to fine-tune the synthesis

Once the synthesis is almost complete the reviewer seeks out additional studies to test those further and revised programme theories that often emerge in the course of the review. Realist synthesis is selective in terms of its focus on particular mechanisms and contexts within an intervention, but its understanding of these features is bound to develop in the course of the review. For example, in the review of mentoring programmes (Chapter 6), the spotlight was always on the relative status of mentors and mentees. However, it became apparent only relatively late in the review process that such an angle could be further teased out by examining the unusual configuration of patient support groups for serious illness, in which the mentor is embedded rather more deeply in the (low-status) out-group than is the mentee. Such decisions are clearly not premeditated and, once again, the exercise of judgement is paramount in the extent and the manner in which searches are expanded.

I stress again that this is a very orderly presentation of the prolonged and repetitive agony of locating appropriate primary materials. The most obvious simplification is that a study identified earlier in the sequence (for example, in the theory-building stage) will, in some cases, also pass muster as a useful member of the later samples. The key point is that each of the searches, and all of the samples uncovered, are defined in terms of the use to which they are put. As such, they might be thought of as relatively pragmatic and unpremeditated tasks. However, no criticism is intended in the use of these labels. The logic is that of purposive sampling, aiming to retrieve materials purposively to answer specific questions or test particular theories.

In may be useful to rehearse some of the time-honoured characteristics of such an approach. Purposive sampling is iterative in that it is usually repeated as theoretical understanding develops. In a qualitative case study a researcher may discover the importance of a key actor or group of actors relatively late in the day. They can be approached and given a voice as and when this occurs. In the same way, research synthesis needs some flexibility to allow for supplementary searches that fine-tune a developing line of explanation (Long et al., 2002).

Purposive samples have a progressive focus as understanding unfolds. Ethnographers learn to navigate their way around communities and come to understand the significance of certain events over time. In doing so, they learn that one useful encounter often begets another and that key informants are often a key source of advice on where to proceed. There are parallels with realist synthesis. Search strategies and terms used are likely to evolve as understanding grows. Because useful studies will often make reference to companion pieces that have explored the same ideas, purposive searching makes as much use of 'snowballing' (pursuing references or authors by hand or by means of citation-tracking databases) as it does of conventional database searching using subject keywords. In a recent systematic review (Greenhalgh et al., 2004) conducted along realist lines, the authors took the trouble to chart this balance. They found that 52 per cent of all empirical studies referenced in the final report were identified through snowballing, compared with only 35 per cent through database searching and 6 per cent through hand-searching.

Purposive samples achieve closure through 'theoretical saturation' (Glaser and Strauss, 1967). In qualitative case studies the sampling of actors, events or actions ceases at the point when it seems that it is unlikely to add new knowledge. Realist synthesis is an exercise in identifying, testing out and refining programme theories, and an almost infinite set of studies could be relevant to such a task. Consequently, a decision has to be made, not just about which studies are useful in developing explanations but also about when to stop looking. The same rule of thumb – cease when sufficient evidence has been assembled to satisfy the theoretical need or to answer the question – applies. For instance, in the mentoring review (Chapter 6), scores of enquiries demonstrated the facility of one of the four mechanisms identified, that is to say 'befriending' appears to come relatively easily. The sheer weight of numbers on this score was not particularly useful (and the search for further instances curtailed), the main point of the review being to examine the balance across all four mechanisms.

Note, however, that the principle of theoretical saturation may offer a different and more salutary lesson to the reviewer. In practice, it is rare to find an overabundance of usable primary studies. As soon as an intervention is subdivided into its different processes and components, the search becomes targeted at quite specific theories and it is often difficult to find material that meets the precise specification. At certain points, the process often feels more like scavenging for information than picking the plums from an embarrassment of riches.

As far as the mechanics of searching goes, realist reviewers use bibliographic databases, libraries, the Internet and personal contacts as sources of information, as in conventional systematic review. They also employ the same techniques to extract useful data, including keyword and citation searching of databases, search engine explorations of the Internet, hand-searching of key journals and so forth. There are some different points of emphasis, however, which can be summarized as follows:

- Because it deals with the inner workings of interventions, realist review is much more likely to make use of the administrative and other 'grey literature' rather than relying solely on formal research in the academic journals (and on the databases that cover this material).

- Because it takes on programme theories rather than programmes *per se*, a much wider breadth of empirical studies may be deemed relevant, and these will sometimes be drawn from different bodies of literature in different settings. For example, studies on the public disclosure of performance data by schools will have important lessons for health care organizations and vice versa. Hence, a tight restriction on the sources to be searched, and the keywords to be used in searching, is often inappropriate.

- Because it looks beyond treatments and outcomes to the processes occurring in the 'black box', the keywords chosen to instigate a search are significantly more difficult to fix. As a rough approximation, one can say that in terms of their ability to score definite and useful hits on a bibliographic database, proper nouns (such as Big Brother) outstrip common nouns (such as mentor), which in turn outdo abstract nouns (such as relationship). However, theory-building and testing utilizes these terms in the opposite proportion. Accordingly, if one is trying to locate material on, say, what makes for a good 'match' between 'mentors' and 'mentees' of different 'status', snowballing is likely to be significantly more fruitful than plugging these often imprecise terms into a search screen.

Stage three: quality appraisal

The next, and time-consuming, stage in traditional systematic review involves the quality appraisal of each candidate primary study. The methodological stakes are upped at this point, and the traditional call-to-arms is as follows: if evidence is to have its say, then it should be based on primary studies that have been carried out to the highest methodological standards. Whilst I applaud the underlying sentiment – the commitment to quality – I have spelled out already some of the profound difficulties in applying it. And I argue uambiguously that the hierarchy of evidence descending from biomedical interventions, with RCTs sitting imperiously atop, has to be abandoned.

The evaluation of interventions of interest in realist synthesis (complex systems thrust amidst complex systems) has to draw on complex bodies of evidence, interrogating programmes both in terms of process and outcomes, and delving at their micro-, meso- and macro-levels. Such an evidence base will inevitably draw on the whole repertoire of social science research and the approach to quality appraisal has to be sensitive to the entire range. The ostensible alternative, namely to manufacture quality checklists for every conceivable brand of social research and apply them collectively prior to the synthesis, is also fatally flawed. Thus far it has resulted in quality frameworks that are gargantuan, abstract and permissive (Spencer et al., 2003). They involve a wholesale grilling of the primary inquiries and still fetch up with no more than a considered opinion on quality. The dream of cross-matching hundreds of primary studies with dozens of indulgent appraisal tools, often drawing on more than one yet-to-be-devised checklist per study, will only end in unadulterated nightmare.

The realist solution is to maintain the commitment to the methodological scrutiny of a wide-ranging evidence base but to cut much more directly to the judgement on quality. The guiding principle is the one used throughout, namely, that the appraisal criteria should be subordinate to the usage to which the primary study is put. The reviewer should not attempt to line up and appraise every candidate study on its own terms and as a whole but, rather, appraise the contribution that each one makes to the developing synthesis. That contribution is unlikely to stem from the entirety of a study.

The realist approach to synthesis has at its heart a model of programme theory, but primary studies are very unlikely to have been constructed with an exploration of that particular theory as their *raison d'être*. More probably, they will have been conducted across the multiplicity of banners under which evaluation research and policy analysis are organized. However, in so far as they have a common commitment to understanding an intervention, few of these investigations will have absolutely nothing to say about why programmes work. In the case of qualitative research, for instance, there is a reasonable expectation that key programme theories will get an airing alongside descriptions of everything from stakeholders to implementation hitches. In a quantitative study, there is likely to be emphasis on net outcomes but there may also be discussion of relative success across subgroups and, perhaps, a judgement on the integrity of implementation. Some distillation of this information may provide useful clues on a particular programme theory.

The focus on programme theory raises a completely revised expectation about the nature of research synthesis, namely that evidential fragments or partial lines of inquiry rather than entire studies should be the unit of analysis. In terms of research quality there is a parallel transformation down to the level of the specific proposition. Quality assessment should be review-specific; research appraisal should be theory-driven. Because realist synthesis takes a specific analytic cut through the evidence, it is not a sensible requirement that every clause and every paragraph of every one of the many-sided claims in a cross-disciplinary, multi-method evidence base has to be defensible. What must be warranted, however, are those elements that are eventually put to use in the overall synthesis.

How might this revised expectation be put into practice in the course of realist synthesis? As with the search for primary studies, it is useful to think of quality appraisal as occurring by stages. The reviewer asks, 'is this study good enough to provide *some evidence* that will contribute to the synthesis?' and there are two grounds upon which to deliver an answer, and two crucial moments to do so.

Assessment of relevance

The first decision is to resolve whether a primary study has the appropriate content to add to the review. Is it relevant in the first place? Is it in the right ballpark? Does it connect at all? The preceding discussion of realist search procedures stressed that they, too, are driven by similar questions. The purposive task is to hunt down studies that are relevant to the programme model under scrutiny, and searches typically involve the progressive focusing of keywords and more pronounced usage of snowballing. These techniques alone are insufficient, of course, to ensure that the study identified is indeed fit for the purpose of interrogating the theory under review. One simply cannot take on trust titles, abstracts and secondary discussion. It is necessary to read the material!

This initial scrutiny marks the turn from search to assessment, and the first point of reference is to judge whether the primary research is relevant *at all* to the particular line of inquiry being pursued. Can it even begin to deliver inferences that are useful to the review hypothesis? Once again, there is no exact formula for making such a judgement. Some of these decisions will be relatively broad-brush. Searches on 'youth' and 'mentoring' will fetch up studies in which young people are both providers and recipients of advice and, having done some initial reading to decide which study belongs to which category, the axe will fall according to the slant of the review.

As the synthesis develops, such decisions become much finer-grained. Realist synthesis builds models about how programmes work and the assessment of the relevance of a primary inquiry has to be made against the specific propositions involved. For example, part of the model investigated in reviewing Megan's Law (Chapter 5) was about whether media influence distorts the intended mode and official means of disclosing the identity of the ex-offender to the community. Does 'the news' go beyond the intended message, which stresses the need for surveillance and vigilance but warns against intimidation? The only studies I could find that came near to addressing this issue were about the media's treatment of released sex offenders in general and not specifically about those released under the law. Here, one faces a much tougher call on the relevance of available material.

Appraisal on the grounds of relevance has to proceed case by case and, in general terms, it is likely that there will be a large (and auditable) wastage of primary investigations that have nothing pertinent to say about the review hypotheses. However, the matter of relevance is far from the last hurrah of quality assessment.

Assessment of rigour

There always comes a point in any research synthesis when a proper methodological appraisal is required. The first eligibility hurdle for a primary research study is relevance, but it is also vital that it is trustworthy. The realist approach takes the same line on both relevance and rigour, that is to say, both are subordinate to the overall strategy of the synthesis. Judgements about rigour are made not on the basis of pre-formulated checklists, but in relation to the precise usage of each fragment of evidence within the review.

The notion of explanation-sensitive standards will ring alarm bells in the homogenized world of meta-analysis, but there is nothing alien to scientific inquiry in such a notion. The iterative relationship between theory and data is a feature of all good inquiry. All investigation starts with understanding E_1 and moves on to more nuanced explanations E_2, E_3, ... E_N absorbing and rejecting many different kinds of evidence in the process. There is gradual change in what is sought by way of evidence, and the data have to meet different challenges. Applying this model to research synthesis introduces an alternative primary question for quality appraisal, namely, is it of sufficient quality to help in clarifying the particular explanatory challenge that the synthesis has reached?

The best way to explain this is to picture the synthesis and any particular primary study as two parallel inquiries. Both are investigating the complex systems that are the subject of the review. They will share some common objectives but by no means all. The primary study will bring together a particular suite of evidence to support a particular set of inferences. The synthetic study will not pursue an identical explanatory agenda, so will only use a subset of that initial bloc of evidence to support its own set of inferences. The test of research quality to support such a manoeuvre can only be this: does the primary subset of evidence support the secondary inference?

The synthesis builds by accommodating further primary studies, and the same procedure is followed. Primary study number two will bring together a somewhat different concatenation of evidence to support its unique set of inferences. The synthetic study will not pursue an identical explanatory agenda, so again it will only use a subset of this second tranche of evidence to support its developing set of inferences. And the test of research quality to support such a manoeuvre remains the same: does the new subset of primary evidence support the emerging secondary inference?

For illustration, take an example from the review of youth mentoring (Chapter 6). Two qualitative studies were deemed particularly relevant in testing the 'phasing model', which postulated that engaging disaffected youth requires a mentoring role that progresses from befriending to confidence-building to coaching to advocacy. Study 1 provided evidence of a programme in which the mentor is able to fulfil all of these functions. Study 2 provided evidence in which mentoring fails to proceed beyond the initial, affective domain. Both studies, however, commit a rather common methodological sin in qualitative research in that they over-generalize, implying that theirs is the common fate of all mentoring programmes.

The quality assessment of these two studies concluded that the grand inferences were unwarranted, but that the primary data on the respective success and failure of the two schemes provided a valuable contribution to an overall model seeking out the conditions for successful engagement mentoring. In this example lies a significant and decisively different tenet of research assessment, compared with the standard approach to systematic review. Studies that are technically deficient in some overall sense may, if inspected closely, still provide trustworthy nuggets of information to contribute to the overall synthesis. The attempt to remove bias procedurally (by admitting only one mode of research) is replaced by the goal of safeguarding inferences (by inspecting the precise usage of evidence).

📖 **Supplementary reading** Further analysis of this principle, and of the illustration, may be found in R. Pawson *Digging for nuggets: how 'bad' research may yield 'good' evidence*, which is included in the web page support materials. ✪

Thinking ahead to the review template (Figure 4.3), there is a further timely lesson here about the rhythm of the appraisal exercise. I have argued that there is an inevitable difference in the usage of each primary study in the synthesis. It follows that the test of research quality must be tailored to each specific usage. And from this it follows that the methodological assessment can only be made in and alongside the synthesis. This is a rather radical departure from the running order in the traditional model. Meta-analysis likes to get its quality appraisal over and done as a single exercise. I am suggesting that primary studies be assessed in two different ways at different points in time. There should be an assessment of relevance, following in the tailwind of the search process, but the assessment of research quality has to be part and parcel of the synthesis itself. It should occur there in the text, right alongside the substantive analysis. The worth of a study is determined in the synthesis, and judgements on this score will occur as each study, from first to last, is written into the synthesis. This is how quality assessment is timetabled into Figure 4.3.

Stage four: extracting the data

The next stage in systematic review is its most characteristic. Given that it is generally an uphill, time-consuming slog, it is also the aspect that reviewers most dread. Conventional reviews proceed at this point by lining up primary studies that have made it through the quality filter; fine-tuning the set of characteristics on which to compare them; combing through the studies to extract precisely the same items of information from each; and, finally, recording these data onto a standard extraction form. In the simplest meta-analysis, the information retrieved is relatively sparse, namely information on the modalities of the treatment, its effect size and spread of impact. The extraction form becomes, so to speak, a data matrix from which the overall conclusion on net effects is calculated. In 'mediator and moderator' reviews, a range of additional information is collected from the primary studies about further attributes of participants, settings and interventions. This information is mined in the form of variables, since a data matrix remains the intended product of the exercise. Perhaps more surprisingly, qualitative reviews often conform to this expectation about uniformity of data extraction. A crucial difference, however, is that grid entries take the form of free text, consisting of short verbal descriptions of key features of interventions and studies.

The good news, for anyone who has performed this thankless task, is that the data extraction exercise as described above has no exact equivalent in realist review. The bad news is that the hard labour in question gets transferred to other points in the process. It is perhaps worth re-emphasizing that all research synthesis involves a thorough reading and detailed processing of information from primary studies, with the consequence that after carrying out a couple of reviews many researchers yearn for retirement or a new career.

There are two reasons, quite familiar by now, why realist synthesis has little use for standardized data extraction forms: first, the original sources are used for *quite different* purposes in the course of the review and, second, each source is expected to contribute *quite different* information to the synthesis. Accordingly, realist synthesis has a more elongated model of extracting (or, more accurately, processing) the information from primary sources. The reviewer is not loading uniform bits of information onto the review conveyor belt, but erecting an explanation, and so the amount, detail and form of materials excavated varies through the process. It is useful to think of this close encounter with the primary texts as having three stages and an extended timetable, which is noted in Figure 4.3.

Annotation

First, as discussed above, some primary sources are asked to do no more than provide potentially relevant concepts and theories. If the reviewer is in this theory-tracking mode, documents are scoured for ideas on how an intervention is supposed to work. Here, the extraction of primary materials begins with nothing more profound than marking the relevant passages with a highlighter pen. These are then noted and given an approximate label. Further documents may reveal neighbouring or rival ideas.

These are mentally bracketed together until an initial model is constructed of key aspects of the intervention theories. Take, for example, the process of developing an understanding of how mentors and mentees interact, discussed in detail in Chapter 6. This is a long-term, relatively unplanned exchange and is described, moreover, in hundreds of different ways in the literature. Nevertheless, there are similarities and difference between these pen pictures, and what emerged from immersion in the primary sources was a basic typology differentiating affective, cognitive, aptitudinal and positional mentoring. In summary, when in theory-tracking mode the reviewer is reading primary materials in order to marshal ideas. Ideas are not lodged uniformly through the literature and so realist reviews begin the processing of primary information by note-taking, annotation, conceptualization and abstraction.

Collation

When the review turns to theory-testing mode, the processing of evidence becomes more complex but still operates in purposive mode. Here the reviewer is dealing with empirical studies that have passed the test of relevance. Note is first made of which review hypothesis or hypotheses they address, what claims are made with respect to which theories, and how the apposite evidence is marshalled. Again, processing begins with highlighting and annotating the passages containing the key evidence. These extracts are then pigeon-holed together as being appropriate to the testing of a particular feature of the model under review. Once again, there is no uniform technical trick for creating the appropriate classification. In the Megan's Law example (Chapter 5), the synthesis is conceived in terms of testing out the strength of a long and linked implementation chain. Accordingly, the processing of evidence consists of identifying which bits of data speak to which linkages: which passages of which studies test the 'accuracy of the initial registration of high risk cases' hypotheses; which segments of which research interrogate the 'accurate maintenance of registers' hypothesis; and so on though the half dozen key links in the chain. The retrieval of data is about creating a tracking system to apportion appropriate evidence to the different parts of the overall model, not a task that can be undertaken using the standardized extraction form of the conventional systematic review. In general in explanatory reviews, different bodies of evidence using different modes of inquiry, drawn from different fragments of a primary study, are required to test different parts of the model under review.

Reportage

There is one further feature of data retrieval in realist synthesis that distinguishes it from the standard procedures, and which also takes it on from simple annotation, classification and note-taking. Significant portions of the primary evidence are propelled into the synthesis itself. Synthesis, by realist lights, is all about trying to draw careful inferences from evidence and this requires that vital (and often lengthy) extracts of that evidence have to find their way into the synthesis. Many,

many examples follow in later chapters. The general point made here is that if, say, intervening variables are deemed vital to understanding the working of a programme then the path analysis in which they are uncovered has to be presented in some detail. Alternatively, if the testimony of particular subjects is deemed significant, then summaries of their reasoning should be extracted. The objective is to extract and present enough of the original data to ensure that the reader knows the basis on which inferences are made. The strategy mirrors and supports a previous principle about the value of a study being determined in the synthesis.

Two further aspirations of the realist reading of evidence are worth noting. The first is the attempt to remain true to the difficult principle of transparency. As with any mode of synthesis, there is a tendency to end up with piles of paper on the floor as the reviewer tries to recall which bit of which study speaks to which bit of the developing theory. These heaps will have already survived another ordering in which the reviewer tries to chart whether a source is useful for theory-tracking or theory-testing or both. Just as a conventional review will append a list of studies consulted and then give an indication as to which contributed to the statistical analysis, so too a realist review should trace the usage and non-usage of primary materials. However, the archaeology of decision-making is more complex and thus harder to track in an explanatory synthesis. One is inspecting multiple theories, and specific studies may interrogate none, one, more, or all of them. Nevertheless, as realist synthesis moves beyond a developmental stage, reviewers should expect to develop a record of the different ways in which studies have been used (and omitted).

A second point is to recall that the steps involved in realist review are not in fact linear; studies are returned to time and again and processing occurs all the way down the line. Note in particular that there always comes an unspoken point in the sifting and sorting of primary materials where one changes from model-building to model-testing and from theory-construction to theory-refinement. The reviewer experiences a shift from divergent to convergent thinking as ideas begin to take shape and the theories underpinning the intervention gain clarity. Accounts of systematic review which insist on its reproducible and thus mechanical nature are being economical with the truth in not recognizing this ineffable point of transformation and defining feature of good scientific inquiry.

Stage five: 'synthesizing the data'

The defining moment, the point of it all, has now been reached, namely, the act of synthesis. I have already signalled a major difference in underlying philosophy: realist review eschews the notion of delivering summative verdicts and, instead, perceives the task of synthesis as one of refining theory. Interventions are theories employing highly complex, non-linear sets of ideas that envisage different roles for individuals, teams, institutions and structures. Realist synthesis inhabits the real world of policy formation in which decision-makers know that, in attempting to prompt change, programmes operate through highly elaborate implementation processes, passing through many hands and unfolding over time. Realist review starts with a preliminary understanding of such processes, which it seeks to refine by bringing empirical evidence to bear on the various highways and byways of the initial theory map. It begins with theory and ends with – hopefully – more refined theory. What is achieved in this signature stage of the review is fine-tuning of the reviewer's understanding of an intervention and so 'synthesis', by these lights, refers to making progress in explanation.

Such an explanatory quest is inevitably complex. Gains may be sought on a number of fronts. The act of synthesis may carry a range of objectives and the initial task in this section is to spell these out. Recall, first of all, that the diversification of potential goals stems from the realist understanding of causality. Realism eschews the mechanical model of cause and effect, replacing it with a configurational puzzle. The traditional 'does it work?' question transforms instantly into at least five different lines of inquiry: *what* is it about this kind of intervention that works, for *whom*, in what *circumstances*, in what *respects* and *why*? The why? question remains paramount in any realist synthesis, of course, and there is no expectation that every aspect of every other theme can be covered. For instance, a 'for whom' synthesis may lean towards questions about the optimal targeting of an intervention. The review would consist of a close inspection of the evidence on the inner workings of an intervention and this would be married to the available data on the pattern of beneficiaries. Sustainability might be the trigger issue for an 'in what respects' review, in which evidence would be marshalled on implementation and the long-term pattern of outputs and outcomes.

A further glimpse of the scope of realist synthesis was offered in Table 4.2, labelled a compendium of explanatory tasks, and which was itself drawn from Figure 2.7, a diagram in Chapter 2 that reveals the complex anatomy of social interventions. These summaries sketch out the broad landscape of realist explanation, the point being that synthesis cannot capture everything about everything. It must make a choice on where to focus its efforts. Freedom from the unanswerable 'does it work?' question can lead realist synthesis to some quite unusual and yet perfectly salient issues from the compendium. There is no reason, for example, why realist synthesis cannot address the ubiquitous question about the need for 'joined-up thinking' on modern interventions. Many, many services are delivered by multiple agencies and it should be possible to produce a theory about the optimal arrangements by reviewing material on joint working arrangements. And at the outer limits, what about this one? Since no family of interventions has ever failed to generate perverse consequences, would it not be possible to review the collected mishaps and seek to discover whether unintended effects are, to some degree, predictable!

This clamour of potential focal points is daunting and will, no doubt, be anathema to the 'one question, one answer' school of systematic review. At the risk of imposing a straitjacket on a research strategy in its development stage, these doubts may be assuaged by identifying some of the more characteristic issues on which realist synthesis settles.

Synthesis to question programme theory integrity

This approach to synthesis aims to discover the typical weak points and major stumbling blocks in the implementation of the interventions under review. It addresses the issues represented in Figures 2.2 and 2.3 in Chapter 2, namely that implementation chains are often long, thickly populated and reliant on the actions of many different stakeholders. In such cases, as the theories-of-change literature suggests, programmes are only as strong as their weakest link. Using primary studies to identify data on each linkage is thus a powerful analytic strategy, and the nature of synthesis bears precisely upon the breaking strength of the overall apparatus. The review of Megan's Law in the next chapter follows this strategy and discovers some vital points of strain.

Synthesis to adjudicate between rival programme theories

Although realist review stresses that interventions are theories incarnate, there is often dispute about precisely how they work. This state of affairs should come as no surprise because programmes are often based on simple, and thus contestable, theories about human nature. To achieve longevity, programmes need broad appeal and thus usually have the capacity to accommodate different ideologies. In such circumstances, a realist synthesis interrogates the evidence in order to adjudicate between rival theories of how interventions work. Marshall et al.'s (2000) review of hospital rankings and report cards is a good example. This focused on whether such public disclosure impacted on hospitals through consumer choice, purchasing decisions, enhanced regulation or practitioner shaming. The notion of synthesis as arbitration can clearly be seen in one of its telling conclusions: 'currently available report cards are rarely read by individual consumers or purchasers of care and, even if accessed, have little influence on purchasing decisions'.

Synthesis to consider the same theory in comparative settings

This approach to synthesis assumes that particular programme theories work in some settings and not others, and aims to make sense of the patterns of winners and losers. In many ways it is the quintessential realist strategy in that it focuses on contextual constraints on the action of programme mechanisms. It also allows for some out-of-the-box policy learning, in that such hypotheses are likely to lead the reviewer across policy domains and responsibilities. Policy ideas are frequently borrowed in the corridors of power and, as new problems crop up, old ideas are dusted down in devising potential solutions. A worked example explored in Chapter 7 looks at one such ubiquitous policy in the form of public disclosure, or 'naming and shaming'. To emphasize the point again, the intention is not to reinstate the verdict business, pronouncing that public disclosure programmes work in sector X but not in agency Y. The goal is to produce a general theory of the conditions that support and hinder the programme theory.

Synthesis to compare official expectations with actual practice

This approach to synthesis aims to compare the 'official' intervention theory and what goes on in practice. It is a particularly useful framework for analysis if the intervention under review has a clear legislative or regulatory foundation. Criminal justice programmes often carry such a birthright, and this analytic strategy is used to supplement the 'implementation chain' synthesis carried out in the Megan's Law example in Chapter 5. The theory to be tested is drawn quite directly from the legislative documents and mission statements underpinning the law. Note, incidentally, that this 'formal theory versus informal practice' motif is a characteristic of many primary studies, for example, investigations of service delivery in health and care settings (Shaw et al., 2004). Thus raw materials for this style of review are often plentiful.

This elaboration of the choice of analytic framework returns us to the well-worn theme about the elongation of the traditional stages in a review. The selection of one or other of the above explanatory motifs occurs in the foundation stages of a review: synthesis is not just a wrapping-up operation and its major theme has to infuse the whole process. Whilst reviewers are still considering priorities, when they are busy tracking down and annotating programme theories, they will have at the back of their minds some of these major analytic frameworks (a point reinforced in Figure 4.3).

So much for goals – what of the deed itself? The dominant activity at this stage must have at its core a practical means of handling each piece of evidence and bringing them together for the purpose of theory-testing and refinement. The technical process of realist synthesis is illustrated in Figure 4.2. The raw materials of this process are explanatory propositions and explanatory inferences, and the preliminary theory to be tested is depicted at the top of the figure. This initial model (the great circle) is itself a set of propositions explaining in abstract terms how certain key aspects of an intervention work. Each primary study is then inspected for evidence, according to how it supports, weakens, modifies, supplements, reinterprets or refocuses the preliminary theory. This process is depicted in the second stage of the figure, as the gathering of smaller circles around the main explanation. These are spread around the explanatory whole in order to show that primary inquiries are quite likely to impact on only a portion of the working model. The smaller and large circles intersect as a simple representation of the idea that only a portion of the evidence marshalled in a primary study is likely to be relevant to the synthetic explanation. Three of the primary studies overlap in order to illustrate that the synthesis may also involve squaring one instance with another. Synthesis, in other words, is not a simple, one-study-at-a-time process. The absorption of primary materials will also require attention to their sometimes contradictory and sometimes complementary evidence.

The dynamics of synthesis itself are represented in the third section of the figure. Adaptive theory is the product of realist synthesis and this gradual transformation in understanding the intervention is depicted as a movement from an initial to a revised model. The shift in explanatory power is mimicked by the changes in the shaded silhouette from perfect to battle-worn circle. There is no uniform mode of adaptation on each encounter with empirical material, and it is not a case of thumbs up or thumbs down for the explanatory model. In order to describe the

Initial explanation: the basic model

Encounters with primary studies

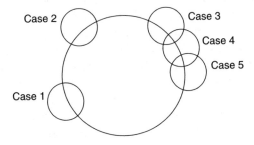

Synthesis: revised explanation

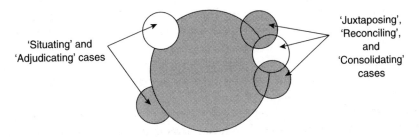

FIGURE 4.2   *Synthesis as 'accumulating explanation'*

practice of synthesis, it is useful to return to the domain principles announced at the start of this chapter. Evidence speaks to theory in contradistinctive tones, and in moving from case to case, reviewers are involved in juxtaposing, adjudicating, reconciling, consolidating and situating the evidence.

The reviews presented in the next three chapters will resonate with such reasoning, but let us follow a couple of illustrations schematically, as in Figure 4.2. Cases 1 and 2 represent primary studies in the mentoring review that is described in detail in Chapter 6. This begins with a model anticipating severe difficulties for an individual mentor in trying to provide support in the affective, cognitive, aptitudinal and positional domains. Case 1 says otherwise and provides qualitative case history materials of very successful growth through these stages. The review does not collapse in a heap at this news but absorbs the evidence by paying special attention to the contextual conditions pertaining in the case. In other words, it *situates* the data. It uses information on the characters and communities involved to better specify the model in respect of for whom and in what circumstances the programme works. This growth in understanding is represented in the lower portion of Figure 4.2, which bulges at this point in recognition of a significant addendum to the model.

Case 2 in this particular review also involves qualitative case histories and presents evidence showing that mentoring fails to get beyond the affective domain. Indeed, the author claims that success in befriending actually negates progress in orthodox education and career terms. Once again, the findings are absorbed into the review by noting the personal and institutional conditions pertaining in this particular programme, which in terms of the emerging synthesis take a bite out of the overall understanding of contextual contingencies.

Also evident in these two cases is another key synthetic manoeuvre, namely that of adjudicating between studies. Alongside synthesis comes quality appraisal and, as noted earlier, such assessment is part of the synthesis. Both studies were considered to fall foul of a common error in qualitative research, namely that of reaching a gross verdict on youth mentoring on the basis of highly specific samples. Their overall glosses on youth mentoring (enthusiastically positive and utterly negative) are brought into balance (via the bites and bulges) in the developing model.

Cases 3, 4 and 5 in the figure represent another sequence of synthetic reasoning. This illustration will be treated in depth in Chapter 5 on Megan's Law but, for the present, we commence with Case 4. This trial shows that matched samples of offenders, released before and after the enactment of the law, reoffend at the same rate. This disappointing evidence creates a sizeable but unexplained bite out of the programme theory about how the law will provide increased protection for communities. However, the same study also shows that arrest rates quicken after the introduction of the law, hinting at the paradoxical outcome that the programme improves the detection rather than the deterrence of repeat offences. This revised explanation is hardened by Case 3 (which shows that that the opportunity for the preventative surveillance of a sex crime is remarkably low) and by Case 5 (which maps out the upgrading of probation and police record-keeping as a result of the law). After consideration of three cases, there is a developing, adaptive theory that what actually happens with the enactment of the law is improvement in the classic apparatus of locating and hunting down suspects. Methodologically speaking, whole tranches of evidence are being juxtaposed, reconciled and consolidated – and this is synthesis laid bare.

It remains to locate this revised understanding of the act of synthesis into the overall template in Figure 4.3. Looking down the fifth column, one sees that synthesis begins early by establishing an overall theme, by devising a particular explanatory model of the programme in question. Thereafter, synthesis is the act of spelling out the current state-of-play of the model upon each encounter with a primary study, and this is reflected in the way the synthesis is presented. Studies are written up as a consideration of the model in the light of each empirical interrogation. The lessons learned are not singular and discrete, as illustrated by the combined usage of evidence above from Cases 3, 4 and 5. Accordingly, by the time the mid-synthesis stage is reached, the presentation must also convey how successive suites of primary material have been absorbed into the evolving model, and this developmental analysis in evoked in the figure.

Finally, the synthesis reaches a resting point and this will consist of an abstract summary of how the model has been revised across the whole empirical piece. The Megan's Law review concludes with a summary of the entire implementation chain and an assessment of the breaking strength of the overall apparatus. The mentoring review builds a model of the totality of relationships that must be present for long-move, engagement mentoring to succeed. The public disclosure review constructs a theory of the key contextual conditions that need to be present in order to attempt to name and shame.

Throughout the fine-tuning of the model, every adjustment in reasoning must be evident within the presentation of the review. Realist synthesis heeds the advice of the maths teacher to always 'show your working'. This little motto is reinforced if one reads across the template in Figure 4.3. The key act of synthesis is described as 'absorbing primary materials into developing synthesis'. In order to do this transparently, reviewers have to justify the inferential shifts to the reader and, to do so, they must provide an intelligible account of the original empirical material and a justification of why it can be relied upon to warrant the inference made. In other words, key aspects of data extraction and quality appraisal are carried out in harness with synthesis.

Stage six: disseminating the findings

The act of synthesis may be the *coup de grâce* in research terms, but the ultimate finishing blow has to be delivered in the policy arena. Judgement on the big issue of whether the findings of systematic review can deliver decisive policy thrusts, or whether they are bound to remain pin-pricks, is delayed until the final chapter. Here, the focus is on the mechanics of dissemination. Contemporary accounts (Walter et al., 2003) stress that, for research to be properly utilized, this concluding stage should go well beyond the submission of a final report to the commissioner. The situation in which the systematic review jury retired for several months and appeared with a verdict many steps removed from the real world of policy is becoming less common, and two important changes for the better are in hand.

The first is for commissioners of reviews to be much more closely involved in the production of the research synthesis, a state of play that Lomas (2000) has called linkage. Researchers can only address themselves to a question, and decision-makers can only find pertinence in the answer, if that question has been adequately honed and left without major ambiguity. The second form of redemption is for reviewers to bring their technical expertise closer to the policy issue in question. Research synthesis needs to be able to locate recommendations in relation to the policy options on the table, and this objective is supported if the research takes cognizance of the practical needs of a range of stakeholders in the shaping of an intervention. Both requirements place a premium on avoiding overly technical language in dissemination, cutting instead to the quick and using the parlance of decision-making.

Realist synthesis is comfortable with both of these innovations. Indeed, it raises the status of linkage from a recommendation to a methodological requirement. Realist synthesis is theory-driven. The tasks of identifying the review question, articulating key theories to be explored and choosing an overall analytic theme cannot occur meaningfully in the absence of input from practitioners and policy-makers, because it is *their* questions and *their* assumptions about how interventions work that form the focus of analysis.

Similarly, and by its very nature, realist synthesis is well placed to meet the second desideratum. It eschews the notion that reviews deal in political arithmetic and it operates automatically with the cautious and contextualized grammar of policy discourse. Realist reviews deliver models, which in policy terms are not the end but the beginning of the story. They initiate a process of thinking through the tortuous pathways along which a successful programme has to travel, and their conclusions take the form of reflections on how to navigate some significant highways and byways. Accordingly, what the recommendations describe are a series of key decision points through which an initiative has proceeded, and the findings are put to use in alerting the policy community to the caveats and considerations that should inform those decisions. For each decision point, a realist synthesis should be able to proffer the following kind of advice: 'remember A'; 'beware of B'; 'take care of C'; 'D can result in both E and F'; 'Gs and Hs are likely to interpret I quite differently'; 'if you try J make sure that K, L and M have also been considered'; 'N's effect tends to be short lived'; 'O really has quite different components – P, Q and R'; and 'S works perfectly well in T but poorly for U' The review, inevitably, will also reflect that, 'little is known about V, W, X, Y and Z'.

Only time (and perhaps Chapter 8) will tell whether such a strategy may find favour in the policy community. There is, however, a strong rationale for why this middle level of abstraction might prove the most useful. Chapter 3's critique of the standard model of systematic review warns of the perils of over-confidence. Trying to offer decision-makers concrete verdicts on whole families of interventions can only produce simplistic advice, which is usually inaccurate to boot. Chapter 2 warns of the untold levels of complexity that lurk in any policy question, but there is little utility in describing to decision-makers the thousandfold reasons why they cannot make a decision. The solution described in this chapter shows how realist synthesis can take some strategic cuts through the implementation swamp. It does not take on the full A-to-Z of programme complexity but concentrates on a subset of the lexicon. The four priority themes described in the previous section (analysis of weakest links, rival explanations, rival targets and departure from official expectations) provide feasible and modest goals for evidence-based policy. Prioritizing specific programme theories in research synthesis delivers a further dividend, moreover, in that it allows policy-makers to insert a priority of their own into the basic designs – namely, that realist synthesis should concentrate on the policy levers that can actually be pulled.

It remains to place these ideas on dissemination and utilization onto the realist review timetable. When should the liaison between reviewers and decision-makers occur? The popular and growing recommendation is that they should hold hands throughout the review. However, this prospect is usually somewhat unrealistic and the tryst is surely best located at the beginning and end of the process. In practice, this means the commissioner coming to the reviewer with a broad list of questions about an intervention. The reviewer questions the questions, and suggests further angles that have resonated through the existing literature. Then there is more negotiation and, eventually, a firm agreement about which particular lines of inquiry to follow. This process is thus assigned to the template in Figure 4.3 alongside other preliminary steps involved in navigating through the initial conceptual swamp.

As well as this initial meeting of minds, realist synthesis also anticipates that the review itself will partly reorder expectations about what is important. Realist thinking on unintended consequences must also be applied reflexively. This means that room for further rounds of negotiation must be left open about whether, say, an unforeseen chink in the implementation chain deserves closer inspection. When and how often these adjustments should take place is itself a matter for negotiation, but for illustrative purposes one such reorientation period is depicted on the template. Note, however, that at several intermediate points there are long periods when reviewers should be left to their own devices. They should, for example, be able to apply their expertise on matters such as the methodological rigour and relevance of the primary research materials.

The final, and by definition still most crucial, act of dissemination occurs with the propagation of the findings of the review and this is marked at the terminus of the time and task dimensions in Figure 4.3. Realist synthesis has the traditional role of providing an independent and dispassionate overview of an intervention through the existing research. Conclusions and recommendations have to reflect this objective and this standpoint. However, the end product is a more refined theory rather than a final theory. The progress made in a realist review is not one from ignorance to answer, but from some knowledge to some more knowledge. As a result, extraordinary care must be taken at the point where findings are transformed into recommendations, and close liaison with decision-makers is once again required in thrashing these out.

The intended outcome of the dissemination process, as with all systematic review, is that those on the ground take note of the findings and implement them. In the case of meta-analysis, such changes might be monitored in terms of simple behaviour changes in the direction of particular recommendations (for example, are clinicians prescribing therapy X for condition Y?). However, implementation of the findings of a realist review is a complex process involving multiple actors, multiple processes and multiple levels of analysis. Furthermore, implementation is not a question of everyone stopping doing A and starting to do B. Rather, it may involve subtle shifts of emphasis in a programme in one setting, expansion of that programme as it stands in another setting, and the withdrawal of exactly the 'same' programme in a third setting. Quite different decisions may flow as more informed judgements are made about what works, for whom, how, in what circumstances and in what respects. The ultimate goal is that individuals, teams and organizations take account of all the complex and inter-related elements of the programme theory that have been exposed by the review and apply these to their particular local contexts and implementation practices.

Conclusion

The conclusion to the chapter is, of course, the long-awaited Figure 4.3, which sets out an agenda and a timetable for realist synthesis. All systematic reviews start with a question and end with an answer, but the sequence and tempo of the intermediate steps – as well as the nature of the answer – are different in realist synthesis.

The figure attempts to summarize the entire apparatus of a synthesis but it is important, however, to clarify some expectations about the template. In trying to set down research designs, the methodologist always confronts the twin perils of over-simplification and over-prescription.

Hectic as it is, Figure 4.3 is still an over-simplification. I have stressed all along that realist synthesis is an iterative process, and that throughout the mission the reviewer has to make judgements on where next to turn. This means that the 'time' and 'task' locations on the template are approximate. Realist synthesis has to be able to respond to new data and to new ideas, and no one can say precisely when a new lead will surface and where it will take the review. In short, a maze of feedback loops and repetitions will be encountered in bringing a real realist synthesis to completion. By and large these are not depicted on the figure. The willingness to acknowledge such thinking on one's feet as an integral part of the design will be disconcerting to many in the review community who regard procedural uniformity as the be all and end all. My view is that such pauses for thought occur in all reviews and their suppression in the classic protocols is 'brutishly destructive of some of the most important aspects of research and scholarship' (MacLure, 2005).

Because it is so hectic Figure 4.3 is also over-prescriptive. I have this little nightmare of the tyro researcher trying to conduct a realist review by working through this chapter, navigating across the template and fretting, 'well, it must be time to be getting on with stage four, phase three'. Such ritualism would be a mistake, and a sign that this book has failed, for what I am trying to describe is not some esoteric ceremony in which the routines must be exact for the magic to work. The core is quite simple. Programmes are theories about how to change behaviour. Primary research provides evidence on the utility of those theories. Systematic review draws together that evidence in order to refine the theories. If the reviewer keeps the spirit of this little sequence of postulates in mind, then many of the practical steps on the way will follow automatically.

Tasks →

1 Identifying the review question	2 Searching for primary studies	3 Quality appraisal	4 Extracting the data	5 Synthesizing the data	6 Disseminating the findings
Map key programme theories	Background familiarization search				
Prioritize key theories for investigation	Search for sources of programme theory		Annotation, note-taking on candidate theories	Prime focus of synthesis selected and formalized	Negotiation with decision-makers on analytic and policy focus
Formalize model of subset of hypotheses to be tested	Search for empirical studies to test model	Assessment of relevance of primary inquiry to inform model	Collation of materials from selected primary studies		
		Assessment of rigour of primary data to test theory	Detailed reportage of evidence from each case study	Absorbing primary materials into developing synthesis	
	Search for further empirical studies consequent on revisions to model	Further assessment of rigour as each study enters the synthesis	Differential reportage of evidence from each case study	Juxtaposing, adjudicating, reconciling, consolidating and situating further evidence	Consultation on which emerging lines of inquiry should be followed
				Revised model of the complex and inter-related elements of programme theory	Summary theory to initiate process of 'thinking through' future implementation decisions

Time

FIGURE 4.3   *A task-and-time template for realist synthesis*

This is not to say, of course, that there is no point in formalizing the method. Quite the contrary; it is vital to do so because the ability to 'rationally reconstruct' method lies at the heart of any claim to be scientific (Popper, 1972). All of the steps in this chapter describe a 'logic of discovery', and to defend the conclusions of a synthesis is, in the last analysis, to be able to defend that logic. The strategy described in Figure 4.3 is thus not only a research design but a repository of all the previous arguments about the nature of social interventions and realist explanation. Doing realist synthesis is not just a question of following the above logic but of fashioning the very text of the review in terms of that logic. This returns us to the venerable principle of transparency, although in the case of realist synthesis one is transparent about explanatory processes that other methods cannot reach. This thought provides the last word of advice on how to conduct and how to write a realist review. Above all else, what must remain clear is the process of theory-building and refinement.

5

Reviewing Implementation Processes:
Megan's Law

From now on, every state in the country will be required by law to tell a community when a dangerous sexual predator enters its midst. We respect people's rights, but today America proclaims there is no greater right than a parent's right to raise a child in safety and love. Today America warns: If you dare to prey on our children, the law will follow you wherever you go, state to state, town to town. Today, America circles the wagons around our children. Megan's Law will protect tens of millions of families from the dread of what they do not know. It will give peace of mind to our parents. (Levi, 2000: 582, quoting remarks by President Clinton (1996) in the Bill signing ceremony for Megan's Law)

This chapter is the first of three providing detailed, practical illustrations of realist synthesis. This review is an attempt to see if the evidence base can make itself heard in one of the most emotionally and politically charged areas of public policy, the US sex offender registration and community notification programmes. These interventions have quite a long history and in their present form have been harnessed via several pieces of federal legislation including the 1994 Jacob Wetterling Crimes Against Children and Sexually Violent Offender Registration Act, the 1996 Pam Lychner Sexual Offender Tracking and Identification Act, and the 1996 President's Directive. However, the great moral driving force behind the legislation was Megan's Law in 1996. Megan Kanka was raped and killed by Jesse Timmendequas, one of three released sex offenders who, unbeknown to her parents, lived in their neighbourhood. Within months, following an enormous public outcry, New Jersey passed emergency legislation for a mandatory community notification system for convicted sex offenders. Within a very short number of years the other 49 US states had all followed suit.

It is a programme that continues to be implemented in a policy hot-bed, and the review attempts a cool look at the evidence in order to review to what extent and in what respects and in what circumstances it has worked. The example is chosen for a range of methodological reasons. First is the nature of the evidence base, which is lopsided, disparate and contested. There has been an avalanche of commentary on dealing with sex offenders in the 'plague or panic' genre, but only two quasi-experimental studies offering estimates of effectiveness. Accordingly, there is insufficient material to conduct a meta-analytic review, especially as these two studies are decidedly inconclusive. Nevertheless, there is copious material of quite different methodological provenance that does permit a rigorous analysis.

Megan's Law is also chosen on grounds much rehearsed in the previous chapter. It is a classically complex intervention that traces a long implementation path and passes through many hands in doing so. It is, moreover, a prime example of the mutating specimens that emerge from the laboratory of public policy that is the US federal system. The legislation passed into the statute books in 50 different ways, each state making slightly different decisions on the practical details. Megan's Law is, in short, a complex system thrust amidst an existing complex system, and requires the reviewer to prioritize ruthlessly in establishing a focus for the synthesis. Accordingly, the review takes on two of the motifs described in the previous chapter. The programme theory is articulated in the form of a theories-of-change sequence chain (Connell et al., 1995) represented in Figure 5.1, which maps the intended course of the intervention through its initial, intermediate and ultimate aims. The review strategy is to examine the integrity of the overall sequence. Studies pinpointing each phase are probed for weak points and stumbling blocks in the implementation of the law.

FIGURE 5.1   *Reviewing the implementation process*

This way of framing the review question also evokes another element of the realist approach to synthesis, in that it aims to compare the 'official' intervention theory with what goes on in practice. Thus the theory for this review is drawn directly from legislative documents and mission statements underpinning the law.

A final foreword should also be noted. Reviews, by their very nature, aim to be exhaustive, and a truly comprehensive review cannot be accomplished at chapter length. The following is a summary of a 60-page original and concentrates on explicating the review theory and analysis using a limited number of primary studies. It is basically an account of stage one and stage five in realist synthesis, as laid out in Chapter 4, and much detail on the original sources as well as on their selection and quality assessment is lost in this synopsis.

📖 **Supplementary reading** Readers interested in the 'full' review should consult R. Pawson *Does Megan's Law work: a theory driven systematic review* which is included in the web page support materials. 🕮

The 'theory' of Megan's Law

A wide variety of information sources was used in surfacing and articulating the programme theory of Megan's Law:

- procedural guidelines on the enactment and enforcement of the sex offender registration laws, produced both at federal and state level
- commentaries and opinions in the *Law Reviews* of the major US law schools
- official notification bulletins used to identify specific offenders
- publications of key agencies such as the National Institute of Justice (NIJ) and the Center for Sex Offender Management (CSOM)

The theory of Megan's Law obtained from these documents, formulated in a manner that acts as the review hypothesis, is summarized in Figure 5.2.

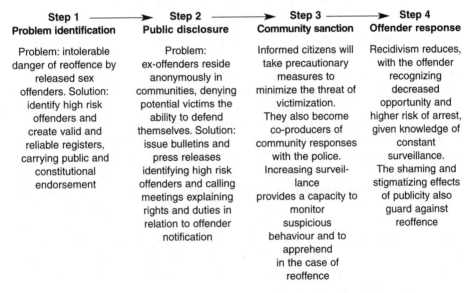

Step 1 **Problem identification**	**Step 2** **Public disclosure**	**Step 3** **Community sanction**	**Step 4** **Offender response**
Problem: intolerable danger of reoffence by released sex offenders. Solution: identify high risk offenders and create valid and reliable registers, carrying public and constitutional endorsement	Problem: ex-offenders reside anonymously in communities, denying potential victims the ability to defend themselves. Solution: issue bulletins and press releases identifying high risk offenders and calling meetings explaining rights and duties in relation to offender notification	Informed citizens will take precautionary measures to minimize the threat of victimization. They also become co-producers of community responses with the police. Increasing surveillance provides a capacity to monitor suspicious behaviour and to apprehend in the case of reoffence	Recidivism reduces, with the offender recognizing decreased opportunity and higher risk of arrest, given knowledge of constant surveillance. The shaming and stigmatizing effects of publicity also guard against reoffence

FIGURE 5.2   *Megan's Law: basic programme theory*

Step one: problem identification

Creating registers of potentially dangerous sex offenders about to be released from prison is far more than an administrative preliminary to the task of protecting the community. One of the major theories driving the registration process is that of risk to the public. Megan's Law assumes that there is a group of released offenders who are beyond treatment and are to be considered permanently dangerous. It also assumes that registration is capable of identifying this minority based on a 'statutory definition of the sexually violent predator' (Poole and Lieb, 1995). Implementation of this first theory is unlikely to be easy, with the New Jersey Attorney General's guidelines giving an example of the kind of tricky distinctions the law has in mind:

> If, for example, one is dealing with a compulsive exhibitionist, although there might be a high likelihood of recidivism, the offense itself is considered a nuisance offense. Hence the offender's risk to the community would be considered low,

consistent with the low legal penalties associated with such offenses. Conversely, with a violent offender who has a history of substantial victim harm, even a relatively low likelihood of recidivism may result in a moderate or high risk to the community given the seriousness of reoffense. (Whitman and Farmer, 2000: Exhibit E: 2)

This gives a first indication of some of the technical complexities with which risk classification has to deal. Not only have there to be some clear definitions of what constitutes the high risk offender, there also have to be reliable and valid operational procedures to put them into practice in appraising each offender. In addition there are practical steps to be undertaken to ensure that the process is efficient, and that all high risk cases are entered and maintained on the register.

Step two: public disclosure

Step two of the programme theory is the bridging point at which registration information is disclosed, prior to the public becoming involved in the management of high risk offenders. The first objective of public notification is a continuation of the risk theory identified at step one. The assessment of risk has to be articulated and explained to the public through a high fidelity communication process that warns of the threat posed by high risk offenders. The message 'should reach the widest possible audience in the least amount of time'; it 'should give community members concrete information about the offender'; it 'should ensure that all vulnerable citizens have been reached'; and so on (CSOM, 2001: 8). However, there is also a qualitative aspect to such communication. Part of the challenge is to summon nascent moral condemnation of sex offenders, and to channel it appropriately. Thus notification procedures also tend to have a public information and education function. For example, in the extract from a notification bulletin reproduced by Matson and Lieb (1996b: 22):

THIS NOTIFICATION IS NOT INTENTED TO INCREASE FEAR, RATHER IT IS OUR BELIEF THAT AN INFORMED PUBLIC IS A SAFER PUBLIC

In case readers should mistake the bulletin for a 'wanted poster', they are also told firmly:

HE IS NOT WANTED BY THE POLICE AT THIS TIME

The bulletin anticipates some unintended consequences of the stir of emotions caused by such publicity, and warns that 'Citizen abuse of this information to threaten, intimidate or harass registered sex offenders will not be tolerated'. Many policy-makers in the area also stress that notification is a key moment for public education (CSOM, 2001: 15).

Step three: community sanction

Step three concerns expectations about the safeguards and sanctions that are envisaged as a result of notification orders. At one level, the programme theory is based on simple avoidance of danger: 'by informing the public about the presence of a sex offender in the community, neighbors will be able to protect themselves from sex offenders by keeping themselves – and their children – out of harm's way' (NIJ, 1997). In general, however, the public and police are seen as active co-producers of measures against released offenders, working together to prevent what are often concealed and infrequent offences. The most basic intended consequence of notification is to open eyes. Police surveillance can be much expanded through informal public scrutiny, or as Bedarf (1995) puts it, '... under hundreds of watchful eyes it is more difficult for a sex offender to escape into anonymity'. In addition, citizens are given powers to inform upon and raise doubts about subjects, adding yet another defensive layer (NIJ, 1997).

If the defences are breached and reoffence occurs then notification is expected to perform a rather different role: 'if a sex offence is committed and no suspect is located, the registry can be used to identify potential suspects who live in the area, or who have a similar pattern of crime' (Matson and Lieb, 1996a). It is also anticipated that notification data can assist further down the line in police action. Alabama state law puts it thus: 'the lack of information shared with the public may result in the failure of the criminal justice system to identify, investigate, apprehend and prosecute criminal sex offenders' (CSOM, 1999).

Step four: offender response

In the final step of the Megan's Law programme theory a diverse reaction is expected, based on varying degrees of rational calculation and self-reflection on the part of individuals. Situational crime prevention attempts to imbue the potential offender with knowledge of the increased risk of being caught, and the increased effort needed to continue with the offending behaviour. Both notions can be found in the Megan's Law literature. For example, 'it is believed that such laws will reduce the likelihood that the sexual offender will reoffend because everyone will know of his past, and because of this, he will have a more difficult time luring his potential victims' (Freeman-Longo, 1996).

Notification is also said to provide an incentive for offenders to admit to crimes and show improvement under treatment in order to demonstrate that they no longer deserve the highest levels of notification ('acceptance of guilt' is taken as a classic sign of rehabilitation). The same mechanism can be invoked against released offenders at lower levels of notification: 'The threat of [full] community disclosure is the greatest contribution of notification as a tool for managing sex offenders in the community' (English et al., 1996). Another psychological theory argues that a brush with Megan's Law will have a far more direct consequence: 'there is much reason to think such offenders will suffer a hard psychic blow regardless of the setting in which they are exposed. The fact that one's sexual activities have been exposed has a way of lodging itself inescapably in one's consciousness' (Whitman, 1998: 1065).

The final potential action of the programme on the offender is neither prevention, nor cure, but arrest. It is assumed that in some, perhaps very few, cases the offender cannot be deterred (Presser and Gunnison, 1999: 303). In such instances, it is expected that the information trail created by Megan's Law will make re-arrest and reconviction more likely.

Synthesizing the evidence

The above constitutes the basic 'theory' of Megan's Law as seen through the eyes of its key architects. Programme theories are always contested and it would be perfectly possible to provide an alternative to the 'official line', which hypothesizes the ways in which Megan's Law mis-identifies offenders, mis-communicates risk, mis-applies sanctions and mis-controls recidivists. Indeed, as implementation has unrolled in the 50 states, much of it has been concerned to iron out unintended effects (CSOM, 2001). There is, however, no need to spell out these alternative paradigms, for this is neither a philosophical nor an ethical inquiry about the nature of sex offending. This is a review of what happens to Megan's Law in practice rather than on paper.

As will become immediately obvious, the following does not resemble a Cochrane or Campbell review. There is no data extraction form, no attempt to assess each study against a hierarchy of evidence, and no attempt at statistical aggregation. There have been only two outcome trials of Megan's Law, and so evidence is culled from very diverse sources, including administrative, legal and educational documents as well as formal evaluations. The review uses each source as a fragment of evidence about precise points in the implementation chain described in the previous section. There is only one criterion for inclusion, namely that a piece of evidence is 'fit for purpose'. Does it illuminate understanding of the theory-of-change assumed at each point of the chain? Again, the full results of the review should be consulted for detailed analysis of the evidence. This account focuses on selected examples to illustrate the power of a theory-driven approach to synthesizing evidence.

Step one: problem identification

Sex offences are many and varied, and sex offenders come in many shapes and forms. Accordingly, the questions to be asked and the choices to be made at registration are numerous and subtle, and there is considerable diversity in the way the US states approach problem identification (Matson and Lieb, 1996a). The programme theory hypothesizes that this stage of the process works well if decisions are viewed as technically valid and reliable, in particular if they assess 'the offender's risk to the community with more precision than is possible when someone is identified simply as a sex offender'.

Is this how registration works? To take just one of the questions to be asked – who should be registered? – Presser and Gunnison (1999: 301) describe the range of methods in play at the time of submission of their paper as follows:

> Some states (e.g. California) rely solely on criminal history. Some states defer to the determination of one law enforcement official, such as the county prosecutor. Some (e.g. Georgia) automatically subject certain sex offenders, such as paedophiles, to notification requirements. Finally, some states use actuarial risk instruments.

Further analyses (Hebenton and Thomas, 1997; Poole and Lieb, 1995) give details of similar over-time and cross-state changes in assessment systems. The key point about such classifications, however, is that in themselves they cannot carry absolute indications of future risk of offending. Indubitably, the likelihood of committing a sex offence is shaped by previous behaviour but it will also depend on the offender's dispositions on release, whether he has received or learned from treatment, his current mental health, his position in the life-course and, of course, opportunity. Given these additional factors, the chances of making mistakes in risk assessment are ever-present. For example, Lonbom quotes an Assistant Bureau Chief in the Illinois State Police as follows:

> We have some great stories. We registered an 86-year-old man in a nursing home, a quadriplegic and an individual in the Federal Witness Protection program. We even registered a man currently in a coma, so I think the program has been pretty aggressive. (1998: 72)

Risk estimation has become more sophisticated since the early days of Megan's Law (Whitman and Farmer, 2000), but with professionalism has come expert recognition of its limitations. Actuarial calculations can carry information on more and more variables but they remain actuarial calculations in that they are based on population tendencies rather than individual assessments (Winick, 1998). If the other route is travelled, namely individual clinical and psychological profiling, variation in classification is still a problem because of the inadequate specialist clinical resources available and the diversity of personnel and psychological paradigms applied (Quinsey et al., 1998).

The gap between theory and reality in respect of the reliability of risk assessment is also evident in other decisions taken at the registration step. Take, for example, the decision on what information to record about offenders. Matson and Lieb's (1996a) review of state laws reveals wide discrepancies in the volume of information recorded about offenders, ranging from minimal data on name, address and offence to much more detailed information including fingerprints, palm prints, blood and saliva samples, and scars and tattoos. More recent advice in Washington State (Hebenton and Thomas, 1997: 10) also recommends the addition of data such as social security number, employment history, previous criminal contacts and favoured *modus operandi*.

Recall that, in step two of the implementation chain, the theory posits that disclosure of information will help the public maintain surveillance over released offenders. Yet much of what is recorded in step one is redundant for this purpose. The public cannot keep tabs on offenders on the basis of palm prints and saliva samples. The full records resemble, and are indeed based upon, the index systems and offender profiles used in all policing processes to assist in hunting for suspects. But this is not the encircling barrier that the Clinton address had in mind for Megan's Law, for such information serves the purpose not of crime prevention but of crime detection.

From these brief examples of two preliminary decisions it is apparent that the step one theory – that sex offender registers reflect accurate and consistent assessment of risk – is hard to maintain in the face of the evidence. However, as the illustration on the varying volumes of data recorded shows, decisions made at this first stage of the implementation chain will ripple through the entire process. The dice are already loaded as we move forward to step two.

Step two: public disclosure

The innovatory element of Megan's Law was not the idea of registering sex offenders. Police, probation and prison authorities have held such records for many years. What was new was the idea of public disclosure of such records as a way of enabling citizens to protect themselves and their families against a potential threat. The theories in play at this point are about effective communication – how to optimize the reach of notifications and how to ensure that the intended message is communicated. Thus the evidence to be considered here relates to the decidedly tricky transmission path from authorities to the public. How was the official view of the threat, and of how to deal with it, encoded in the notification procedures? How was this risk-and-response theory transmitted, and was the medium of release conducive to its successful transmission? How was the official message decoded by the public on the receiving end of the notification?

Evidence on the first two of these questions is relatively abundant and treated in depth in the full report of the review. As it was with registration, the message and medium of notification is complex and varies across the states. A tiered system of Special Bulletin Notifications is the norm, with disclosure required only at the higher levels of risk (with all the attendant variation caused in assessment methodology). Disclosure itself ranges from 'passive' (where records are simply made available) to 'restricted' (where access is granted only to those who need-to-know) to 'active' (in which there is a general broadcast of information). There is also variety in the specific means of disclosure, which include media releases, Internet access, mailed flyers, door-to-door notification and community meetings (CSOM, 2001).

Answers to the third and perhaps most crucial question – how the public comprehends the messages embodied in disclosure – are much more difficult to come by. However, there is some evidence relating to community notification meetings, which are perhaps the most considered strategy of the law enforcement authorities. These meetings capture a key stage in the Megan's Law programme theory because they embody the change from the identification of the problem to the identification of a solution, as well as the move from the criminal justice system to the general public. They encapsulate these shifts in a concentrated session of an hour or so, and so provide well-positioned evidence on this phase of the programme theory.

Matson and Lieb's (1996b) account of a community meeting shadows the pro-gramme theory, checking out whether there is a meeting of minds on the desired results as perceived by the authorities and residents. Information on the specific offender is, of course, provided at the gatherings but broader educational goals come to the fore in this particular jurisdiction. Disclosure is thus designed to inform community members 'which crimes require an offender to register', 'that theirs is not the only neighbourhood with a resident sex offender'; 'that large numbers of sex offenders will not reoffend ...'; 'that you cannot identify a sex offender by looks, race, gender, occupation or religion'; and 'that a sex offender can be anyone so precautions need to be taken at all times'.

And how do audiences react to this message? Matson and Lieb's (1996b: 13–14) reportage on this is brief and seemingly obtained from audience 'evaluation sheets' as analysed by the police authorities. These show a 'high degree of support regard-ing the community notification law at the meeting', namely 8.5 average rating on a scale running from 1 (extremely critical) to 10 (fully supportive). However, a more varied and circumspect response is revealed in another piece of data that iden-tifies four grounds for 'dissatisfaction' with the meeting:

- Some audience members did not want sex offenders living in their neighbourhoods in the first place.
- Some felt that notification was tantamount to picking on the offenders who (particularly if young) were not being given a fair chance.
- Some felt that the policy amounted to, and resulted from, lack of direct super-vision given to offenders.
- Some felt that information should be released on all sex offenders, including Level I (those posing the lowest risk).

A further study from Zevitz and Farkas (2000b) confirms the picture of significant support for the concept of community notification meetings, combined with signif-icant variation of opinion on their purpose. It also found that 38 per cent of the participants surveyed were more concerned about the specific offender after the meeting than before it and that, of these, 67 per cent were those who attended in the expectation of placing blame on public officials and/or preventing or removing the offender from local residence.

Perhaps the most interesting feature of these responses is the cheek-by-jowl clash of liberal sentiment and conservative reaction. Step two of the review delivers clear evidence of variation from the theoretical expectation of a notification process that reaches the widest possible audience in the least amount of time, and delivers its intended message. There is variation in the extent of public disclosure, variation in the media used for passing on information, and variation in the public's response to it. In short, communities on the receiving end of notification appear to take deliv-ery of mixed messages and they respond in equally mixed, and not necessarily 'appropriate' ways, which have the capacity to filter into subsequent steps of the implementation chain.

Step three: community sanction

The review now turns to evidence of how communities react to the presence of a notified sex offender in their locality. The programme theories under inspection assume that notification should increase opportunities for a community response in partnership with law enforcement and, in particular, that the prospects for surveillance, protective action, preventative action, evidence-building and prosecution are all increased. Among the sources of evidence that shed light on how well these theories correspond to reality is a survey of Wisconsin probation and parole officers with day-to-day responsibility for supervising sex offenders (Zevitz and Farkas, 2000c). Questionnaires were distributed to 128 officers, 77 of whom responded. Questions (closed and open-ended) focused on training, responsibilities and workload, and particular reference was made to the changing duties brought about by Megan's Law in terms of how Special Bulletin Notification cases (SBNs) added to caseloads.

Megan's Law, as the probation officers emphasized, is an 'unfunded mandate' and this new obligation diverted the balance of their daily activities towards SBN cases: for example, 'I don't think management understands the huge number of collateral contacts necessary for a sex offender caseload – family of defendant, victim's family, D.A., clinician, employer and so on'. Perhaps the most significant comments on caseload (in respect of both magnitude and feelings) refer to the problems of having to manage the community's reactions to offenders. Minor harassment is routine, housing problems commonplace, death threats occasional. All of this is rather nicely summarized in the sardonic observation of one probation officer: 'there is more pressure to spend greater amounts of time (baby-sit) with SBN cases, simply because they are SBN cases'.

A key theoretical assumption of step three of the theory – that the community will work in partnership with the law enforcement authorities to co-produce a surveillance apparatus – seems far from the reality facing practitioners. On this fragment of evidence, they spend a substantial amount of time in 'collateral contacts' with the purpose of protecting the offender from the harsher edge of the community's attention. This may, perhaps, be an unintended consequence of step two notification meetings. Zevitz and Farkas (2000b: 404) conclude the study examined above, reasoning that: 'many emerge from such meetings better informed, but with their anxiety and frustration still intact. However, now such feelings are focused on the offender.'

A second piece of evidence to shed light on one of the step three theories is a 'prospective simulation' by Petrosino and Petrosino (1999), who take on the difficult task of trying to estimate the difference Megan's Law makes to the capacity of the public to defend itself. The inquiry was conducted in Massachusetts, the last of all states to bring Megan's Law to the statute book, and the researchers had no current registrations with which to work. Given these difficulties, their ingenious response was to work forward from a current set of actual offences, seeking to

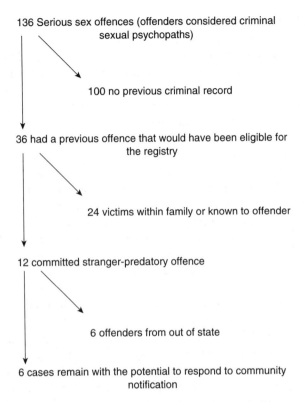

136 Serious sex offences (offenders considered criminal sexual psychopaths)

100 no previous criminal record

36 had a previous offence that would have been eligible for the registry

24 victims within family or known to offender

12 committed stranger-predatory offence

6 offenders from out of state

6 cases remain with the potential to respond to community notification

FIGURE 5.3   *The diminishing target of Megan's Law in Massachusetts*

discover how many current offenders *would have been* under surveillance *if* the law had been in place. Their estimate is summarized in Figure 5.3.

Of the 136 offenders, only 36 had a prior conviction that would have triggered the notification process. Of these, 12 had committed a stranger-predatory offence and 24 had offended against family, friends or co-workers. It must be supposed that notification has little protective effect on offenders' associates who, in all likelihood, already know of previous convictions. Thus attention focused on the 12 stranger-predatory offenders. In six cases it was deemed very unlikely that the victim could have been forewarned by notification because these offenders were from out-of-state. The simulated notification chain thus ends with just six victims who might have had a realistic chance of responding to warnings, and thus warns of the perils of a programme theory pinning its main hopes on public surveillance.

Step four: offender response

Ultimately, the answer to whether Megan's Law works lies in step four but, again, the review has no simple answer to draw about offender response. Sex offenders, even high risk sex offenders, are diverse and so are their reactions to the spotlight of publicity. The obvious starting point is data on reoffence and this brings us to the two outcome studies (Adkins et al., 2000; Schram and Milloy, 1995) that approximate to the so-called gold standard of the controlled comparison. Both evaluations fail to discover a significant effect on recidivism. However, the small print of their findings provides an interesting refinement to the programme theory, which can be pursued via the former study.

Clearly, this is a field in which the random application of subjects to experimental and control groups is utterly impracticable, it being impossible to focus legislation on only a portion of released offenders. The researchers therefore use a quasi-experimental design. In the first study, this took the form of a comparison of the recidivism rates of members of the first group of offenders released under Washington's notification regime (1990–1993) with those of a matched sample selected from those released prior to the enactment of the new law. The key comparison focused on the percentages re-arrested for a sexual offence within 4.5 years of release. The headline results from the study are as follows:

- At the end of the 54 months at risk in the community, the notification group had a slightly lower estimated rate of sexual recidivism (19%) than the comparison group (22%). This difference was not found to be statistically significant.
- Although there was no detectable effect on recidivism, the timing of re-arrest was significantly different for the notification and comparison groups. Offenders subjected to community notification were arrested for new crimes much more quickly than comparable offenders who were released without notification. (Schram and Milloy, 1995: 3)

This suggests that Megan's Law has little impact on the propensity or ability to commit repeat offences: the rates of sexual recidivism, at approximately 20 per cent over 4.5 years, were depressingly consistent with other studies of adult sex offenders. There is, however, a stunning clue in the second, speed-of-arrest finding about an evident outworking of the law. Recall that evidence on the earlier steps in the chain suggested that whatever else was or was not achieved through the legislation, significant dossiers and profiles were being amassed. A strong suggestion emerges that registration and notification harness a capacity for detection rather than prevention.

Process evidence from in-depth interviews with 30 designated Level III offenders in Wisconsin also brings flesh to the bare bones of the outcome research. This study by Zevitz and Farkas focuses on offenders' post-release experiences of work, housing, family and friends, and their overall reactions to the law. It finds that 'only a few thought that the new law on community notification would prevent reoffending'. Respondents reach this conclusion in totally different ways:

If you're going to reoffend, it doesn't matter if you're on TV, in newspapers, whatever, you're going to reoffend. And there's nothing to stop you. It's a choice you make … The only person that can stop it is the sex offender himself.

> If these people know you're a sex offender and keep saying – keep pointing at you and everything else. Everything breaks under pressure, everything. No matter what. No matter how strong he thinks he is. You taunt a dog long enough, no matter how calm and cool – calm and collected that dog might have been the whole time, it might have been the most loving dog with children and everything else, but if you taunt that dog long enough, it's going to bite. (Zevitz and Farkas, 2000a: 387)

The above quotations give a flavour of a classic qualitative study, providing eloquent testimony of one group of offenders' opposition to Megan's Law. But, they would say that, wouldn't they? So how should such a study be judged alongside other, more 'scientific' evidence? The foolish inference is the instant one that because these 30 men say that Megan's Law will not reduce offending, then it will not reduce reoffending. The valid and transferable lesson, once again, is about disparity of reasoning under the law. These men have intense theories of their own about notification and the nature of sex offending that contradict squarely those of the policy-makers that infiltrate the law. Megan's Law is about physical containment but it is also an attempt to plant ideas. This and other studies in the main review demonstrate that offenders are not at one in terms of their emotional response – but there is relatively little evidence of 'shame', 'contrition', 'acceptance of guilt' and 'readiness for treatment'. This, together with the 'disappointing' outcome studies on reoffence, calls into question another of the deeper-rooted aspirations of Megan's Law.

Policy lessons of the review

Realist synthesis shuns the idea of verdicts and so no decision or decree is offered on the efficacy of Megan's Law. If there is an overall conclusion it is, perhaps, a much higher level one about the inadvisability of marshalling policy though public opinion, and then assuming that the populus will conform to expectation. The grand lesson here the mirrors Rousseau's argument about another attempted shaming campaign (to reduce duelling!):

> The state could never order members of society to regard private persons either with respect or contempt, for public opinion formed its own opinion about the merit of private persons over which the state could not have the slightest influence.

This insight, owed to Whitman (1998: 1055), provides an interesting parallel for registration and notification programmes.

The review emphasizes that Megan's Law is a programme with subtle underlying theories that passes through many hands in the attempt to transform moral condemnation into offender management. It is iterative in its impact. One decision follows another, and at each stage stakeholders must decide how to respond. The review has shown clearly that these are almost always split decisions. Sometimes the key stakeholders behave in keeping with the policy-makers' underlying theories, and oftentimes they do not. The overall outcome of Megan's Law is thus multiplicity. The complexity of decision-making compounds at every point, with the result that there is little guarantee of uniformity between cases as they proceed through the registration and notification process. Differences in implementation occur from state to state, county to county, official to official, neighbour to neighbour.

The previous sentence is perhaps the ultimate statement on the contingencies of policy and, classically, the last thing the policy-maker wants to hear. The exception, perhaps, is the senior decision-maker considering whether to implement a notification programme in the first place. The UK does not have 50 different state jurisdictions but its criminal justice system, its practitioners, its communities and its offenders are hardly uniform. As many will recall, the UK did teeter on the question of whether to introduce a 'Sarah's Law' (following the killing of Sarah Payne in distressingly similar circumstances to the Megan Kanka case). The crucial issue confronting such a decision is whether it is possible to devise an assessment, management and containment framework to deliver outputs that are sufficiently reliable and predictable to ensure the more effective control of offenders. In this respect, the review's evidence about the perils of complexity is entirely to the point, and it only scratches the surface. Betwixt and between the major decisions that are considered here – on risk levels, registration requirements, notification strategies and so on – lie the dozens of minor adjustments and practical judgements needed to put them into practice. The ensuing unpredictability of delivery is a point not to be disguised from policy-makers.

Realist synthesis aims to test and refine programme theory and wrap up with an evidence-informed model of how programmes work. The conclusions with a more precise policy pay-off are thus outlined in Table 5.1, which is based on the findings of the full review. Actions and decisions made in the early stages of the process reverberate right down the implementation chain, and the review has uncovered many instances where inconsistency at one point triggers an unanticipated outcome later in the sequence. Table 5.1 can be regarded as a summary of the evidence on Megan's Law although, to be precise, it is a summary of the fate of some of the key programme theories of Megan's Law. It also speaks to the matter of how the Law may be improved in its operation, for example by tightening the procedures at each of the decision points to reduce inconsistency and ambiguity.

It remains a matter of judgement as to whether tinkering with the parts will make the whole sufficiently strong. And it remains a matter of political judgement as to the level of acceptable performance. There is a political voice echoing through the entire process which says that one life saved by Megan's Law is enough to make it worthwhile, and on the merits of that proposition the evidence cannot decide.

And back to method

This exercise is intended to show that there is more than one way of doing a review, and more than one way of doing it systematically. It exhibits some, but not all, of

TABLE 5.1   *Megan's Law – decisions and consequences*

Decision point	Immediate, intermediate and long-term consequences
Risk assessment	If risks could be assessed perfectly there would be no need for Megan's Law. Risk assessment tends to the piecemeal and goes well beyond the original target of predatory offences against children. Large amounts of management resources and emotional energy are drawn into the containment of so-classified 'high risk' cases that may be better handled via a more diverse response.
Registration maintenance	There have been difficulties in maintaining complete registers, with loss of compliance over time and on change of address. This provides an opportune loophole for dangerous offenders who are the very target of the law.
Registration details	Depth of record-keeping varies significantly. The nature of comprehensive registrations is such that they are more likely to assist detection than prevention, and there is some evidence that Megan's Law operates more successfully to this end.
Registration legitimacy	Megan's Law champions public safety over offenders' rights to privacy. This moral authority has survived many constitutional challenges and it legitimizes the shaming of offenders. Much of the public (but few offenders) accept the legal basis and moral force of such denouncements.
Notification – active or passive	Notification practices vary widely from 'aggressive, proactive publicity' to 'legitimate interests and inquiries only'. This represents a trade-off in consequences, with the former risking increased levels of community harassment and the latter risking failure to reach the vulnerable.
Notification – mode	Notification is by bulletins, flyers, meetings, door-to-door visits, press, radio and television releases, and Internet access. These have similar trade-offs to the above, plus a further one - the more public the media, the less control of the message.
Community response – partnerships	Megan's Law is an 'unfunded mandate'. It requires a complex multi-agency response but provides few extra resources to this end. The notified communities differ and some lack the culture of concerted community action, with the result that response is left mostly to practitioners and individual members of the public.
Community response – practitioners	Practitioners remain pivotal in enacting the law. There is a gearing-up of depth and breadth in supervision, as well as new duties in emergency response to adverse consequences of the law. Containment and control become more intensive and there is enhancement in public safety promotional activities.
Community response – the public	Public testimony reveals responses varying from red-handed witness of further offence to bloody-minded attack on former offenders. Estimation of the balance of responses is unclear but the opportunities for surveillance are low given the inefficiency of the registers and the pattern of offending. Harassment is significant, but practitioner and offender estimates of its seriousness differ.

(Continued)

TABLE 5.1   *(Continued)*

Decision point	Immediate, intermediate and long-term consequences
Offender response	The main effect of the law lies with the offender-at-large. All of its measures meet with complex and diverse reactions. Compliance with registration differs. Efforts at more intensive supervision meet with mixed response. Treatment does not sit easily with public surveillance. There is little evidence of a 'shaming' effect of the intervention. The impact on recidivism seems slight, but rates are still unknown.

the strengths of the realist approach (especially in the present condensed version) and it is worth constructing a methodological balance sheet to conclude the illustration.

In particular, the review addresses the advantage and the challenge of trying to use different types of evidence, for this particular effort would have stalled on the starting blocks if the gold standard of randomized controlled trials had been a requirement. All manner of evidence is synthesized, without methodological melodrama, by the simple device of using the data to interrogate a carefully articulated theory.

The review also demonstrates that the basic unit of analysis in realist synthesis is not the whole primary study but individual and selective findings. Such an approach rests on the extremely high probability, in this case well founded, that no one report on a complex intervention can be comprehensive and cover every aspect equally well. An important corollary is that insights may also be culled with profit from otherwise slight or even partisan reports, which nevertheless contain some nuggets of very solid evidence. For example, on the matter of parole and probation officers' implementation of the Law, the review takes on board Zevitz and Farkas's (2000b) evidence about their tactical response (that they become baby-sitters). There is no acquiescence, however, with their decidedly rosy conclusion that morale was high and recidivism was under check.

> 📖 **Supplementary reading** Further examination of the merits of the primary research discussed here may be found in R. Pawson *Assessing the quality of evidence in evidence-based policy: why, when and how?*, which is included in the web page support materials. 👑

The review does, however, have limitations. The first is a question on the status of the provisional programme theory, which forms the backbone to the review. It is referred to as the 'official theory' and whilst it is true that it is derived from formal documentation, this claim to executive legitimation is not entirely founded. First, such a model can never match the detail of the full set of assumptions embedded in the programme. In the present example, for instance, not only does there have to be a decision on the medium for notification, there has to be a pronouncement on the precise area to be covered (in Chapter 2, I discussed some prominent – and exotic – theories on this score). Second, is the fact that the official theories always change, not least in the attempt to iron out perceived difficulties within the programme. A better description of the background hypothesis in Figure 5.1, therefore, is that it is the reviewer's 'reconstruction' of the official theory. In other words, in this and all realist reviews the process builds from hypotheses formulated as abstract 'ideal types' or 'prototypes'. Whilst this clarification is useful, it does not undermine the main logic of the review, which is to show how much the implementation routines depart from a common logic, from the prototype. If the starting point had been a somewhat different theory-of-change, the conclusion would still hold.

A second limitation is the relatively light and residual usage of the key realist notion of context. In the analysis above, contextual variation is mostly expressed and understood through the idea of difference, in that it is shown that different programme theories operate to different effect across different states, different jurisdictions and different practitioners. Contextual influences do indeed pervade the intervention and the review provides scores of examples, leading to the main conclusion that implementation variation undermines the law. What is not possible, however, is to gather evidence systematically on these contextual influences. The fragments of evidence about variation within step one of the process are not culled from the same states/counties/officials as those that tell of differences at step two, and so on. Some jurisdictions keep cropping up in the materials, some appear less frequently, and some do not appear at all. The lack of data providing systematic contextual comparisons precludes a comparative-style realist review, but the analysis has still allowed a broad conclusion to emerge: that Megan's Law works more successfully through parole management and detection than it does through shaming or public surveillance. These may turn out to be significant inferences, but the evidence cannot provide us with the precise configurations of legislation, law enforcement and community action that generates optimal progress on all fronts. Reviews can never bring finality to policy deliberation, but the deliberations prompted by this approach might be rather more fruitful than those in which programme theories do not get an airing.

6

Reviewing Inner Mechanisms: Youth Mentoring

Mentoring is one of those bright ideas that take a periodic grip on the imagination of the policy community. Everyone appreciates that one learns from experience and so much the better if one can trade on the wisdom of others. Here, then, is the kernel of the mentoring movement. Creating a close relationship with a knowledge-able guide is seen as an all-purpose resource offering both opportunities for advancement and solutions to disadvantage. These are the small beginnings of a brain-child that has grown up in many social and public policy homes from the prison wing to the boardroom, and from the maternity ward to the hospice.

Because of this ubiquitous quality, and because of the surface plausibility of its pri-mary theory, a review in the area of mentoring is selected as the second example of realist synthesis. Whilst there is a not quite the moral press of the Megan's Law exam-ple (Chapter 5), there is a certain messianic quality about the literature with which the reviewer has to contend. The primary research, moreover, is huge in proportion, wide-ranging in method, and all over the place in quality, presenting a veritable dog's dinner of evidence for the synthesizer to chew upon. Then there is the nature of the intervention itself. Put simply, a 'relationship' is the intervention. Accordingly, men-toring programmes are essentially spontaneous, decidedly mixed term and usually in a state of flux. This is no 'treatment' and the great challenge for the reviewer is to pierce the inner mechanisms, to try to discover what really goes on in a mentoring relationship. Finally, there is the issue of joined-up thinking. Mentoring is often offered as part of a wider package of interventions, and attribution can be problem-atic. For all of these reasons, mentoring is a promising subject for the realist reviewer.

Again, I emphasize that because of space restrictions this chapter is a synopsis of a much, much longer review, and concentrates entirely on evidence about youth mentoring – the pairing of disadvantaged and, often, disaffected youth with an experienced adult. This is perhaps mentoring's most challenging task and it throws into relief the kinds of social forces that a relationship has to withstand if it is to succeed. The original review also examined other kinds of pairings, the better to understand the dynamics of partnerships. Here, however, this evidence on youth-on-youth peer support, workplace mentoring and self-help interventions to support the ill is omitted.

Note also that, as in Chapter 5, the full methodological regalia of realist synthesis are not on display. The focus is on analysis, and the line of development through theory-articulation to theory-testing to theory-refinement is clearly on show. This chapter also finds space for a fuller exposition of the primary research in order to give a sharper indication of the nature of the extraction phase in realist synthesis. Each primary study is subject to basic exposition, quality appraisal and data (re)analysis as part and parcel of the synthesis. Discussions on the search for and selection of material are omitted.

> 📖 **Supplementary reading** The 'full' review, R. Pawson *Mentoring relationships: an explanatory review*, is included in the web page support materials. ⍟

A theory of youth mentoring

In stage one of realist synthesis the ground is cleared and terms of reference are defined, and these preliminaries are executed alongside an initial consultation of the literature. I have already indicated the broad and high expectations for close and caring mentoring partnerships but, clearly, there are an infinite number of ways in which such newly honed, one-to-one, open-ended relationships may operate and develop. Equally clearly, the precise way in which the mentoring bond is configured will make a potential difference to any outcomes. So what initial sense of mentor and mentee interactions does one derive from the literature?

As a pilot exercise I pulled together a rough and ready inventory of the way researchers have described the activities that take place under the name of mentoring. It is a rather daunting compendium. Mentoring, it seems, may be any of the following: helping, coaching, tutoring, counselling, sponsoring, befriending, bonding, trusting, role-modelling, mutual learning, direction-setting, progress-chasing, sharing experience, respite provision, sharing a laugh, widening horizons, resilience-building, showing ropes, informal apprenticeships, providing openings, kindness of strangers, sitting by Nellie, treats for bad boys and girls, the Caligula phenomenon, power play, tours of middle-class life, and so on and so forth.

It seems that all human life lurks in this catalogue and I have made no attempt to tame it in this list, other than to register towards the end that some commentators discern a dark side to mentoring. There is, however, no utility in research or policy terms in the message that success in mentoring lies in the balance of scores of such little imponderables. So are there some shared themes, some core properties, some common denominators that underlie a successful relationship and contribute to successful mentoring programmes? This brings the reviewer to the exercise in theory-mining, digging through the literature for key terms, abstract ideas, middle-range theories and hypotheses that might provide explanatory purchase on the multifarious differences identified in the preceding paragraph.

The results of that exercise are summarized in Figure 6.1 which presents an initial model of how youth mentoring may work. The starting point, already established, is that there are many different objectives and many different modes of mentoring. The conceptual literature has tried to capture this diversity in a number of typologies of the forms of mentoring. Best known perhaps is Kram and Isabella's (1985) distinction between 'career', 'psycho-social' and 'role model' mentoring. The first consists of aptitudinal coaching in relevant tools-of-the-trade. The second operates in the affective domain, encouraging the mentee into emotional equilibrium. The third marshals the combined forces of leading-by-example and following-the-leader. Another venerable, and perhaps self-explanatory, distinction that crops up in the mentoring literature is that between 'formal' and 'informal mentoring' (Noe, 1988). One of the best known expositions of the merits of youth mentoring (Freedman, 1993) keys into this same distinction, advocating 'voluntarism' (over state provision) as the key motor of mentoring.

Further adaptations of these ideas by Philip and Hendry (2000) and Colley (2004) create another raft of useful distinctions such as that between 'engagement mentoring', 'achievement mentoring' and 'identity mentoring'. Identity mentoring operates through emotional contact and befriending, supporting and cultivating the ideas of mentees, particularly in terms of how they see themselves. Achievement mentoring promotes gains in status by fostering and assisting in the development of qualifications, skills and job opportunities. Engagement mentoring is an ambitious combination of the two, nurturing the hardest-to-reach youth, and aspiring to wholesale gains in both fortitude and fortune.

These classifications are borrowed and adapted in Figure 6.1, which is an attempt to tease out the inner workings of mentoring schemes designed to promote engagement. An initial theory is put forward in answer to the question, 'what does it take to engage the disengaged, what form must mentoring take to achieve this task?' The young person at whom engagement mentoring is aimed is located at the bottom left of the figure. In the UK many such programmes are aimed at youth captured by the acronym NEET – Not in Education, Employment or Training. These young people are not only outsiders on these measures; they are also likely to be disaffected and disengaged, and may well be hostile to the whole 'system', which they perceive to be responsible for their plight. The model in Figure 6.1 goes on to hypothesize how a mentoring programme might work to address their actual and perceived exclusion from mainstream society.

It is assumed that there will not be one almighty leap into training, employment and equanimity, but that mentoring will facilitate this in different modes and by stages:

1 **Befriending**: creating bonds of trust and the sharing of new experiences so that the mentee recognizes the legitimacy of other people and other perspectives.
2 **Direction-setting**: promoting further self-reflection through the discussion of alternatives so that mentees reconsider their loyalties, values and ambitions.

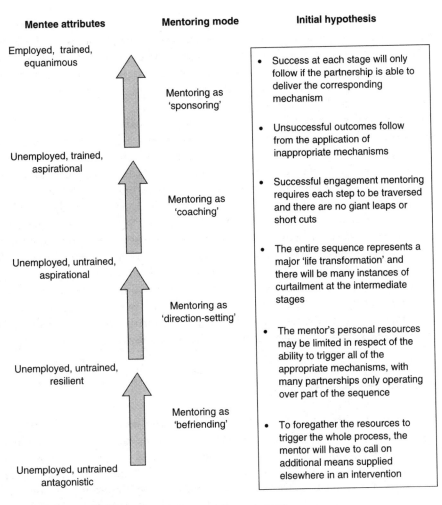

FIGURE 6.1   *Initial model of 'engagement mentoring'*

3 **Coaching:** coaxing and cajoling the mentee into acquiring the skills, assets, credentials and testimonials required to enter the mainstream.
4 **Sponsoring:** advocating and networking on behalf of the mentee to gain the requisite insider contacts and opportunities.

These four steps are depicted as the upward column of arrows in the figure. The expectation is that clambering through them will encourage a parallel, step-wise set of changes in the disposition and position of the mentee. These shifting personal outcomes are summarized in the rolling sequence of attributes in the left-hand column of the model.

   This is the framework of the programme theory to be tested, but it is only the chassis, since this is a realist review. It is assumed that the process articulated in

Figure 6.1 will come to pass only in certain respects for certain mentors and certain mentees on certain mentoring programmes in certain social contexts. The basic model is thus buttressed by a series of hypotheses and questions about limiting conditions, which are summarized in the six bullet points on the right-hand side of the figure. These introduce a series of caveats, which on closer investigation will allow us to better capture the factual scope of a policy passion.

Before taking this model back to the primary studies, it is worth issuing a brief methodological aside about its status. The framework and theories are drawn from the literature but, unlike the initial Megan's Law model in Chapter 5, they are not derived from 'official expectations'. Many of its ideas are to be discovered directly in the programme rubric but in the last analysis it is my model, my distillation of some of the key ideas that inform both the construction *and* critique of such programmes. It would be perfectly possible to commence the review with a somewhat different, but entirely legitimate, set of questions. The point to be stressed is that the review does not set out to prove or disprove the model, but to refine it. The justification for the initial hypotheses, therefore, is that they are sufficiently close to the extant ideas on youth mentoring, and sufficiently complex to recognize the intricacy of the task, for their interrogation to be informative for the policy and practice community. The other characteristic of the model, as in all realist syntheses, is that it employs sufficiently abstract middle-range terms to be testable via a range of primary inquiries, employing quite different research strategies.

The evidence – nine key studies

The following studies were selected purposively, as an optimal set capable of putting to test the review theory. All cover programmes that deal with disaffected, high risk youth, attempting to move them into the mainstream via value *and* positional shifts. But, to repeat for emphasis, this review is not a synthesis of youth engagement mentoring as such. In the realist approach the studies are interrogated for what they say about the inner mechanisms of engagement mentoring. They are dissected in order to throw light on the precise changes engendered in successful youth mentoring, on what the relationship must contrive to do to bring about change, and on who is best placed to deliver and receive the apparatus of change.

Study 1: de Anda, D. (2001) 'A qualitative evaluation of a mentor program for at-risk youth: the participants' perspective', *Child and Adolescent Social Work Journal*, 18(2): 97–117

This is an evaluation of project RESCUE (Reaching Each Student's Capacity Utilizing Education). Eighteen mentor–mentee dyads were investigated from a small, incorporated city in Los Angeles with high rates of youth and violent crime. The aims of the programme are described in classic engagement terms:

> The purpose of this relationship is to provide a supportive adult role model, who will encourage the youth's social and emotional development, help improve his/her academic and career motivation, expand the youth's life experiences, redirect the youth from at-risk behaviors, and foster improved self-esteem. (p. 98)

A curious, and far from incidental point, is that the volunteer mentors on the programme were all firefighters.

It is a qualitative evaluation involving group interview data and case studies. There is a claim in the abstract that the mentees are shown to secure 'concrete benefits', but these are mentioned only as part of the case study narratives, and there is no attempt to measure inputs, outputs and outcomes. The findings are, in the author's words, 'overwhelmingly positive'. The only hint of negativity comes in a reply to a questionnaire item about whether the mentees would like to change anything about the programme. 'All but three mentees answered the question with a "No" response. But two of these malcontents merely wanted more "outings" and the third, more "communication".'

In quality appraisal terms the research could be discounted as soppy, feel-good stuff, especially as all of the key case study claims are in the researcher's voice. For example, 'the once sullen, hostile, defensive young woman now enters the agency office with hugs for staff members, a happy disposition and open communication with adult staff members and the youth she serves in her agency position'. The case studies do, however, provide a very clear account of an unfolding sequence of mentoring mechanisms that evokes closely the core of Figure 6.1:

> Joe had been raised in a very chaotic household with his mother as the primary parent, his father's presence erratic ... He was clearly heading towards greater gang involvement ... He had, in fact, begun drinking (with a breakfast consisting of a beer), demonstrated little interest in school and was often truant ... The Mentor Program and the Captain who became his mentor were ideal for Joe, who had earlier expressed a desire to become a firefighter. The mentor not only served as a professional role model, but provided the nurturing father figure missing from his life. Besides spending time together socially, his mentor helped him train, prepare and discipline himself for the Fire Explorer's test. Joe was one of the few who passed the test (which is the same as the physical test given to firefighters). A change in attitude, perception of his life, and attitudes and life goals was evident ... [further long, long story omitted] He also enrolled at the local junior college in classes (e.g. for paramedics) to prepare for the firefighters' examination and entry into the firefighters academy. He was subsequently admitted to the fire department as a trainee. (p. 111)

This extract provides confirmation of the 'long moves work by little steps theory'. All the attendant mechanisms are mentioned, moving from befriending to direction-setting to coaching to sponsoring. Another interesting datum for the review is that this particular mentor ('many years of experience training the new, young auxiliary firefighters as well as the younger Fire Explorers') was quite uniquely positioned. As Joe climbs life's ladder away from his morning beer, the Captain is able to provide all the resources needed to meet all his emotional, attitudinal, aptitudinal and training needs. This evidence gives the lie to two proto-theories about the rarity of the complete sequence and about the limited compass of mentor resources. The typicality of these achievements and supporting conditions is, of course, a moot point and a worry acknowledged by de Anda only in the final moments of the paper.

The study does, however, provide two more defensible claims, indeed ones that square with the initial hypotheses. There is a constant refrain about precise circumstantial matches and points of interpersonal congruity being required to provide the seeds of change:

> It was at this point [end of lovingly described string of bust-ups] that Gina entered the Mentor program and was paired with a female firefighter. The match was a perfect one in that the firefighter was seen as 'tough' and was quickly able to gain Gina's confidence. (p.110)

There is also an emphasis within the case study format (the narrative) on the holistic and cumulative nature of the successful encounter. 'The responses and case descriptions do provide *a constellation* of concrete and psychosocial factors which the participants felt contributed to their development and success [my emphasis]'.

Read at face value, this study tells us that engagement mentoring works. Read critically it screams of bias. Read synthetically, there is nothing in the account to suggest a general panacea and much to suggest a special case. The key point, however, is that some vital explanatory ingredients (well-positioned mentor, established community base, specific interpersonal connections, holistic programme) can be extracted and taken forward in the review.

Study 2: Colley, H. (2003) 'Engagement mentoring for socially excluded youth: problematising an "holistic" approach to creating employability through the transformation of habitus', *British Journal of Guidance and Counselling*, 31(1): 77–98

In this study we transfer from American optimism to British pessimism through use of the same research strategy. The evidence is drawn from a study of a UK government scheme (New Beginnings) which, in addition to basic skills training and work placements, offered a modest shot of mentoring (one hour per week). This scheme is one of several in the UK mounted out of a realization that disaffected youth have multiple, deep-seated problems and, accordingly, joined-up service provision is required to have any hope of dealing with them. Colley's study takes the form of series of qualitative stories (her term) about flashpoints within the scheme. She selects cases in which the mentor 'demonstrated an holistic person-centred commitment to put the concerns of the mentor before those of the scheme' and reports that, 'sooner or later these relationships break down'. The following quotations provide typical extracts from 'Adrian's story'. This youth spoke about his experience of mentoring with evangelical fervour:

> To be honest, I think anyone who's in my position with meeting people, being around people even, I think a mentor is one of the greatest things you can have ... [passage omitted]. If I wouldn't have had Pat, I think I'd still have problems at home ... You know, she's put my life in a whole different perspective. (p. 85)

Adrian was sacked from the scheme after 13 weeks. He was placed in an office as filing clerk and dismissed because of lateness and absence. Colley reports that, despite his profuse excuses, the staff felt he was 'swinging the lead'. His mentor figured otherwise: 'Pat, a former personnel manager and now student teacher, was concerned that Adrian had unidentified learning difficulties that were causing him to miss work through fear of getting things wrong. She tried to advocate on his behalf with New Beginnings staff, to no avail.' At this point Adrian was removed from the scheme.

Another story betrays an equivalent pattern, with the mentor supporting the teenage mentee's aspiration to become a mother and to eschew any interest in work (and thus the programme). From the point of view of the review theory, there is an elementary fit with the idea of the difficulties entrenched in the long move. Mentors are able to provide emotional support and a raising of aspirations but cannot, and to some extent will not, provide advocacy and coaching. On this particular scheme, the latter are not in the mentor's gift but the responsibility of other New Beginnings staff (their faltering, bureaucratic efforts also being briefly described).

What of quality appraisal? Colley displays the ethnographer's art in being able to bring to life the emotions described above. She also performs ethnographic science in the way that these sentiments are supported by apt, detailed and verbatim quotations from the key players. Compared to Study 1, the empirical material might be judged as more authentically the respondent's tale than the researcher's account.

However, then we come to the author's interpretations and conclusions. On the basis of these two case illustrations, the inevitability of mentoring *not* being able to reach further goals on employability is assumed. This proposition is supported in a substantial passage of theorizing about the 'dialectical interplay between structure and agency', via Bourdieu's concept of 'habitus', which is explained as follows:

> ... a structuring structure, which organises practices and the perceptions of practices, but also a structured structure: the principle of division into logical classes which organizes the perception of the social world is itself the product of internalization of the division into social classes. (p. 92)

Put in more downright terms, this means that because of the way capitalist society is organized the best this kind of kid will get is a shit job and whatever he does will be taken as a sign that he barely deserves that. In Colley's words, 'As the case studies illustrate, the task of altering habitus is simply unfeasible in many cases, and certainly not to a set timetable'. It is arguable that this interpretative overlay derives more from the author's self-acknowledged Marxist/feminist standpoint than from the empirical case studies presented. There is also a further, very awkward method-ological aspect for the reviewer in a 'relativistic' moment often seen in qualitative work, when in the introduction to her case studies Colley acknowledges that her reading of them is 'among many interpretations they offer'.

There are huge ambiguities here, normally shoved under the carpet in a system-atic review. Explanation by theorizing, and an underlying constructivism in data presentation, are not the stuff of study selection and quality appraisal. Realist syn-thesis plays by another set of rules, which are about drawing warrantable inferences from the data presented. Thus, sticking just to the case study evidence in the review, it is a further exemplification of the 'long moves work by little steps' theory. It has particular explanatory value because it exemplifies in close relief some of the diffi-culties of long-move mentoring. In the accounts presented, the mentor is able to make headway in terms of befriending and direction-setting but these gains are stalled or even thwarted by programme objectives on training and employment.

The notion, implicit in the review theory, that there is some sort of linear ladder of engagement is thus called into question. There is a need to insert a supplemen-tary hypothesis at this point about whether and in what circumstances befriending may create forms of self-reflection that serve to consolidate outsider status. At a slightly different angle, the study supports the review theory about the individual mentor's restricted resources and his or her limited capacity to compensate for lives scarred by poverty and lack of opportunity. But it also warns that the hypothesis about the need to 'call upon additional resources' is hardly straightforward and will be in need of further unpacking. These, rather than Colley's propositions about the unfaltering grip of capitalist habitus, are ideas to be carried forward in the review.

Study 3: Philip, K., Shucksmith, J. and King, C. (2004) *Sharing a Laugh? A Qualitative Study of Mentoring Interventions with Young People.* York: Joseph Rowntree Foundation, 60pp

This inquiry compares three Scottish schemes. Two, termed the education and housing projects, used planned mentoring; that is to say, the contacts took place as part of the paid activity of a youth worker. The third, a befriending project, was undertaken by unpaid volunteers managed by a professional co-ordinator. There are further differences in organizational and funding arrangements, but the clien-tele and aims are considered sufficiently similar to make a formal comparison. The means to this end is another qualitative study concentrating on 'an account given principally through the eyes of young people of their experiences of mentoring within these settings'. The conclusions (p. 50) are particularly useful for the syn-thesis as they too are an exercise in teasing out the scope of different mentoring relationships.

Befriending   It may be useful to look at mentoring as a spectrum of intensity, with the volunteer befrienders offering a form of mentoring that focuses on respite and opportunities for shared activities with less troubled or younger children. The voluntary commitment of the befrienders was an important element in making the relationship 'special' and developing the potential for friendship. Equally it is true that relationships could become isolated if befrienders were unwilling to participate in further events, despite the best efforts of the co-ordinator.

Education and Housing   [Both] projects offered a higher dosage of mentoring that ultimately aimed to reintegrate young people into the mainstream. Many of the young people had a complex array of difficulties and had contact with a range of professionals with whom mentors often acted as advocates. Unexpectedly, the status of paid workers did not appear to distance them from their clients although it made for a more problematic relationship with other professionals ... Such an intensive level of support is unlikely to be possible within a voluntary context. Paradoxically it also demands the flexibility of voluntary commitment in promoting a version of '*professional* friendship'. [italics in original]

There seems an approximate fit with some of the review theories here. The befrienders (not surprisingly) have success with befriending and with 'providing a space in which to tell their [the mentees'] story and to rehearse what they would do with their lives' (that is, direction-setting). In contrast, befrienders were unable or unwilling to move on status matters: 'we are not an authority figure, we are not police, we are not social workers, we are purely there to give them a bit of fun and take them out of the home situation for a wee while'. This limited jurisdiction may, however, follow from the tender age of many of the mentees in this particular project. Thus before the review gets swept away with a 'befrienders can only befriend' theory, note that allocations on the housing project were 'generally in the 16–18 age group', the education project was 'for young people in the 12–18 age-group', and the befriending project operated for children 'aged 5–8'.

In line with the review theory, the professional workers attempt to be, and appear to have some success as, sponsors and coaches, but they do this in association with, and, sometimes, after scrapping with, other agencies (compare Colley's hapless mentor in Study 2). However, it is claimed that they operate in this domain having first established high levels of personal rapport with the kids. This 'professional friendship' idea sits well with the initial model in that it recognizes that engagement is reached through progressive stages, but it sits uneasily with the sub-theory about the difficulty of a mentor being all things to one person. The report gives some detailed clues on why the latter might be viable in this particular intervention:

- unusually favourable workloads (to allow frequent contact)
- not 'grassing' ('I wouldn't be rushing to the police')
- natural contact in the locality (key workers often lived in the neighbourhood)
- risky pasts ('being a bit of a tearaway myself')

These conditions give a glimpse of some important individual and institutional contexts that may be required to sustain the progressive leverage of engagement mentoring. They are potential candidates for inclusion in the basic model of the mentoring relationship, on the basis of further investigation in the review. Whilst operating in completely different circumstances, they do evoke some of the advantageous conditions pertaining in the RESCUE study (Study 1).

Philip et al.'s research, however, is not unalloyed good news. It also pays particularly close attention to the roots of youth disaffection and thus to the stop–start mechanics of building up a mentoring relationship (a finding later reinforced in Study 6):

> Striking a balance between raising false hopes and lowering expectations is a continuing issue for those working with vulnerable young people. However, mentoring processes may offer an opportunity to tackle this through building up a launch pad and safety net. However, this demands a long-term commitment on the part of mentors in order to support young people to feel safe enough to take risks, to fail and start again. (p. 50)

This evocation of perpetual strain and impending breakdown leads the authors to emphasize the importance of the role mentoring offers in 'bringing reliance to the surface'. This fits rather neatly with the review hypothesis that mentees only shift from antagonism to aspiration through the stage of acquiescence (the state of being prepared to 'hang in there'). However, this readiness to tough it out seems to hang by a rather thin thread. As one mentor puts it:

> The causes are deep rooted and to iron these out takes time and some of the scars are there and they'll never disappear, they'll always be there. And they'll always affect that person as an individual and it'll either make them fight like hell or [go] various degrees downward ... I think a lot depends on who these young people latch onto and whether they get a leg up or get smacked down. (p. 40)

The report also brings a weight of evidence to bear on the importance of such programmes' going beyond one-to-one partnerships and building bridges to other agents and agencies. As well as battles with welfare agencies, mentors also report an effect on family ties. Despite the fact that family breakdown was commonplace amongst programme subjects, Philip et al. present some evidence to show that mentoring relationships were complementary to family relationships, a point on which to build. Mentoring provided encouragement and some skills to hang on to precarious relations of the following kind: 'If I fall out with my mum, I just go to my room. If I fall out with anyone else World War 3 breaks out.'

This research offers tell-tale signs of several shortcomings in the review's preliminary theory. It typifies the strengths and weaknesses of qualitative evaluation. It is strong on testimony, and the explanatory themes noted above are identified very clearly and supported in quotation after quotation, example upon example. Inevitably, there is no attempt to measure outputs and stepping stones on any of the dimensions identified; in this respect we are left with the authors' impressions that progress is made on one front, not so much on another, and so on. Frustratingly, very little use is made of its comparative structure. Three introductory sketches of the schemes are offered rather than any systematic comparison of processes, inputs and outputs. The synthesis needs further evidence on pattern to rein in these insights.

Study 4: Parra, G., DuBois, D., Neville, H. and Pugh-Lilly, A. (2002) 'Mentoring relationships for youth: investigation of a process-oriented model', *Journal of Community Psychology*, 30(4): 367–88

This is a quantitative study attempting to tease out which aspects of the mentoring relationship have an effect on 'perceived benefits' and 'relationship continuation'. The former is measured in terms of a series of predictor variables (listed in Table 6.1) about the mentor's training, the closeness of the relationship, and the type of activities and discussions that take place. The success of the intervention is measured by perceived gains (as reported by mentor and mentee) and by relationship longevity (whether it has survived or broken down). The study starts at the point when the mentor and mentee were initially matched and takes further measures at 6 and 12 months. It is thus positioned beautifully for the review, in its attempt to figure out what makes the relationship happen.

Participants are enrollees in one of the US Big Brothers Big Sisters (BBBS) programmes and are aged 7–14, with 84 per cent from single adult homes and 69 per cent defined as low income (eligible for school lunch support). More about the BBBS participant profile will be revealed by subsequent studies in the review; here it is sufficient to note that they span a range of status backgrounds. Nothing is reported on their values, dispositions, identity or reference group on entry to the scheme, but it might be inferred from the usual BBBS long screening process that these are not America's foremost rebels (see Study 7 for further details). The main results are presented in a path analysis format but the zero-order correlations in the following, and as simplified Table 6.1, provide the gist of the findings on what these youths value. Note again that these particular outcome measures are not about improved status via educational or behavioural gains, but relate only to 'self-reported benefits' and 'staying with the programme'.

So what do these kids like, and what keeps 'em at it? What the synthesis is looking for in these results is a quantitative footprint giving an indication that certain elements of the mentoring relationship have greater pay-off than do others. Is there a quantitative signature to match the process evidence discovered in Studies 1 to 3? The simplest indication of what is important is contained in the significance levels reported as asterisks in the table. The quality of the mentor's training does not figure (small negative coefficients in the first row). These adolescents do not seem to notice or care much about their mentor's preparation. This contrasts, interestingly,

TABLE 6.1   *Correlations between predictor measures and reported outcomes*

Predictor measure	Perceived benefit Youth report	Relationship continuation
Quality of training	−.10	−.06
Mentor efficacy	.31*	.11
Programme staff support	.09	.21
Relationship obstacles	.04	−.19
Mentor/youth contact	.38**/.42**	.24/.18
Relationship closeness	.29*/.60***	.50***/.29*
Discussion – youth behaviour	.24/.19	.04/.15
Discussion – youth relationships	.16/.17	.17/.22
Discussion – casual conversation	.27/.14	.19/.27
Discussion – social issues	.18/.07	−.06/.23
Activities – sports/athletic	.13/.38**	.26/.31*
Activities – recreation/non-athletic	.29*/.32*	.27/.26
Activities – educational/cultural	.30*/.44**	.13/.26

The cells with dual scores refer to predictor variables that are rated separately by mentors/mentees.
Significance levels indicated by */**/***

with the mentors' perceptions, in which there is a strong association (+ .31*, data not shown) between their perceptions of the quality of their training and their own report on the perceived benefits of the partnership. For the purposes of the review a blank is drawn on whether volunteers or professionals develop more productive relationships.

Relationship closeness (row 6, as estimated by either mentor or mentee) seems to be the most significant factor in terms of utility and bond to the programme. This finding, however, is arguably a tautology, with similar reported measures being utilized as both dependent and independent variables (relationship closeness ends up explaining relationship durability!). Amount of contact is another factor influencing the perceived benefits of, and continuation with, the relationship. Again, this is hardly surprising but the authors note a fit with other research showing that regular and consistent patterns of contact are essential, and that 'more than half of the relationships studied were not maintained at the agency's minimum criterion of at least three hours per week'. A brief reflection on the previous studies in this review affirms the contribution of regular contact to the long haul.

Perhaps the most useful results lie towards the bottom of the table. In general, activities (rows 11–13) seem to outstrip discussion (rows 7–10) in terms of perceived utility and tie to the programme. Mentees who report being engaged in a relationship based on plenty of sports/athletics are significantly more likely to stay with the programme. The study thus begins to pinpoint the precise nature of befriending that nurtures the long move in its formative stage. Non-directive, mutual activities in the form of basketball, music and retail grazing are the mundane starting points of relationship-building.

The study is of use to the review in giving quantitative confirmation of the significance of some of the inner mechanisms of the mentoring relationship that, so far, have only been evoked in qualitative description. The exact nature of the continuing contact that follows on commonplace companionship nonetheless remains somewhat elusive. This study reaches to and beyond the limits of the survey method, and produces associations galore. However, it is very difficult to interpret because so many of the correlations are rooted in self-reports about self-reports, and there is so much overlap (auto-correlation) between the so-called explanatory variables.

Study 5: St James-Roberts, I. and Singh, C. (2001) *Can Mentors Help Primary School Children with Behaviour Problems?* Home Office Research Study 233. London: Home Office Research and Statistics Directorate, 60pp

This is a mixed-method evaluation of project CHANCE, a programme aimed at primary school children referred 'with behavioural problems and other risk factors'. Its key feature was the provision of mentors whose task was to intervene 'before problems became entrenched, to support and redirect children away from antisocial behaviour, social exclusion and criminal offending'. It thus has long-move objectives and is squarely in the domain of engagement mentoring.

The programme theory for CHANCE specified two stages or objectives for mentoring. The first was to 'establish trusting and supportive relationships with the children'. The second was the 'use of an individualised, solution-focused intervention … aimed to teach lifeskills which encourage independence, active learning and a sense of personal mastery rather than seeking to identify the original causes of the problem'. These correspond, most helpfully, to the emotional (befriending) and cognitive (direction-setting) stages of the mentoring relationship that form the basis of this review.

The research involved an intensive process evaluation using semi-structured interviews with all stakeholders (management, teachers who made referrals, mentors, mentees, mentees' mothers). There was also an outcome evaluation using a comparison group study of children with similar high risk backgrounds. This part of the study examined behavioural change using standardized measures of school attendance, school exclusion and academic performance.

In the formative evaluation, the befriending goal is reported to have met with considerable success: children and mentors are shown, with some exceptions, to have got on very well. However, the individualized, solution-focused intervention goal was the cause of some confusion, summarized by the authors as follows:

> To evaluate how successfully the solution-focused stage of mentoring was implemented, mentors were asked about their immediate and longer-term goals for the meetings and how the meetings were designed to meet the goals. Responses varied with some planning their meetings with specific goals and clearly working

with a strategy in mind. Others appeared to turn up for meetings with little overall idea of where they were going or the steps needed to get there. Interviews with mentors identified some uncertainty in what to target and how to deliver the solution focused stage of mentoring. Some mentors saw themselves as the link between school and home, attended school regularly, took part in case conferences and had set up a close working liaison with the children's teachers. Others were uncertain how to help with schoolwork, how much to support the child or whether to support the mother in order to help the child. (p. 19)

The outcome evaluation showed no net impact: 'the mentored children improved in their behaviours but equivalent improvements were found in the comparison group who had not had mentors.' This finding is based on a comparison of only 25 children per group and needs to be treated with appropriate caution on that score. In particular, there is the difficulty, acknowledged by the authors, that this entire group of 'difficult children' had already been singled out for assistance within the local education and welfare services. As always in field experiments, the control group is not 'in repose' but rather 'in the system'. It is, therefore, also difficult to know what levels of attention those who were apportioned to the control group received from within mainstream services. Nevertheless, there were no significant differences observed across a considerable range of measures and, what is more, 'serious problems continued in both'.

This study provides a reasonable fit with the toughest corners of the review theory. As well as socio-economic deprivation, the mentees (97 per cent male, 50 per cent white) scored highly on a standardized measure of behavioural problems (hyperactivity, conduct and peer problems). They are thus outsiders in status terms by very many a measure, and probably more so than in the other inquiries featured here. Furthermore, and unlike the other schemes reviewed here, the mentees were all recruited by teacher referral. On these grounds it may be reasonable to infer that they have already resisted change and are, quite probably, a more detached and antagonistic group than in other cases examined here.

Faced with this situation the volunteer mentors (80 per cent women, 'mostly' white), who were given four days' training followed by 'well-managed' supervision, appear only to be able to make affective shifts (nevertheless deemed important by the researchers). Significantly, their ability to influence cognitive/direction-setting seems mixed and limited. Further, and unsurprisingly, they are not able to promote the climb up the engagement ladder to its aptitudinal and positional rungs. An explanation, perhaps, is given rather eloquently in a boxed section on 'What do mentors do?'.

Mentors generally met their children for two to four hours a week, usually a weekend morning or afternoon, giving an average of 120 hours over a year. The most common activities were walks, sports and activities in the park; visits to the cinema, theatre or zoo; home activities such as cooking (in some cases in the mentor's home), puzzles, making things, computer games; visits to libraries and museums; and just talking. A few mentors involved their mentees in activities with their own children. Most mentors had regular contact with their children's mothers. (p. 17)

These somewhat dismal findings throw useful light on the synthesis. The hypothesis states that unsuccessful outcomes follow from the application of inappropriate mechanisms. Here, a weak array of mentoring mechanisms is aimed at a tough task and outcomes flow accordingly.

Study 6: Shiner, M., Newburn, T., Young, T. and Groben, S. (2004) *Mentoring Disaffected Young People: An Evaluation of 'Mentoring Plus'*. York: Joseph Rowntree Foundation, 92pp

This is a long report of a multi-method evaluation of a complex programme. It is appropriate, therefore, to issue a reminder that this review only pursues material that relates to the model under investigation and that many other important findings on programme implementation, integrity and context are not assessed here. The programme in question is called Mentoring Plus, comprising a pre-programme residential course and a parallel educational and training programme, as well as the mentoring element. The different phases were staffed by a variety of in-house staff and local providers as well as the volunteer mentors.

The mentees exhibited high levels of deprivation and offending, and were outsiders on many counts. The study provides an unusually detailed profile (via a comparison with a national survey of youth lifestyles) of family disruption, education, training and work difficulties, offending behaviour, high levels of drinking and smoking as well as illicit drug use. They came to the scheme through a variety of routes, with pathways from self-referral and word of mouth being considered as significant as formal referral through offending teams and schools. There was an interview and selection process, an induction phase and pre-scheme residential course. Mentees could opt out at any of these stages. Throughout the review, it is noticeable how both position and disposition are crucial in affecting programme success. Between them, self-referral and volunteer-only membership suggest that most scheme members may have been at a post-antagonism stage in terms of reference group affiliation. This is borne out by some data on 'reasons for joining the scheme' in which 'stopping me getting into trouble' and 'help me get a job' top the poll.

A key finding from the qualitative research relates to the nature of the mentoring relationship. Case after case points to the fact that the linear escalator of engagement not only gets stuck at intermediate stages but also tends to bump up and down on the journey. This can be summarized in a three-step model, described in enormous detail (not reproduced here) by the authors as follows (p. 38):

- The basic cycle: contact–meeting–doing
- The problem-solving cycle: contact–meeting–doing–firefighting
- The action-oriented cycle: contact–meeting–doing–[firefighting]–action.

The first stage is similar to befriending or, as the authors put it, 'the mundane stuff of basic human interaction'. Relationships then frequently face the test of a problem

TABLE 6.2   *Main activity at beginning and end of programme*

	Beginning %	End %	% Change
Participants			
Attending school	38	21	−17
Attending further/higher education	6	25	+19
Training scheme or employment	6	17	+11
Regular truanting	10	5	−5
Excluded from school	11	5	−6
Not in education, employment or training	30	28	−2
Non-participants			
Attending school	47	38	−9
Attending further/higher education	15	18	+3
Training scheme or employment	7	12	+5
Regular truanting	7	1	−6
Excluded from school	4	0	−4
Not in education, employment or training	20	32	+12

or crisis, and only progress on the basis of a successful response (hence firefighting). For example, mentoring partnerships were consolidated if they managed to deal with specific and periodic episodes of violence, homelessness, substance misuse and so on. When sufficient levels of trust and mutual understanding were achieved through the first two stages, some partnerships were then able to move to the action agenda and to advance in relation to work and educational plans. The authors show that progress though the stages is far from automatic, that crisis points intervene throughout and that the process is often cyclical, involving numerous returns to square one.

This study also produced detailed quantitative evidence on impact, including the participant and non-participant comparison in Table 6.2. These and other data reveal a complex pattern of outcomes. The authors make two claims in particular, that:

- Programme participants display a greater overall shift from exclusion to inclusion than do non-participants.
- Evidence of impact was most marked in relation to progress in work, training and employment rather than family relationships, substance abuse and offending behaviour (data not shown).

There are attribution problems with this particular methodology. The comparison group is of young people who had initial contact but failed to participate in the (voluntary) programme. This is far from any common perception of a control group. Rather than a like-with-like comparison, voluntary self-selection could render this comparison as one between the aspirational and the antagonistic. Selection effects are the classic bugbear of quasi-experimentation and this *self*-selection effect may load the experimental group with the acquiescent and the aspirational, who, according to the review theory, have better chances in the first place. Opting out of the programme might stem, alternatively, from being sufficiently in control to feel no need for it. Either way, attribution of these changes to the programme is dangerous. Be that as it may, significant gains in the direction of 'inclusion' are made by participants, and the research went on to investigate their own understanding of what was important.

Here lies a rather dramatic result: 'overall the Plus element tended to be rated more favourably than the mentors'. The greater perceived utility of orthodox education and training provision is further evidence that mentoring alone rarely promotes the full range of engagement shifts in the review model. Study 2 showed how there can be tension between mentors and formal providers. In Study 3 by contrast, professional mentors offered both friendship and a guiding institutional hand. This study, however, demonstrates that these are not the only permutations. Perhaps the most interesting fragment of evidence is on the synergy of the mentoring and the Plus elements. Table 6.2 shows that the greatest gains on the programme are made in terms of moves into further and higher education and, in this particular sphere, the mentors' contribution (not shown in the data above) is rated at much the same level as the formal provision. This dual effect is illustrated in a vignette in which a mentor speaks about the confidence-building that prompts and sustains the education hard slog:

> She's gained entry level one in Maths and English and we talked about level two and it was 'no, I'm not doing that, that's too hard'. Like at the presentation the other evening she picked up four certificates and I said to her 'I'm really proud and are you glad you did it now?' and she went, 'yeah I'm glad'. And I said to her jokingly 'well we'll start that level two soon' and she went 'no', but the next day she was on the phone, 'I want to start level two, will you come and help me?'. (p. 51)

Here then is a further refinement of the basic model. Not only is there a clear indication that mentoring fosters reliance by sheer persistence, the nature of mentoring support in promoting aptitudinal and positional support is also made clearer. The mentor's role here, if successful, is likely to be in facilitative mode.

This study approaches book length and offers much greater detail on subprocesses and multiple outcomes than most of the others collected here. This review, therefore, is not exhaustive and further nuances, such as the limited impact on offending, are not reported here. Bulk does not make for perfection, of course, and there are the inevitable difficulties in the study on matters of attribution and the meaning of some of the outcome measures.

Study 7: Grossman, J. and Tierney, J. (1998) 'Does mentoring work? An impact study of the Big Brothers Big Sisters program', *Evaluation Review*, 22(3): 403–26

This is the best-known study of the best-known programme. It takes some of the responsibility for the popularity of mentoring programmes for youth, thanks to its positive conclusion:

Taken together, the results presented here show that having a Big Brother or a Big Sister offers tangible benefits for youth. At the conclusion of the 18 month study period, we found that Little Brothers and Little Sisters were less likely to have started using drugs or taking alcohol, felt more competent about doing school work, attended school more, got better grades, and have better relationships with their parents and peers than they would have if they had not participated in the programme. (p. 422)

Moreover, its methodological credentials are often seen as impeccable. The research strategy employed is a 'field' version of a randomized controlled trial in which the core comparison uses 959 volunteers for the programme who are split into an experimental group and a 'waiting list' control. It is not quite clear what happens in the limbo of the queue but (self-)selection effects are minimized and, according to the authors, programme impact can thus be calculated directly because 'the only systematic difference between the groups was that the treatment youths had the opportunity to be matched with a Big Brother or Big Sister'.

So who are these Little Brothers and Little Sisters? This is the staple question of this review and probably the key to explaining the success of this particular trial. Grossman and Tierney provide a useful description of the mentees' characteristics. They are rather young (mean age 12, with 80 per cent being 13 and under). In terms of race and gender, they are 23 per cent minority girls, 34 per cent minority boys, 15 per cent white girls and 23 per cent white boys. They have some of the characteristics of social deprivation but this by no means applies to the majority: 43 per cent live in a home receiving public assistance; 39 per cent of parents are divorced or separated; 40 per cent have a history of domestic violence; 21 per cent have suffered emotional abuse; and 11 per cent have experienced physical abuse. This is a rather mixed bag. Indubitably, we are dealing with some of America's disadvantaged young people but they do not all possess the multiple, ingrained characteristics of the dispossessed and, crucially, this is not a profile that matches participants in some of the other studies examined.

Information on reference group positions and thus motivation on entry to the programme has to be gleaned indirectly (the authors are concerned only to control for this). The study, however, provides a footnote outlining a clear set of entry and eligibility requirements, and some vital clues on the participants' aspirations lie here. Big Brothers Big Sisters (BBBS) screening involves: an assessment for a 'minimal level of social skills', ensuring that youths and parents actually 'want a mentor'; gaining the 'agreement of parent and child to follow agency rules'; the successful completion of orientation and training sessions; and the fulfilment of residential and age limitations. After the induction period, matching occurred, which itself was a prolonged procedure. Matching with a mentor was achieved for 78 per cent of the would-be mentees, with an average waiting time of 4.7 months, the shortage of suitable mentors being especially acute for minority boys, for whom the average delay was 5.9 months. In addition to these programme requirements, the research created exclusions of its own, namely for more than a hundred youths: those with 'physical and learning difficulties' not allowing them to complete a telephone interview; those on 'special programmes' within the overall BBBS package; and those 'serving a contractual obligation such as Child Protection Service contract'. This welter of self, bureaucratic and investigatory selection is significant. It is not too brave an inference to observe that the programme and the research (and indeed the control group) dealt with a relatively compliant and particularly persevering set of mentees.

The report provides too much detail on programme impact to be easily summarized here, but a pattern of generally positive results across a range of behaviours is exemplified in a whole succession of tables. There is fluctuation, of course. For instance, in terms of 'antisocial behaviour' the programme generates significant reductions in the commencement of smoking and drug usage, and in the levels of 'hitting'. However, no effect is found for stealing or damage to property. Significant impact differentials are also reported for sub-groups (minority/white, male/female). Unfortunately, the sub-group analysis is only reported for the 'face-sheet' race/gender classifications, and the variables more directly indicating deprivation and detachment (for example, public assistance, domestic violence) are not used. A potential test of the differences between those making long and short moves up the ladder of engagement is thus omitted in the analysis.

Another significant and (in)famous limitation of the BBBS impact data is that much of the information on outcomes is collected by self-report via a telephone survey. It is the programme subjects who report on the grades received, on whether they have used drugs, and so forth. In a footnote the authors quote sources which they claim support the view that such 'measures are acceptable by conventional social science standards'. For this reviewer, this is a questionable view, most especially in the context of programme trials, which ever since the discovery of the Hawthorne effect are well known for their capacity to influence respondents to 'fake good'.

In the round, this study provides the most comprehensive basis for the claim that mentoring works to alleviate a range of problems, and improve a range of attitudes and behaviours. Doubts remain, however, about the validity and reliability of some of the crucial outcome measures. Rather more important for the purposes of this theory-testing review is the subsidiary information about mentee position and the nature of the mentoring relations. Despite some solid evidence on (status) deprivation, Little Brothers and Sisters (and their parents) are rather willing horses by the usual motivational standards. By a steady and, perhaps, unintentional process of elimination, more damaged and antagonistic youths are held at bay from the programme and the inquiry. There is no basis here for a generalizable claim that youth mentoring works or that long-move mentoring is easily sustained.

And no such claim is made:

> This study does not provide evidence that any type of mentoring works, but rather that mentoring programs that facilitate the type of relationships we observed in the BBBS program work. In our judgment, the positive impacts observed are unlikely to have occurred without both the relationship with the mentor and the support the program provided the match. (p. 422)

If an additional qualification is made – that BBBS only confronts a sub-set of disadvantaged youth – we are on the way to assessing the proper import of this study.

What remains is the important matter of the infrastructure supporting the mentoring relationship. Previous studies in the review have shown that the relationship with other parties and agencies is crucial to mentoring's success, and Grossman and Tierney's report ends with a description of some of the unique features of BBBS (pp. 422–33):

- ... volunteer screening that weeds out adults who are unlikely to keep their time commitments or who may pose a risk to youth.
- Matching procedures that take into account the preferences of youth, his or her family, and the volunteer, and that use a professional case manager to analyse which volunteer would work best with each youth.
- Close supervision and support of each match by a case manager who makes frequent contact with the parent/guardian, volunteer and youth and provides assistance when requested, as difficulties arise.
- Training that includes communication and limit-setting skills, tips on relationship-building and recommendations on the best way to interact with a young person.

This list arguably omits one of its key features. A glance at the history of BBBS shows that is a 'sturdy programme', surviving in different forms for a whole century (Freedman, 1993). This particular inquiry was only possible because it concentrated on those agencies that were popular enough and had sufficient capacity to create a waiting list for places. In other words, it is a study of the sturdiest bits of a sturdy programme. Given the queue for places, it is quite likely that there was some local kudos in being a graduate of these particular schemes and, perhaps, that they were regarded as a passport out of social deprivation. Grossman and Tierney's caution on matters of generalizability is thus particularly well founded, because there is a world of difference between repute on this level and that of being referred compulsorily to a small-scale trial of an untried government scheme such as that reported in Study 5.

Even though this reappraisal of the study has questioned some of the authors' conclusions and the general wisdom that has grown around them, the findings are not inconsistent with the overall set of hypotheses under review. Steady gains (or at least reported ones) in family relationships and educational success, and movement away from minor criminal behaviour, testify to the engagement of this particular group. Such transformations are easier for the well motivated and there are grounds for supposing that this is the cohort being dealt with here. Mentors have generally been found to need considerable additional support, and this is evident even in the well-oiled BBBS programme.

Study 8: Rhodes, J., Grossman, J. and Resch, N. (2000) 'Agents of change: pathways through which mentoring relationships influence adolescents' academic adjustment', *Child Development,* **71(6): 1662–71**

This study provides further evidence on the side-play in successful mentoring relationships, and is included because it provides a quantitative analysis of some key

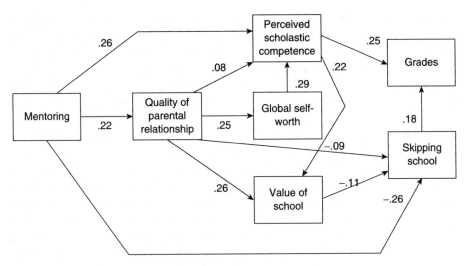

FIGURE 6.2   *Path model of direct and indirect effects of mentoring*

facets of that relationship. Normally, a reviewer may expect process information to be found in qualitative studies and outcomes to be described in quantitative analyses. This division of methodological labour is not entirely watertight, however. Multivariate studies that examine a range of measured changes associated with a programme may provide some clues about the pattern and sequence of those changes and thus give an indication of how they are triggered. The research strategy involved is similar to that of the previous study in that it uses the same design on a very similar sample drawn from the biggest BBBS agencies (quick-eyed readers will note overlap in the research teams). The key difference is the attempt to model the pathways of change.

As we have seen in Study 7, before/after comparisons of the BBBS cohorts show a wide, if uneven, range of gains associated with the programme. Study 8 uses a method of analysis known as LISREL to arrive at a statistical model of the pattern of change in output and outcome measures associated with participation in the programme. This is reproduced in Figure 6.2.

What the model attempts to do is to show which of these intermediate changes is direct or indirect, and give a weighting to the strength of that influence. For example, according to the upper portion of the model, mentoring does not influence grades directly (no arrow) but only by building a youth's perception of his or her scholastic competence, which platform then goes on to influence actual school performance. Although they show very neatly the uneven and developmental nature of the changes associated with mentoring, these models are notoriously difficult to interpret.

There is no space to enter into all the technicalities of LISREL (which can be found in the full review). The reported coefficients are prone to minor variation according to how the model is configured, so it is often wiser to concentrate on parts of the more general picture obtained through such models. In this respect it is safe to endorse the broadest finding of the survey, namely that 'the effects of mentoring are partially mediated through adolescents' perceptions of their parental relationships'. This is a rather cautious and thus relatively safe inference, gained from a large sample of successful cases. It does not say anything about the actual process at work: the pattern is statistical, namely that the mentees who report a variety of educational gains (they value school more, they are less likely to skip class, they consider themselves to be improving) tend to be the ones who also report improved relationships at home.

It is this inference – 'if parents feel involved in, as opposed to supplanted by the provision of additional adult support, they are likely to reinforce mentors' positive influences' – that I want to add to the review. A further reason why it is a safe inference is that it buttresses earlier, qualitative findings about successful mentoring relationships extending beyond the one-to-one and insinuating themselves into other relationships and agencies. In particular, it gives support to the earlier illustrations about how the most able mentors can assist in hanging onto and building upon often tenuous family relationships (recall the 'World War 3' quotation in Study 3). It is probably one of the unsung early components of the affective relationship, marking the beginnings of the long haul of engagement mentoring.

This study thus adds a very specific piece to the mentoring relationship jigsaw. What is perceived in the initial review hypotheses as a process of personal change generated in the 'dyad' may well be rooted in the 'triad' (in this instance with other family members). The model of befriending as personal solace needs supplementing. A beneficial mentoring relationship is not just the medium of individual change, it is also the bridge into further successful associations.

Study 9: DuBois, D., Holloway, B., Valentine, J. and Cooper, H. (2002) 'Effectiveness of mentoring programmes for youth: a meta-analytic review', *American Journal of Community Psychology*, 30(2): 157–97

This is a long, highly technical meta-analysis, pooling the results of 55 experimental and quasi-experimental evaluations of mentoring programmes in the United States. As such it may appear a strange choice for inclusion in this theory-driven review. The purpose is two-fold. The first is to add to the technical range of studies covered. Realist synthesis tries to make sense of data patterns, be they found in primary studies (of any methodological stripe) *or* in secondary analysis. The second rationale is to demonstrate the idea of explanatory refinement. Because it operates at high levels of aggregation, DuBois et al.'s review throws up results that seem somewhat out of kilter with previous analyses. Can they be synthesized into an explanatory whole? In some cases, as the subsequent discussion shows, this involves the reviewer in re-interpreting or even discounting claims in the original research.

The meta-analysis draws on literature from 1970 to 1998 and aims to assess the overall effects of mentoring programmes on youth as well as investigating impact variation in relation to key aspects of programme design and implementation. There is evidence that mentoring programmes are effective, but impact is declared to be 'relatively small' or 'modest'. This result is estimated via several forms of the weighted and unweighted d-index, but in a more digestible form is rendered thus: 'the outcome for the average participant in a youth mentoring programme surpassed that of approximately 55% of the control group'. This indubitably tame influence is of no special interest to the current explanatory analysis, although entirely consistent with it. DuBois et al.'s net impact measure gathers up and pools together data on a wide diversity of programme goals, operationalized in 44 different ways. As such, the overall verdict melds all manner of victories and defeats, and the analysis to date has taught us to expect net effects 'to crawl asymptotically towards zero' (Rossi, 1987; see Chapter 3).

The moderator and mediator analysis provides more analytic purchase in that it tries to provide statistical estimates of some of the characteristics of those programmes and personnel associated with the more positive effects. Two are of special interest from the perspective of understanding partners and partnerships.

(I) The strongest empirical basis exists for utilizing mentoring as a preventative intervention for youth whose backgrounds include significant conditions of environmental risk and disadvantage. (p. 190)

There is a suggestion here, much welcomed incidentally by the mentoring fraternity, that mentoring works best for high risk youth. However, the statement needs careful unpacking, especially for the present review, in that it seems to run counter to some of the previous evidence showing the difficulty of 'rags to riches' mentoring. In terms of destination, the outcome measures for the youth in question include training and academic gains, and positive shifts on these dimensions are demonstrated in DuBois et al.'s analysis for the group in question (although the proviso remains about many of the primary studies using 'perceived scholastic gains' as the benchmark).

The crucial question is about origin: in what sense are these high risk subjects? There is one sense, of course, in which all subjects in programmes such as BBBS are high risk in that programme publicity, referral and screening are usually directed at those with needs for the additional support that mentoring may bring. Within this group, DuBois et al. distinguish between those suffering 'environmental' and 'individual' risk, with the meta-analysis revealing that only the former reap the enhanced gains. Operational definitions are not provided in the journal report but convention suggests that environmental risk might be measured in terms of demographic location within deprived groups as measured by poverty, race, welfare support, parental circumstances and so on. Individual risk is often located within a record that includes elements such as behavioural disruption, substance abuse, criminal activity and being a victim of abuse. In this respect, the review hypothesis about the relative rarity of engagement for high-risk youth with behavioural problems (as well as the evidence on this score from Study 5) is supported.

This leaves us with the positive evidence for the 'environmental risk only' sub-group. Whilst it is reasonable to suppose that they are high risk in demographic terms, we do not know whether this is the case in terms of aspirations and dispositions. Several authors have criticized the evaluations of BBBS interventions for not acknowledging sufficiently the 'filtering out' of unmotivated families and young people (Lucas and Liabo, 2003). As noted in the discussion of Study 7, there is a screening element often involving written elements, referral is controlled and there is often a lengthy waiting list to start the programme given the perpetual problems of finding and training suitable mentors. The data required for meta-regression can only be obtained from large-scale programmes and so these features may well reoccur across the whole sample (see Jekielek et al., 2002 for a description of other major US mentoring programmes). Thus one way of accounting for the finding is that this sub-group of relative successes may be materially deprived but are also a forbearing lot who have already climbed a couple of rungs on the aspirational ladder before encountering the programme.

Yet another interpretation of the relative success of the environmentally deprived might be the classic floor/ceiling effect. Materially better-off youngsters have better 'grades' on entry and may have less room for improvement. Meta-regression cannot, however, provide an explanation for this particular association and we need to look elsewhere in the review for the appropriate clues.

> (2) ... whether mentoring was provided alone or as part of a multi-component program was not a significant moderator of effect size. Similarly, neither the comparison of BB/BSA versus non-BB/BSA programs nor the comparison of programs according to psychosocial or instrumental goals yielded significantly different effect sizes. (p. 177)

All of these null results are surprising and run counter to some of the earlier findings. They are startling in that they seem to suggest that however a youth mentoring programme is packaged, it will have broadly similar and very modest impacts. They do not square with any of the previous analyses, which suggest that the sequencing of mentoring resources is vital. Reviews face such puzzles and contradictions all the time and it is important in an explanatory synthesis to be able to account for the discrepancies.

In this case, there is a methodological explanation and it is likely that the high levels of aggregation in meta-analysis account for the inconsistency. The 55 different trials are compared in terms of effect sizes and it will be recalled that the raw data that DuBois et al. use in coming to this calculation are based on different permutations of the 44 outcome indicators used in the primary studies. Variations in programme effect are then accounted for in the moderator analysis which itself takes into consideration 49 variables describing the myriad characteristics of the programmes. Each of these moderators takes a single and simple cut at the variable of interest. For instance, in the case of programme make-up, each trial is categorized as 'mentoring alone' or 'multi-component'. The result is that when it comes to making an assessment of the importance of a particular programme configuration, the meta-analysis is making a crudely drawn comparison assessed in terms of highly assorted measures.

Earlier case studies have shown that multi-component programmes take on a variety of forms. In Study 1, the different facets were embodied in the mentor. In Study 2, mentors acted as an adjunct (and seemingly in opposition) to a training programme. In Study 3, mentoring was carried out as an extension of professional youth work. In Study 6, there was a separate education and training programme, which mentors supported synergistically. In Study 7, case managers rather than mentors were tasked with weaving programme components together. These studies show that one of the keys to youth mentoring lies in the ability to dovetail the components of engagement, and DuBois's aggregate data cannot make the subtle discernment to assist in such an analysis.

A similar question may be raised in relation to the apparent non-significance for impact of whether the programme was 'psycho-social', 'instrumental' or 'both'. Details are not given about how such a classification was operationalized but, again, this is a very tough measurement call; mentoring relationships develop and blow with the wind and this key function might be better judged at the level of individual partnerships rather than a public statement about programme ethos. One suspects that the impact of these different mentoring styles is better interrogated by a locally sensitive analysis rather than the crude three-fold distinction. This conclusion is reinforced by a further, contradictory result from the meta-regression. One recommendation of the authors is that the use of 'mentors with a background in a helping role or profession (e.g. teacher) tends to be associated with positive results'. Note that this positive mediator suggests, in contrast to the previous classification, that mentors capable of providing instrumental assistance may have more clout than those trading on psycho-social loyalties. Like much of the rest of the telescopic analysis, this remains an interesting possibility but one which it would be unwise for decision-makers to follow without reservation.

Conclusion

This synthesis is selective and theory-driven in highlighting the particular role played by the basic orientation of the mentor and mentee, and the nature of their relationship. Quite diverse research studies have been brought into the analysis by concentrating on this particular theoretical thread, and by pulling out the empirical evidence that relates to some simple hypotheses about different mentoring relationships and for whom and in which circumstances they function (Figure 6.1).

The review thus moves, in realist synthesis style, from some knowledge to more knowledge and the findings are expressed, quite deliberately, in the form of a model (Figure 6.3). It takes the form of a diagram of the pathways that youth mentoring has to take if it is to realize its most daunting ambition of engaging with disaffected youth and reintegrating them into the mainstream world of education and work.

The balance of evidence is that this ultimate goal is met infrequently and only in the special circumstances described in the model. The model itself is expressed as a network of flows, blockages and slippages. The metaphor of snakes and ladders comes to mind in representing the ups and downs of a mentee's progress, but we shall continue in more prosaic fashion, with four concluding bullet points:

- Starting at the bottom left of the diagram, the model remains faithful to the initial idea that in order to fulfil the overall ambition of engagement a mentor must accomplish a whole set of functions, summarized and simplified as befriending, direction-setting, coaching and sponsoring. The evidence shows that moving up this ladder gets progressively more difficult and many relationships get no further than a close bonding based on the sharing of mundane activities. The arrows decline in volume as an indication of this waning effect (it is not possible, however, for this or any other review to quantify this diminution of outputs and outcomes). There are positive exceptions, in that some programmes report a solid ascent from emotional and cognitive gains and into skill and career progression for a significant number of mentees. Such progress, however, is much more likely for mentees who arrive in a programme with in-built resilience and with aspirations about moving away from their present status. Whether this is considered a success story or a soft target depends on the overall objectives of a programme.

- Turning to the second column, one sees that mentee progress is not only halting, it is non-linear. Given the circles in which they move, many disadvantaged young people have frequent and repetitive battles with authorities, bust-ups with family, and brushes with the law. In such circumstances (the lightning symbol) mentoring relationships will tend to collapse along with everything else. Accordingly, the best available micro-data on the mentoring relationship reveal a persistent firefighting element. This rebuilding of mentoring functions also follows a stepladder of ascent in which relations of trust have to be regained, in which mentees are imbued with resilience against repeated stumbling blocks, and in which they are instilled with confidence in the face of new hurdles.

- Turning to the third column, this indicates that the mentor's relationship is not just with the mentee. Mentors have to bring Muhammad to the mountain, but also vice versa. In respect of each mentoring function there exists a reception committee of other agents and agencies, and the function is better accomplished if the mentor makes steps to bring along members of that committee. Thus befriending and trust-building work better with, and to some extent through, the development of support to, and exchange with, the family and close friends of the mentee. In moving up the ladder, the mentor will parley with other members of the mentee's community and, after that, all manner of welfare, training and career guidance professionals. Bridge-building to other agents and agencies is shown to be a key facet of success. Clearly, different mentors will have quite different access to and experience of these different networks. There is some evidence to demonstrate the utility of having a mentor who has 'been there and done that', but in ransacking these studies it is rare to find cases in which the single mentor operates routinely across all channels.

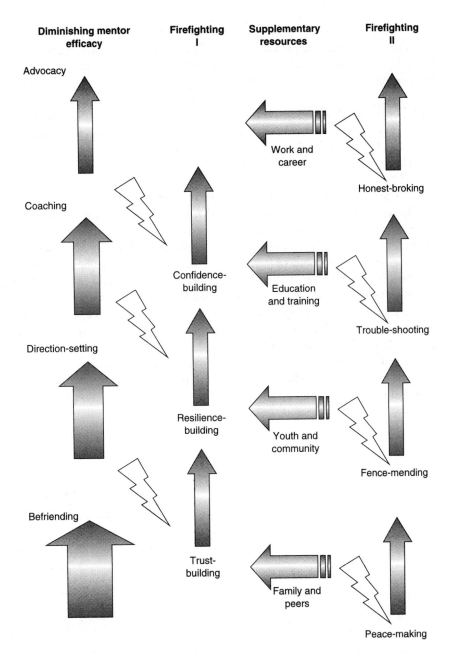

FIGURE 6.3   *Pathways of youth mentoring*

- This leads us to the finding that mentoring works better if it is embedded in a programme offering further support, especially in terms of some of the loftier training and career aspirations of mentoring programmes. But once again, there is no given and guaranteed formula of 'mentoring plus'. Some studies show that relationships with other agencies can be marked by a lack of co-ordination or insufficient resources, or even mistrust and hostility. Accordingly, lightning can strike here too, and this may involve the mentor in a rather different round of firefighting with a rather different group of incendiaries (illustrated in column four). Here the literature describes another of the mentor's supplementary tasks, namely placating the various authorities of whom his or her protégé may have fallen foul. Needless to say, relatively few mentors will have the equipment or stomach for this battle and these interfaces mark another set of potential culs-de-sac for the mentoring journey.

Figure 6.3 and the four-point summary above represent the conclusion to the review. It does not tell the policy-maker whether to buy in or opt out of youth mentoring programmes (it is assumed that this decision gets made on other grounds). However, it does try to encapsulate what has been learned about why such mentoring programmes work and why they fail. The conclusion is deliberately offered in the form of a model, in the belief that policy-makers think in model-building terms when they plan and develop programmes. They aspire to change. They know that change inches along. They know that a variety of pulls, pushes and supports is needed to sustain an intervention. Accordingly, the figure is a sketch map of the pathways along which mentoring flourishes or flounders, all of which need to be anticipated in the management of a programme. It offers a blueprint of the mechanisms that need to be embedded in the construction of a programme, in the selection and training of practitioners, and in the targeting and motivation of subjects.

7

Reviewing Outer Contexts: Naming and Shaming

There is not a crime, there is not a dodge, there is not a trick, there is not a swindle, there is not a vice, which does not live by secrecy. Get these things out in the open, describe them, attack them, ridicule them in the press, and sooner or later public opinion will sweep them away. (Pulitzer, 1978, quoted in Fisse and Braithwaite, 1983: 1)

In Chapter 3, I made the observation that some programme ideas are ubiquitous and that one can find the same underlying mechanism at the heart of interventions operating right across the policy waterfront. The above epigraph in Pulitzer's name is a positive prize-winner on this score. All manner of human failings exist and endure, he argues, because they are hidden from public view. And the resolution, he goes on to claim, is a matter of getting the underlying truths out in the open and allowing public opinion to apply the corrective.

This grand thesis constitutes the subject matter of the third illustration of realist synthesis. Decision-makers have apparently warmed to Pulitzer's maxim to the extent that there is hardly a field of public policy in which 'public disclosure' has not been tried in the attempt to overcome recalcitrant behaviour. One reason for its ubiquity is that the very idea carries substantial public and media support. It is blessed with a catch-phrase, 'naming and shaming', that is both easy on the ear and easy to promote, for who would oppose ceding knowledge to the people?

In contemplating this review I began by looking for examples, and immediately entered a mire. The following are just a brief selection of some of the main public disclosure initiatives, which should be recognizable from these basic descriptions:

- US sex offender registration (Megan's Law)
- Naming prostitutes' clients ('outing johns') (US/UK)
- School 'league tables' (on exam performance, absence rates, etc.) (UK)
- Identification of, and special measures for, 'failing schools' (UK)
- Hospital 'star ratings' (UK) and mortality and surgeon 'report cards' (US)
- 'Pub-watch' prohibition lists for the exclusion of violent drunks (UK)

- European Commission (EC) beach cleanliness standards and 'kite marking'
- Local press adverts for 'poll tax' non-payment and council rent arrears (UK)
- The Community 'Right-to-Know' Act on Environmental Hazards (US)
- Car crime indices and car safety reports (UK/EC)
- Mandatory (public) arrest for domestic violence (US)
- Roadside hoardings naming speeding drivers (UK/US)
- Posters naming streets with unlicensed TV watching (UK)
- UK rail company SPAD (signals passed at danger) ratings
- EC 'name and shame and fame' initiative on compliance with Directives

The indicative sub-sample used in this review shows that disclosure initiatives have been aimed at everything from criminal behaviour to poor work performance, and at targets ranging from isolated individuals to mighty corporations. Public disclosure is also used around the globe and is not, despite the UK/US/EC designations, somewhat crudely applied to the above list, a purely Anglo-Saxon preoccupation.

This notion of widespread cultural susceptibility to the idea of naming and shaming provides the focus for the synthesis. One of the great preoccupations of the realist approach is the contextual sensitivity of the impact of interventions. The review thus selects for closer examination a set of public disclosure programmes played out in contrasting settings. The core exercise is to build a theory, in this case a model of the interpersonal, institutional and cultural conditions, which are required to support successful shaming sanctions. Learning from failure is another motif of realist synthesis, and implementation misfires are deliberately included in the purposive sample. Another inevitable characteristic of this illustration, with its broad policy remit, is that the primary studies consulted include a complex mix of methodological strategies and designs. There is relatively little on show in this chapter about the search, vetting and extraction of the original evidence, and no full-scale review to support the account. This pilot exercise is all there is but this status hopefully does not detract from its singularly important message. To date, systematic review has concentrated on asking tightly defined questions about closely delimited interventions. The aim here is to show that transferable policy lessons may flow from asking ambitious questions about overgrown interventions.

Public disclosure: a theory

> Sunlight is the best disinfectant: electric light the most efficient policeman. (Brandeis, quoted in Fisse and Braithwaite, 1983: vii)

This is an appealing rendition of public disclosure theory, but the realist needs to transform metaphor into model in order to start the process of review. Although the basic idea behind such schemes is often rendered as a couplet (naming and shaming), there are at least three prime stakeholders (shamed subjects, responsible bodies, wider public) and at least four major stages in public disclosure programmes. The intended programme theory, let us call it Plan A, is to transform under-performance or deviant behaviour through the application of the following sequence:

- **Identification:** in which the performance or behaviour in question is observed and then classified, measured, rated, ranked, verified, etc.
- **Naming:** in which information on, and the identity of, the failing or deviant party is disclosed, publicized, disseminated, notified, published, broadcast, registered, etc.
- **Public sanction:** in which the broader community acts on the disclosure in order to shame, reprimand, reproach, censure, control, influence, supervise the named party.
- **Recipient response:** in which behavioural change follows the sanction, with the subjects being shamed, regretful, penitent, contrite, restrained, re-integrated, etc.

Attentive readers will recognize this as a more abstract version of the model which underpinned the Megan's Law review in Chapter 5. This is a deliberate ploy to show that realist synthesis is not formulaic. The same model can be tested in different ways, and the same evidence can be deployed in different ways. The Megan's Law review has already taught that such long and complex processes have many potential weak spots as they pass from stakeholder to stakeholder. This negative conjecture may also be built into the preliminary model, for failure also has a pattern. With this balance of fortunes in mind, some initial reading on the perverse (let us call them Type B) consequences of such interventions was brought together as follows:

- **Culprit misidentification:** in which the performance or behaviour in question is classified inappropriately, with the measure being over- or under-discriminating, lacking in 'risk' or 'value-added' adjustments, or failing though inadequate monitoring or registration.
- **Dissemination dissimulation:** in which the disclosure is poorly managed by sparse or excessive publicity, over-restricted or over-stretched targeting, over-complexity or over-simplification in presentation, or wrangles about the meaning of the information.
- **Sanction misapplication:** in which the wider public applies measures that go beyond shaming, such as humiliation, deprivation, vigilantism, defamation, banishment; or falls short of shaming though disapproval, stoicism, apathy, sympathy, collusion.
- **Unintended outcome:** in which the individual or institution under sanction reacts to shaming by accepting the label and amplifying deviant behaviour, or by ignoring or rejecting the label and continuing existing behaviour, or by reinterpreting the label and adopting a perverse modification to behaviour.

As with all social initiatives, naming and shaming programmes sometimes succeed, sometimes fail, and sometimes end up with a medley of the two. How can differences in the efficacy of disclosure sanctions be accounted for? When do they work (according to Plan A) and when do they fail (with Type B outputs and outcomes)? The review begins by hypothesizing some contextual factors that might account for these diverse destinations. These theories are found scattered through the literature, often embedded in polemical pieces arguing for and against such interventions, and the reviewer's task is to formalize them in such a way that the available evidence can adjudicate between the contrasting claims. There are a great many potential circumstantial differences between the array of programmes noted above, and five are chosen to illustrate the method:

1 **Authority and susceptibility:** Shame turns on blameworthiness. Shaming possibilities will thus vary according to the extent that the 'shamer' can command moral authority, and to the degree of vulnerability of the 'shamee' to such pronouncements. Somewhere in the middle of this ethical continuum lies public opinion, and potential differences in the levels of opprobrium directed against the deficient or offending behaviour in question. These can range from 'moral panic' (for example, sex offenders) to 'there but for the grace of god' (for example, speeding). The review needs to examine the balance of norms and values operating around the social problem addressed, and consider how formidably they gather in support of shaming sanctions.

2 **Nature of the sanction:** Naming and shaming is often regarded as 'pure communication' in that it works as a chain of reactions to what is said about whom, to whom, by whom. In practice, however, disclosure sanctions are rarely solely reputational, but often operate through complementary mechanisms such as economic backlash or increased surveillance or revised management mechanisms. The review needs to examine different applications in order to discover what are shaming's best allies.

3 **Control over the information agenda:** Public bodies are normally in charge of gathering and releasing information but have imperfect control over its onward dispatch and interpretation. Other parties, most notably the public and the named group, may have a degree of day-to-day control over the flow of information. The review needs to examine how and when this blunts the intended effect of the disclosed data.

4 **Control over the media:** A fourth party is often involved in the communication chain, one that may carry and perhaps distort the intended message. Shaming opportunities may go unheeded if the message is not newsworthy, or the intended interpretation of the disclosed information may go astray if it does not fit with existing media frames. The review needs to examine who controls the information flow.

5 **Power and application of the arsenal:** As well as moral authority, shaming sanctions rest on political clout. Important contextual differences may reside in the extent of the authority of the disclosing body (is it a government department, local authority, governing body, trust, consumer watchdog, purchaser,

whistle-blower?). The exercise of that authority may also be significant (is the release of information active, passive, vituperative, benign?). The review needs to examine the power behind the message.

The evidence: five key contrasts

In the main body of this review fragments of evidence are extracted from six contrasting applications (fragments is the operative word, affirming that this chapter reports on a pilot rather than a full review). The review is set its standard explanatory quest, and the developing explanation is interwoven through the synthesis. The five core questions above give some overall sense of when and why public disclosure might work, and critical comparisons are used to test this programme theory to destruction. In all these comparisons, one particular case (the Car Theft Index) is used as the 'positive' in order to track down its virtues in contrast to the five 'negative' cases. However, readers should note that this is merely a presentational device, allowing me to pursue programme diversity with a minimal number of cases. In a full-length synthesis, many more hypotheses would be tracked and dozens of cases would be applied to each developing hypothesis.

Comparison 1: Susceptibility and status of the named party

The Car Theft Index

At their peak in 1993 car theft claims to the UK insurance industry numbered almost 600,000, compared with half that figure in France, and a quarter of it in Germany (Roberts, 1997). So soft was the target and so popular was 'joy riding' that car crime accounted for over a quarter of all crimes reported to the police. The cost of car crime is not borne by manufacturers, with the result that, other things being equal, they will sell vehicles that are particularly valuable and remarkably vulnerable. One potential mechanism for addressing this problem was shaming, and the introduction by the Home Office of the Car Theft Index (Houghton, 1992) was an attempt to make the idea manifest. It brought to the public's attention the make, model and year of vehicles most at risk of being stolen. The CTI was recalculated in 1997, renamed the Car Crimes Index, and has since become an annual production.

From 1993 there has been a steady decline in car theft, following the introduction by manufacturers of a range of security features. In the early period of the Index, new and recent models were stolen more often, the pickings being obviously much greater. The position has now reversed, with cars lacking the now standard, manufacturer-installed, high-tech immobilizers becoming the favoured target. The shaming initiative, it seems, was a success. There is, however, an attribution problem. These aggregative shifts are insufficient to demonstrate the efficacy of the CTI or that it had a shaming causal nexus. The real and direct effect of disclosure is to be found in the reactions of particular companies to the first wave of publicity and in the close texture of the CTI. One manufacturer in particular was caught in an avalanche of statistics. Seven ranges of cars were identified as high risk in the original 1992 report and Ford made six of them. Following this disclosure, the company took a decision to transform vehicle security by introducing an entirely new key system, and from 1992 to 1994, the Index revealed a 60 per cent improvement in the rate of theft across the Ford range.

Publicity for 'poll tax' protesters

Disclosure for non-payment is one of the classic targets for shaming sanctions. It is used in the UK, largely by public authorities, to name individuals in arrears for payment of TV licences, council tax bills and, most notoriously, the 'poll tax' or Community Charge. Naming, in this instance, took the form of final warnings followed by listing of the names and addresses of defaulters in the local papers. It is the historical and political context of the measure that is of interest here. The Community Charge had an (in)famously difficult legislative passage. It was subject to much protest (Burns, 1992), was subsequently amended and eventually withdrawn, being deemed 'uncollectable'. In the midst of this action, local qualitative accounts (Reynolds, 1992) reveal that many defaulters were overjoyed when their names appeared in the local papers. There was a craving to be shamed in these circles. Disclosure, in this context, became a badge of honour.

It is appropriate to make a brief aside here on the nature of the evidence that public notification of non-payment failed to stifle the poll tax protest. There are no RCTs, time-series analysis or even head counts of how many people named in the newspapers actually paid up. The only evidence, but compelling nevertheless, is of the chain of action and reaction between enforcement and resistance. Having ceremonially 'burned their bills' in an initial propaganda counter-attack, ardent protesters then faced (Burns, 1992) a reminder, a 14-day notice-to-pay, a second letter, a summary warrant, a court appearance, a frozen bank account, wage arrest, poinding, and warrant sale. Accounts of the protest show how resistance was mounted at each stage. Defaulters traditionally try to ignore as many sanctions as possible but in this case there was a deliberate Turn Up In Court campaign, aimed at facing magistrates with protesters galore in order to over-stretch and filibuster the legal system. It is this picture of the accumulation of opposition strategies that provides the evidence base, for it is against this picture that one appreciates the futility of the disclosure sanctions aimed at this particular group.

Emerging theory

These starkly contrasting outcomes are readily explained using a standard, middle-range sociological theory. According to Elster (1999) '... shame belongs to a bundle of "self-conscious emotions": embarrassment, shame, guilt, pride, and pridefulness'. Disclosure thus carries the capacity to trigger any one of these emotions, and which one surfaces depends upon the aspirations and allegiances of the person named. The explanation is a variant on Merton's (1968) theory of reference group behaviour, which shows how 'in-group aspirants' and 'out-group marginals' respond to life's challenges in a completely different manner. Ford is a decidedly aspirational member that does what it can to preserve a reputation under threat, whilst Joe Street-Protest is clearly an antagonistic non-member who seeks repute only outside 'the system'.

Further status comparisons and contrasts are necessary to tease out the full implications of reference group theory for shaming, but here I focus on one aspect of the current juxtaposition, which might appear rather jarring. Ford is a corporation; poll tax protesters are individuals, or perhaps a loose collective. Another self-evident task for any review of disclosure policy would be to discover whether individuals and institutions might equally be shamed. This idea is not pursued here but those who imagine that collectives cannot suffer embarrassment might ponder the words of a highly relevant figure on the significance of corporate reputation:

> To succeed and even survive, Ford Motor Company must have the trust and confidence of its many publics. A good reputation is a priceless asset. (Henry Ford II, 1976, quoted in Fisse and Braithwaite, 1983: 247)

Comparison 2: The balance of sanctions following disclosure

The Car Theft Index
Motor manufacturers compete with each other. They tend to spend on items they suppose will increase the allure of a model to the public and to make savings on matters not estimated to be widespread priorities. Hence, in the early 1990s, it could be said 'the notion that they might compete in developing a more secure vehicle for the better good of the British public was quite foreign to them' (Laycock and Tilley, 1995). This suggests that the shaming action of the CTI could not have had sufficient power to be entirely responsible for the widespread upgrading of vehicle security following its publication. Such a speculation is reinforced by the fact that the public was for a time shielded from concerns about security by the insurance system. However, this context, too, was about to change (Roberts, 1997).

The Index was introduced in response to rapidly increasing thefts. At the same time, the UK car insurance industry was experiencing its first serious losses and beginning to retreat from its practice of spreading risks, to the point where it would refuse to insure vehicles of high risk design. For a time it became impossible to insure particular makes and models except at exorbitant prices and, through its pocket, the public became aware, perhaps for the first time, of the real costs of poor vehicle security. The link from theft rates to market concerns was consolidated, however, with a leap in the rigour of the 'group rating system', which resulted in more steeply graduated insurance premiums. A 'vehicle security assessment' administered by Thatcham UK became a formal part of the grouping process and this had the effect of pitching information on car security directly into the cost of car ownership. Realism always questions what it is about a policy that makes it work and in this case the mechanism may well have been double-headed, with shaming sanctions giving way to consumer forces. It is likely that only the first CTI had a significant impact, which was then consolidated by the insurance infantry. There is little reason to believe that on its sixth and seventh outings the CTI contained fresh information capable of high levels of shaming, and this transformation of causal powers may be entirely typical of a successful disclosure initiative.

Hospital report cards

Here an entire, existing review is used as the comparison case. Marshall et al. (2000) examine the response to the release of health care performance data in the United States. This is a particularly useful example in respect of testing the second review theory because its self-appointed task is to examine the applicability of the 'public accountability', 'market orientation' and 'professional orientation' models of public disclosure. Much of the political rhetoric and published programme theory on report cards in the United States anticipated that disclosure would bring discipline to health provision via the second mechanism, that is to say, by better informing purchasing decisions. The reviewers conclude, however, that 'currently available performance data has little impact on consumer choice'.

There is a prima facie case for considering that publicity holds a similar sway over car manufacturers and health providers. In the United States there is quite a robust health market because of the substantial purchasing power of employer-managed care plans. However, the finer print of Marshall's review reveals that these users seem to prefer 'process to outcome data' (patient satisfaction scores over performance data) and are more impressed by 'utilization rates over clinical measures' (turnstile turn-around to mortality measures). Market-inspired changes seem to be restricted to the 'provision of entirely new services' rather than 'adjustments to clinical practices' (Longo et al., 1997). In other words, a hospital only responded economically when report cards revealed complete inactivity in a particular health pursuit, to which the only response was to close the 'gap in the market'.

Marshall et al. conclude that whilst provider organizations seem to have been forced onto their toes by the report card phenomenon, its impact seems to work largely through non-market mechanisms. Demonstrating how report card publicity works its way through labyrinthine administrative and professional structures is no easy task, but this brief glance is sufficient to put another theory in place.

Emerging theory

Naming can trigger off a range of sanctions; the public may avert their eyes or watch ever more closely, they may reach for their wallets or run from the market, they may vote with their feet or send in the shock troops. Instances of pure shaming, in which reputations alone are at stake and status alone is damaged, may turn out to be extremely rare. Public disclosure will normally trigger a combination of actions and reactions. In the car security example, the shaming-cum-economic sanction may have been particularly effective when applied in a reputation-sensitive and market-sensitive situation. In the second case, the information disclosed does not seem to equate closely with the purchasing decisions of actual hospital clients and so the anticipated economic claw-back was lost. In dealing with a quasi-autonomous, quasi-market organization it may be that disclosure is best regarded as a shaming-cum-managerial action in a reputation-sensitive and administratively reactive situation. The subtle shift in sectoral context makes a world of difference to the working of the measure.

It would require many more cases to flesh out this theory, but this comparison makes a start in suggesting that if policy-makers want the public to respond to public disclosure, then 'remedial contexts' need to be chosen that are sensitive and responsive to real decisions made by the public. There is another glimpse here of how the full review could be developed. A key task for the reviewer is to discern whether a particular act of public disclosure generates surveillance, economic sanction, managerial change, self-reflection, or some combination thereof. Once these different implementation pathways are distinguished, the review can then build a picture of which contexts are sensitive to which configuration of mechanisms.

Comparison 3: Control over the information agenda

The Car Theft Index

The CTI itemizes risk of theft in three categories: red (more than 21 cars in every 1,000 on the road stolen); amber (between 4 and 21 per 1,000); and green (less than 4 per 1,000). Actuarial tables are then supplied in a user-friendly way. Manufacturers are distinguished, and colour-coded tables are supplied for every model and year of each car on the road, provided there are sufficient numbers for statistically reliable results. Distinctions are thus very precise. Consumers intent on a quickish 1997 Peugeot 106 are still able to distinguish between the chances of being able to hang onto their Escapade, or GTI or Rallye. Members of the public are nudged towards the purchase of green or amber cars, or investment in extra security measures for high risk red models.

No database is fault-free, and potential errors are indeed noted in the full versions of the inventories. The core information comes from reports to the police of stolen vehicles and there is a small element of false reporting and under-reporting. The CTI also suffers some difficulty in recording error in respect of UK registration numbers, in which suffixes and prefixes have chopped and changed over the years. Such errors, however, are not considered biased against particular model ranges. The review failed to discover any major instance of information distortion (although one might argue that one unanticipated consequence of the Index is to point car thieves precisely and efficiently at motors that provide the easiest pickings – especially if they happen to have a colour printer). Overall, CTI information is pretty unequivocal and the potential for public action clear.

Sex offender registration – Megan's Law

The counter-example in this case is by now well known from Chapter 5, but here the discussion focuses specifically on control over information flow. Immediately, one notes a practical difference that is emblematic of the entire issue. The CTI is designed to identify the vehicle on the road (of which there will be thousands). Sex offender registers are designed to identify the man on the street (literally). Recall that all US states are required to maintain a computerized central registry of sex offenders. A typical record-keeping strategy, from Massachusetts, has the following elements. Registration is required of all offenders convicted of any one of 11 sex crimes: assault, indecent assault and battery, unnatural and lascivious acts, open and gross lewdness, kidnapping and rape (itself divided into six categories). The notification of the offence, residence and work of the offender is required for a period of 20 years. The responsible authorities must maintain registration, unless the offender is no longer under supervision, in which case self-registration is required, with punishment for non-compliance. The level and extent of disclosure are based on a risk classification as follows: risk level I – citizen-initiated inquiries only; risk level II – community organization notification; risk level III – active public notification by leaflet, newspapers, community TV and so on.

The offence–registration–notification–response chain is therefore remarkably long and suffers notable ambiguities, which result in uncertainty about its public safety potential. The main concern emerging from research on the integrity of such a complex implementation chain is that the chances of notification reaching potential victims remain slim. Hebenton and Thomas (1997) summarize the key problems as follows. Compliance with registration requirements for those not under supervision remains low, estimated to vary from 30 per cent to 80 per cent between states. Police procedures for verification of the registers were initially non-existent and remain highly varied. The actual notification procedure varies widely, with no uniformity in the application of risk assessment to extent of disclosure. And finally, there is the classic problem of displacement, with reoffending often occurring out of a state's jurisdiction.

Given all these difficulties, it is hard to know what proportion of offences could, even potentially, be prevented by the notification strategy. Registers are created largely in response to stranger-predatory crimes, which are relatively rare and difficult to predict. Recall in this respect Petrosino and Petrosino's (1999) estimate, detailed in Chapter 5, that of 136 such attacks committed in a given period in Boston, there were only six victims who could have had any realistic chance of responding to notification.

Emerging theory

The two cases demonstrate that information disclosure can be as easy as ABC or involve naming the haystack to shame the needle. Disclosure programmes cannot risk ambiguity and are only as effective as the efforts at conceptualization, observation and corroboration that lie behind the publicized information. The comparison here suggests that an 'inverse law' may be at work: the more complex the behaviour categorized, the less the integrity of the notification procedure, the less a clear public response can be anticipated and controlled. Partly because of the conceptual mist surrounding the registration categories, unintended outcomes are a routine feature of sex offender notification schemes. Because they are isolated and rendered inarticulate, sex offenders are unable to deflect the label. Accordingly, Hebenton and Thomas (1997) report that 'some form of harassment occurs in 10 per cent of disclosure cases'. Readers might also recall the bizarre UK case when information disclosure got entangled with phonetics, with a paediatrician being attacked as a paedophile.

How might other programmes and studies be incorporated? Ambiguities in the information disclosed have a less dramatic but equally significant consequence if one considers the debate that is always aired on publication of UK school league tables and hospital star ratings. Each year of publication brings a set-piece debate on whether the tables are properly adjusted for intake and risk. Further steps in the full review process will no doubt suggest a modification of the simple inverse law coined above. That is to say, not only will complexity of information blunt its impact but so will debate over its meaning. If the named party is powerful and articulate, then any small ambiguities in naming will be seized upon as the first defence against shaming.

Comparison 4: How newsworthy is the publicized behaviour?

The Car Theft Index

Nineteenth-century shaming sanctions depended on the pure public display of the offender – sometimes grotesque, sometimes carnivalesque (Molènes's 'scandalous tableau'). Insofar as they depend on public reprimands modern shaming sanctions still have to reach the appropriate public, and this prompts a consideration of media involvement in shaming sanctions. Key to understanding the reputational and communicative aspects of shaming sanctions is the 'storyline syndrome'. In simple terms, the proposition under scrutiny is that twentieth and twenty-first-century shaming sanctions will only become adequately public, and therefore effective, if the media deem the information sufficiently newsworthy.

Evidence on how the media card was played in the CTI scheme is hard to retrieve, but there do (personal communication) seem to have been concerted Home Office attempts to publicize early results to the media with the specific intent of shaming some large manufacturers who had been slow to budge under direct persuasion. Car theft is not particularly newsworthy. However, large-scale theft epidemics might be, and the 'FORD – One-Key-Fits-All Scandal' was able to command a modest run of TV and newspaper features. The fact that Ford figured so prominently in the high risk index positively invited the Hall of Shame headlines.

Health Care Financing Administration's mortality studies

The contrast here calls on a study evaluating the effects of the release of 'mortality report card' information on hospital utilization. The research is of particular interest because the impact data relate to the timing of 'formal information releases', 'press reports' and 'other publicity'. In other words, there is an attempt to try to separate out the media's influence from this particular information flow. The results are as follows:

> There was only a small effect of the release on hospital discharges ... We found no support for the view that press reports of the HCFA data rather than the information release itself affected discharges ... However, we found evidence of large and significant effects (9 per cent reduction in hospital use) of press reports on *untoward deaths* in hospitals (Mennemeyer et al., 1997: 119); [emphasis in original].

Untoward deaths here refer to events such as a patient falling off a gurney or an aide inadvertently turning off a ventilator, resulting in the death of those in the hospital's care.

This research delivers an important finding on the respective strengths of different mortality messages: the report cards in their original form did not find their way significantly into the public consciousness, and neither in this instance did subsequent press reports. Tales of the unexpected, however, are what catch the imagination. At one stage the HCFA data were withdrawn from the public, with officials pronouncing: 'Regrettably, the publication has come to be regarded primarily as a consumer publication.' Mennemeyer's principal conclusion is quite the reverse, namely that 'HCFA was justified in ending the release of mortality data – not because it had turned into a consumer information vehicle, but because it had not'.

Emerging theory

There is effectively a fourth party in most modern shaming sanctions, namely the media. Shaming sanctions are most likely to be successful in policy domains whose data are sufficiently newsworthy to prompt action, but which can prevent the evidence succumbing to 'scandalous tableau' treatment. This is not an easy proposition to formalize and test. However, sex offender notification represents an obvious further case for comparison, with certain UK newspapers, such as the *News of the World*, attempting to commandeer responsibility for public disclosure (with disastrous results for individuals it chose to name). The difference between reporting and campaigning is not always clear but since public shaming depends palpably on publicity, there is a self-evident significance, and no doubt a pattern, to the media's involvement. The influence of media frames is a key topic for the more extensive review.

Comparison 5: The power and independence of the responsible body

The Car Theft Index

The CTI is produced by the Home Office using theft data taken from the Police National Computer and information taken from the Driver and Vehicle Licensing Authority. CTI documentation contains further advice on vehicle security, and contains links to the Office of Fair Trading, Crimestoppers and local Crime Prevention Agencies. Further sources of data on car security for the insurance industry are provided by Thatcham UK and the Transport Research Laboratory (both non-profit-making organizations). These institutions give authority to the Index, since they signal independence from the car manufacturers and are located clearly within the public service and the 'fight against crime'. All of these features make credible 'watchdog' credentials and act as a buttress against dissimulation and counter-publicity against the disclosed information.

The Home Office considered legislation at the height of the joy-riding epidemic and introduced a number of other schemes to detain, distract and rehabilitate offenders. However, as far as action against manufacturers went, there was a watching brief and the index was allowed to 'speak for itself'. Nor was there legislation, or even a 'guiding hand', for the changes to insurance premium gradients, the Home Office again observing a watching brief (personal communication).

Toxic Releases Inventory

The TRI is a computerized, public access database set up under the Local Emergency Planning Committees established by the US Emergency Planning and Community Right to Know Act (Title III). Rather than imposing specific demands for risk reduction measures on industry, Title III pursued an indirect strategy that relied on providing the public with information. Legislators apparently hoped that requiring firms to share data on their use of hazardous materials would provide a vigilant public with the information it needed to monitor industry performance, and exert pressure on companies to undertake voluntary risk-reduction efforts. A major, multi-site study on the implementation, training and staffing behind this plan found it wanting:

> We see no evidence to suggest that public awareness of hazardous materials issues is being raised to the degree needed to make indirect regulation operative. Most LEPCs in our study have focused on the technical aspects of their job and have not made a concerted effort to bring hazardous material issues to public attention. This is quite understandable given the constraints under which they labor. They generally run entirely on volunteer effort and have little or no independent budget or staff. Their mission has been drafted primarily in terms of developing a technically adequate emergency response plan. As a result, they have few members with extensive backgrounds in public relations, citizen participation, or communications. Most make risk communication a low priority and do not know how to go about obtaining public involvement ... Moreover, most have been given very little direction from state or Federal government concerning their role in non-emergency risk communication, so their responsibility for this important function is seldom clearly assigned at the local level. ... Given the selection processes commonly used LEPC members are likely to regard local government or industry as their main constituency ... Many key members come from emergency planning backgrounds that stress one-way communications with the public (in order to comply with emergency instructions) and make little room for questioning or critical analyses of the options. (Rich et al., 1993: 17)

Emerging theory

Shaming sanctions appear to work best when responsible bodies have good watchdog credentials (namely, a degree of independence from other stakeholders), established legal and moral authority, and a range of other sanctions at their disposal. In the area of corporate regulation theory, such an idea is known as the 'benign big gun' hypothesis (Ayres and Braithwaite, 1992). Regulating agencies usually have a range of injunctions at their disposal, including publicity and persuasion, official warnings, civil and criminal penalties, licence revocation and so forth. Rather than going immediately for the toughest sanctions, the benign big gun hypothesis states that the bigger and more various the sticks, the greater the success regulators will achieve by speaking softly.

In the present case, the Local Emergency Planning Committees were certainly benign but backed, apparently, by a peashooter, whereas the Home Office disclosed the data authoritatively and then packed its pistol. The really interesting test of this emerging theory would be to compare two big guns dealing with a similar problem, one of which blazed away with penalties and one of which simply disclosed information whilst polishing the barrel.

Comparisons 6, 7, 8, 9 onwards

Here the review comes to a halt, although enough has been said to show the potential for shifting from a handful to hundreds of researched instances of disclosure sanctions. Let us take stock. None of the data, none of the evidence, none of the comparisons is deemed to have disclosed the 'secret' of shaming sanctions. All the evidence and all the inferences, however, provide refinement in understanding five conditions that govern their efficacy. Each theory needs to be deepened further by considering many additional cases, bringing further clarification to the understanding of each contextual constraint.

Take, for example, the first theory about the status and susceptibility of the party being identified to the public, and recall the rollicking reaction to the disclosure of poll tax non-payment. The 'prior orientation' of the subject is crucial in another criminal justice initiative, much promoted in the 1990s, requiring mandatory arrest in potential cases of domestic violence. Apart from re-balancing the justice scales towards the victim, it was assumed that beneficial effects would flow from requiring alleged perpetrators to face the ordeal of arrest and ensuing public shame, following neighbourhood gossip about the red face under the blue lamp as the suspect was inserted into the patrol car. Unfortunately, evaluations of the scheme (Sherman et al., 1992) showed that the net impact of mandatory arrests was close to zero (and thus destined for meta-analytic ignominy). This aggregate outcome, however, disguises two counter-balancing effects. Closer inspection of the data shows that being arrested in the public eye brings shame (and decreased domestic violence) in 'respectable' communities, but provokes anger (and even increased domestic violence) in 'marginal' communities. The reference group explanation triumphs again, this time by making a within-programme comparison.

Another promising extension to this review lies in examining further theories of further contexts that might shape the disclosure mechanism. For example, this brief chapter ignores the most famous naming and shaming theory of all, namely that shaming sanctions work best if they are 're-integrative' (Braithwaite, 1989). According to Braithwaite, shaming sanctions should always include the opportunity for restoration, rather than leaving the named party wallowing dangerously in one of the other 'self-conscious emotions'. Although I have no direct evidence to support it (and hence is it not in the review), it seems that car manufacturers do seem to survive the ebbs and flows of bad publicity in the CTI, and Ford was rapidly re-integrated into the fold. Indeed, for a period after the costly introduction of new-style keys, it was eager to boast in newspaper adverts of its prowess on vehicle security. This fits the pattern observed by Fisse and Braithwaite (1983) in a study of the crises following charges of corporate offending against 17 major companies. In the medium term, and despite some notable setbacks to earnings, each company managed to respond with reforms sufficient to restore its reputation. In other contexts, by contrast, the public's resentment is deeper-seated and might well defy attempts at re-integration. Some of the research on sex offender notification raises doubts on whether it can ever sit happily with notions of community re-integration (Presser and Gunnison, 1999).

Conclusion

There is one important methodological point to be made on the back of this example of realist review. I have already acknowledged the lack of any methodological appraisal of the primary inquiries, having exhausted the space available on that matter in the previous chapter. Eagle-eyed readers will, however, have noted some differences in the materials used. At one point I have borrowed raw materials directly from the CTI data rather than using 'available research'. The noted 60 per cent improvement in the rate of theft across the 1992–4 Ford range was calculated for me by a helpful official. In addition, some information was obtained through 'personal communication'. This is a rather formal way of acknowledging materials obtained from interviews I conducted at the Home Office and at Thatcham UK in summer 2001.

None of this would be deemed good practice in a conventional systematic review, but is nonetheless part and parcel of good (and thus iterative) theory-testing. Realist synthesis allows the reviewer to go back and reconsider evidence in the light of a developing theory, and this process is likely to reveal many 'evidence holes' that may quite legitimately be filled by more direct means. When 'more evidence is needed', it is not a bad strategy to go out and get it. Indeed, the commitment of realist synthesis to multi-method inquiry can reach even further than this. Currently, with colleagues, I am seeking funding for a study that combines synthesis with action research. There is no reason why the same body of theory cannot be tested on the page and in the field.

Finally, I return to substantive matters. Although only a little learning about naming and shaming is possible on the basis of the evidence trawl in this chapter, it is the nature of that learning that has to be been stressed. The CTI is used as the 'positive' in a range of comparisons, but the conclusion of this embryonic review is most definitely *not* that this particular disclosure initiative works whilst the other examples do not. The claim is to have produced a tyro, transferable theory that the scheme may have worked because:

- the named party was an aspirational insider
- the shaming mechanism could be dovetailed with market sanctions
- the disclosure carried intense but controllable media interest
- the disclosed data were unambiguous both in content and in suggested remedial action
- the authority had exemplary watchdog credentials, which it operated benignly

Despite this success, there is also a solid case for arguing that the CTI has long exceeded its optimal utility. Its shaming shock was early transformed into a market mechanism and then into a benevolent information watchdog, and the crime problem it addressed is also under transformation. Car theft by conventional means has become sufficiently difficult in the UK that new ways have been sought to acquire expensive new models (for example, fraudulent re-registration of foreign and wrecked vehicles, and house 'walk-ins' in search of car keys). All criminal justice programmes go through such a recognizable life-cycle as prevention mechanisms become exhausted and background contexts transform. However, this matters not, since what is transferable from the evidence, what is portable about the schemes, what is the fruit of the exercise is the development of the underlying theories.

8

Conclusion: Flying 'The Tattered Flag of Enlightenment'

This conclusion returns to the big picture and asks, does this dose of realism about the nature of evidence change expectations about its capacity to infiltrate the policy process? My answer is diffidence itself. One must be modest on the grounds that realist synthesis is only at the development stage and that its potential can be realized only at the hands of other researchers. One must be modest on the grounds of the undesirable but undeniable grip of fashion on social research, which may mean that systematic review en bloc will pass as an infatuation. One must be modest on the grounds, long appreciated, that the polity's appetite for evidence, any evidence, is meagre. Above all, one must be modest in reflecting faithfully the limited authority of evidence itself. Good science is not futurology; we should always be humble about predicting the path ahead on the basis of what we know about the one already trodden.

All that is true, but it does not really complete the picture. There needs to be more grit in the conclusion, and the quotation below puts it perfectly. It comes from Lindblom, who is perhaps more famous for another *bon mot* about policy-making being the 'art of muddling through'. The following discusses the destiny of probing, by which he means inquiry or investigation, broadly understood, but exactly the same sentiment applies to research synthesis:

> The significance of probing lies in the possibility that people can change themselves to a degree, that they can achieve at least small betterment, that they can ameliorate some problems. They in fact often fail and in some dimensions always fail. For between the complexity of the social world and human thinking capacity, there exists a tragic discrepancy. But the possibility remains that sometimes in some circumstances people can to some degree succeed. I confess that the tattered flag of the Enlightenment still stirs a deep response. (Lindblom, 1990: 14)

I confess it too and I hope this book has shown how realist synthesis can achieve a small betterment in the way that social interventions are chosen, designed, implemented and targeted. The purpose of this chapter is to put a measure on modesty and to give an honest picture of what realist synthesis might hope to achieve. I begin with a brief characterization of the nature of policy-making and of the manner in which it utilizes evidence. From this I locate the slim passageway in which evidence circulates, and identify the language it must adopt in order to be heard. This brings me to the main claim, which is that realist synthesis is well placed to move in the right corridors and can indeed talk the talk. The chapter then bids farewell with an *aide-mémoire* about the answers supplied by realist synthesis and a reminder that they are not easy answers.

Policy-making and the utilization of evidence

In describing social interventions I have striven to convince the reader that they are *not* 'treatments' aimed at 'subjects'. Rather, they are complex systems thrust amidst complex systems. So too is the environment in which evidence on them may be used. The way the polity is organized, the way decision-making is structured, is complexity itself. Three much-quoted passages make the case:

> The image of decision-making represented by President Kennedy and his group of advisors thrashing out the nation's response to the Cuban missile crisis is inappropriate to most daily bureaucratic life. Much more commonly, each person takes a small step (writes a memo, answers an inquiry, edits the draft of a regulation) that has seemingly small consequences. But over a period of time, these many small steps foreclosed alternative courses of action and limited the range of the possible. Almost imperceptibly a decision has been made, without anyone's awareness that he or she was deciding. (Weiss, 1980: 401)

> [Decision processes] are characterized by novelty, complexity, and open-endedness, by the fact that the organization usually begins with little understanding of the decision situation it faces or the route to its solution, and only a vague idea of what that solution might be and how it will be evaluated when it is developed. Only by groping though a recursive discontinuous process involving many different steps and a host of dynamic factors over a considerable period of time is a final choice made. (Mintzberg et al., 1976)

> A British prime minister says: 'there is just a build up of big and small events, of big and small factors, and they may not be brought to your notice until the issue has already been decided; and, when you eventually have to decide, it may be in response to the smallest of them all'. (Lindblom, 1990: 276, quoting Henry Farlie)

This is the arena in which research evidence seeks to gain attention. As the producers of one of the 'smallest factors of them all', evidence compilers may see a glimmer of hope in the final quotation. On balance, however, it may be wiser to read the passage as intended, and for researchers to accept the distinct possibility that their painstakingly crafted systematic reviews may be brushed aside in the clamour for the attention of key decision-makers.

The plot thickens if the matter is viewed in reverse and one considers what we know about how policy-makers use evidence on those rare occasions when they do so. The original, and still perhaps the best, source on this is again Weiss in her study with Bucuvalas, which paints the familiar picture of politically aware bureaucrats busily watching the polls, the media and their backs but having little time for serious contemplation of the evidence. Evidence enters the equation in pre-digested lumps and, even when they do take the plunge, policy-makers prefer the 'instant summary' and the 'potted history'. Most crucial, however, is the manner in which that information is digested:

> [Decision-makers] talked in general terms about using research to gain general direction and background, to keep up with developments in the field, and to reduce uncertainties about policies and programs. They discussed broad purposes, not specific decisions, specific aims, or the specific content of research studies. (Weiss and Bucuvalas, 1980: 156)

This 1980 study was the foundation stone for an entire school of thought on utilization that also cherishes the e-word. Research, argues Weiss (1986), provides 'enlightenment' as opposed to 'political arithmetic' or 'partisan support'. Her metaphor describes rather well the working relationship between research and policy: slow dawning – sometimes staccato, sometimes dormant and sometimes antagonistic. Enlightenment's positive prospect, for which there is by now a great deal of empirical evidence (e.g. Deshpande, 1981; Lavis et al., 2002; Dobrow et al., 2004), is that the influence of research on policy occurs through the medium of ideas rather than of data. This process is characterized by Weiss (1980) as 'knowledge creep' or 'percolation', terms that describe the way research actually filters into the decision-maker's brain. Research is unlikely to produce the thumping 'fact' that changes the course of policy-making. Rather, there are many days of reckoning and it is through general 'direction and background' that research makes its impression. Policies are born out of the clash and compromise of ideas, and the key to enlightenment is to insinuate research results into this reckoning (Exworthy et al., 2002).

Here lies the room for manoeuvre for realist synthesis. The models that form the end product of realist reviews are designed to speak directly to the choices that have to be made in devising or reforming a programme. The conclusions are already refined. They are not simply evidence, they are explanations. They bring to life the reasoning to be gone through in making decisions. Consider in this respect the following contrast. Policy-makers are likely to struggle with data that reveal, for instance, the respective statistical significance of an array of mediators and moderators in a meta-analysis. They are more likely to be able to interpret and to utilize a full-blown realist explanation of why a programme theory works better in one context than another. Although these two investigatory thrusts serve to answer rather similar questions, the one that focuses on sense-making has the advantage. This is especially so if the investigation focuses on adjudicating between rival explanations, thus providing justification for taking one course of action rather than another. This is the very stuff of political decision-making.

Whilst I have expressed due caution about the sway of evidence, there is a stirring message on research utilization. Realist reviews throw light on the decisions in decision-making and they are not only consonant with, but add substance to, the enlightenment model. However, the vision of research-as-illumination tells us rather more about the medium than the message. We are, it is true, rid of the ludicrous idea that evaluators and reviewers are able to tell policy-makers and practitioners exactly what works in the world of policy interventions, but we are still in need of clarity on the proper content of evidence-based policy advice. How should counsel proceed? What should we expect a programme of theory-testing to reveal?

What the realist approach contributes is a process of thinking through the tortuous pathways along which a successful intervention has to travel. What is reproduced in a realist synthesis is a whole series of decision points through which an initiative has proceeded, and the findings can be put to use in alerting the policy community to the caveats and considerations that should inform those decisions. I used the metaphor of the alphabet of decisions in introducing this idea in Chapter 4, but an alternative may be equally instructive. Imagine the research process as producing a sort of highway code to programme-building, alerting policy-makers to the problems that they might expect to confront and some of the safest measures to deal with them. The code does not explain what works in particular situations (such as how to make that tricky right turn out of Foxhill Avenue to Weetwood Lane) but it does provide the ground rules, informing the driver of matters that should be taken into account. Of course, a realist review programme code could never provide the level of prescription or proscription achieved in the analogy. The point of the parallel is that the highway code does not tell you how to drive but how to survive the journey by flagging situations where danger may be lurking and extra vigilance needed.

Realist synthesis and knowledge management

Let me now attempt to refine the enlightenment principle by providing a more detailed map and a couple of examples of the manner in which realist synthesis can inform decision-making. Nowadays, many policy-making bodies are investing in knowledge management strategies. As new programmes become the main vehicle for policy delivery ('interventionitis') and as the forms and sources of evidence multiply ('exformation'), some way is needed of trying to keep knowing and doing abreast of each other. The realist interpretation of knowledge management is illustrated in Figure 8.2, which is developed as a contrast to the meta-analysis model in Figure 8.1.

Meta-analytic logic says that evidence accumulates by pooling together the findings of each primary study (the funnel in Figure 8.1), which knowledge can then be directed at fresh incarnations of the same programme. Although this manoeuvre gets the evidence horse before the policy cart, there remains an assumption about a one-to-one-to-one relationship between each past intervention, each evaluation and each future intervention. As explained in Chapter 3, this is a foolhardy supposition. Social interventions are complex, active systems thrust into complex, active systems and are never implemented the same way twice. Non-equivalence is the

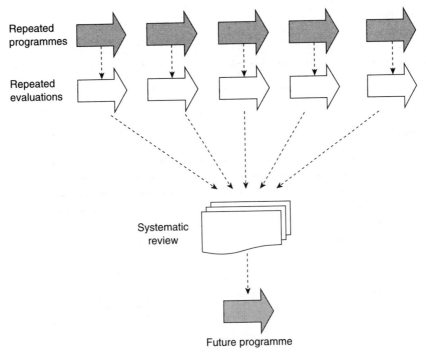

FIGURE 8.1   *Knowledge management according to meta-analysis*

norm. Isomorphism is the myth, morphogenesis the reality. Inexorably, the 'future programme' is only partially in our ken.

A more adaptive mode of knowledge management is required to cope with the vicissitudes of complex systems. Realists envision interventions as whole sequences of mechanisms that produce diverse effects according to context, so that any particular intervention will have its own particular signature of outputs and outcomes. Understanding how a particular intervention works requires a study of the fate of each of its many, many intervention theories. This disaggregation of a programme into its component theories provides the impetus for a new look at knowledge management, which is provided in Figure 8.2. The starting point, stage one in realist synthesis, is the initial mapping of interventions into their component theories and this is illustrated at the top of the figure. The various flows and feedback lines represent the negotiation, the borrowing, the leakage, the user involvement, the self-affirming or self-denying processes and so on that typify social interventions.

The only way to synthesize the evidence on such programmes is to review the primary sources programme theory by programme theory, rather than study by study. This change in the unit of analysis is depicted at the second level of Figure 8.2. Evidence is accumulated in respect of each component process, with the variable

Programme

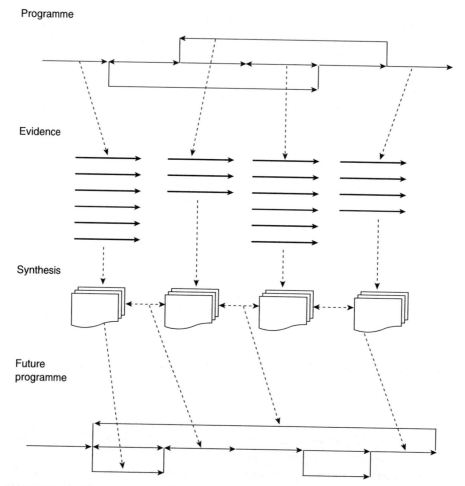

FIGURE 8.2   *The realist approach to knowledge management*

concentrations and assorted modes of available information represented by the piles of 'evidence arrows'. Figure 8.2 then moves down to the synthesis stage. Realist synthesis has no uniform mode of synthesis, and there is no parallel to the uniform funnelling of evidence in conventional systematic review that is depicted in Figure 8.1. The synthesis tests the validity of the component theories separately and then amalgamates them (linking arrows) by considering *if* (Chapter 5), *how* (Chapter 6) and *when* (Chapter 7) the component ideas fit together.

Moving to the foot of Figure 8.2, one gets to the business end of evidence-based policy. The intended function of realist review remains the same as that of conventional review, namely, to be used in decisions about whether and how to implement future interventions. The crucial difference is that, in the realist approach, there is no assumption that any future intervention will be configured in precisely the same way as those included in the review. Obviously, there will be a family resemblance and the success of any fresh intervention will turn on some of the same theories. However, it is assumed that it will be staffed and implemented differently, that it will be conditioned by a distinct institutional culture and political climate, that it will sit side by side with a kaleidoscope of different initiatives, and so on. The future intervention that realist review bears in mind thus depicts broadly the same run of programme theories but anticipates that they will meet a different pattern of negotiation, resistance, bloom and fade.

The policy advice of realist review is passed on phase-by-phase, theory-by-theory of an intervention. This is depicted in the dashed 'recommendation arrows' feeding into the prospective programme in Figure 8.2. Advice may chime in at any point of the implementation chain, and so might concern: the best legislative framework to handle such innovations; the staffing and personnel requirements of such initiatives; the internal opposition, resistance and likely points of negotiation in such schemes; levels of co-operation required with outside agencies in delivering such programmes; and so on. The next incarnation of the intervention may bear no close resemblance to any of the versions whose evaluations provided the raw material for the review, but the reason why a realist review of interventions A, B, C, D and E can inform the design of an entirely new intervention F is that the synthesis works at the level of *ideas*. Since the evidence base is built at the level of programme theories, it follows that research synthesis is able to draw in and advise upon a heterogeneous range of interventions.

The relationship between past programmes, the evidence base and future programmes is thus 'many-to-many-to-many' and, as such, the realist method is uniquely relevant to the creative design phase of policy interventions. No longer need it be supposed that the future design of anger management courses will only be supported by reviews of existing anger management courses; that learning about road safety schemes will emanate only from bygone studies of such schemes; that a synthesis of evidence on health advice/help lines is just what is needed to inform a tyro NHS Direct intervention, and so on.

Rather than assuming that knowledge management will lead decision-makers to imitate schemes lock, stock and barrel, realist review trades on the transfer of ideas. In this respect, its ability to stray deliberately outside the policy domain in question may give a powerful boost to utility, and thus utilization. Heterogeneity is normally considered the curse of systematic reviews but from a theory development perspective much can be learned, for example, about the utility of league tables by comparing their application in schools and hospitals. If researchers suspect that the efficacy of such schemes depends on, say, the readiness of consumers to transfer allegiances and on professional bodies' ability to challenge the key indicators, then a comparison of the evidence on different sets of consumers and professional associations is an ideal testing ground for that theory.

Finally, let me push this thesis on sources of evidence to an even more radical conclusion. We know that quite diverse interventions share common components.

Most obviously, they all need designing, leading, managing, staffing, monitoring, reviewing, redesigning and so on. They all suffer from problems of communication, reward systems, staff turnover and resistance, competing priorities, resource constraints, and so forth. At the very extreme, there are probably some common processes (such as how people react to change) and thus generic theories (about human volition) that feed their way into all interventions and all services. If synthesis were to concentrate on these middle-range mechanisms, then the opportunities for the utilization of reviews would be much expanded. Insofar as they concentrate on these very general levers, reviews could potentially be recycled to inform all manner of future programmes.

An example of how this might work was suggested by a recent review by Greenhalgh et al. (2004), which drew on some principles of realist review. The topic was the 'diffusion, dissemination and sustainability of innovations in health service delivery and organization'. Here indeed is an abstract, generic topic. The review unearthed a complex model of the mechanisms and contexts that condition the transmission and acceptance of new ideas, and successful diffusion was found to rest on the specific attributes of the innovation, the characteristics and concerns of potential adopters, the lines and processes of communication and influence, the organizational culture and climate, the inter-organizational and political backdrop, and so on. The key point for present purposes is that this model (which had been painstakingly constructed from primary studies on a range of interventions) was then tested on four quite different and highly diverse interventions, namely, integrated care pathways, GP fundholding, telemedicine and the UK electronic health record. Despite extracting the ideas from studies unrelated to these interventions, the authors were able to make sense of the rather different footprint of outcomes and outputs associated with each of them. The very heterogeneity of these case studies signals the potential for using a theory-based explanatory framework to inform the development of upcoming initiatives.

... meanwhile back in the corridors of power

It would be wrong to give the impression, that just because evidence-based policy operates via a competitive to-ing and fro-ing of ideas, the playing field is level in that particular clash. I began this book with recollections of my own evaluation experience in which the policy axe had fallen before the research had even gained its stride. Is there any reason to suppose that the balance of power between 'knowledge' and 'power' changes with the advent of systematic review? Consider, in this respect, the following exhibit, an *e-bulletin* from the *iConservatives*:

> A few social scientists with vested interests, and meddlesome politicians who need to be seen to do something, can make some sort of argument for almost anything ... Too often policies are introduced with little or no firm experience to back them up.

An example was the widespread replacement of traditional phonetics with whole word and sentence teaching. The latter also called 'look and learn' almost displaced older methods in the British state education system in the 1960s and 1970s. Parents were sceptical, but the experts who liked the new methods because they were easier to teach, reassured them ... It now turns out that the 'experts' had not bothered to do the correct experiments, or if they had, had not bothered to read the results. Fortunately a new international organisation, the Campbell Collaboration, has been launched to collect the best evidence for this and many other social policies. (www.iconservatives.org.uk/campbell_collaboration.htm)

The question, of course, is whether meta-analysis, or any other form of review, should rush into such a welcoming political embrace. Is this a clarion call to thrust the sword of truth into the heart of policy-making, or a more sinister quest for the 'scientific' justification of ideologically pre-determined decisions? Part of the enlightenment ethos is also about scepticism. My own impression of my own efforts to get my own reviews noticed is that much of the recent governmental head-nodding to evidence-based policy is mere lip service. As one moves up the policy-making ladder through 'analytic divisions' to 'policy divisions' the appetite for evidence dwindles. As one ascends the intervention hierarchy from practitioners to managers to bureaucrats to the political classes, the capacity to absorb complex information dwindles by the bullet point. Evidence can inform policy but it can also be used as a tool to 'park' policy in much the same way as indecision is disguised by the need to await review and committee reports. It can, of course, also be used to misinform policy through sifting, selection and simplification.

Accordingly, there will be moments when the researcher must shout 'foul!' There will be occasions when the enlightened reviewer of evidence must insist that 'it really is more complex than that'. There will be a perpetual need to push home the point that 'there are no easy answers'. Oftentimes these protestations will go unheeded, and we will scratch our chins thinking, like Peter Ustinov, 'I couldn't be a politician – I couldn't bear to be right all the time.' Occasionally, we will encounter living proof of Simon Cameron's thesis that 'an honest politician is one who, when he is bought, will stay bought'. And, at the back of our minds, we will sometimes hear Claude Cockburn snarling, 'when are you bloody liars going to stop lying to me'. The 'realistic' assumption remains that politics, in the last analysis, will always trump research.

Such cynicism, however, should not be unbounded. To repeat, the position adopted here is that decision-making is, to recall Mintzberg et al.'s (1976) phrase, a 'recursive discontinuous process involving many different steps and a host of dynamic factors over a considerable period of time'. Accordingly, evidence can enter this complex realm – by stealth, through persistence, in small doses, in selected venues, and in the right guise – and, despite all, via the pursuit of reasoning.

The previous seven chapters have been about the nature of evidence in evidence-based policy. They argue that evidential truths are partial, provisional and conditional, and they show that systematic review cannot browbeat the evidence into delivering unconditional and universal verdicts on the efficacy of interventions. In this chapter, the viewpoint changes to the policy in evidence-based policy and the negative case gathers strength. Even if the evidence base delivered unimpeachable truths, there are no linear and judicial decision-making processes into which they might feed. The positive case, however, also gains momentum. Realist synthesis can deliver an explanation base that reflects upon the multitude of decisions to be gone through in building social interventions and, when it does start to trickle, the flow of ideas from research to policy and practice can occur along a number of different rivulets – down through institutions to individuals, along the implementation chain, across stakeholders, through the short, medium and long term, and so on.

In short, I concur with a great many commentators who argue that evidential reviews must trade broadly across the entire policy and practice terrain, and that we must apply a 'whole systems approach to research use' (Walter et al., 2003). There are so many potential meeting-points between evidence and policy that the sensible strategy is to strengthen them all by employing a whole variety of strategies and tactics to encourage research utilization (Hanney et al., 2003). Among the tricks of the trade number: long-term liaison, evidence brokers, evidence champions, change agents, diffusion networks, organizational embeddedness, communication training, multi-media diffusion and so on. It goes without saying that each of these ideas will work only in particular circumstances and respects, and I leave to others the task of appraising the balance (e.g. Hemsley-Brown and Sharp, 2003).

The point to stress is that realist synthesis can easily adopt much of this machinery and indeed oil the wheels of much of this proposed exchange. The realist approach is iterative and processual. It is predicated on the steady accretion of explanation rather than the decisive accumulation of data. Its inclusivity in the treatment of evidence demands inclusivity in the treatment of users.

In practical terms, I have called for this liaison between reviewer and other stakeholders at several stages in the realist template in Figure 4.3. The sequence begins with the search for programme theories and this invites into the review, from stage one, all the varied, situated expectations for the programme. Further linkages with decision-makers and with commissioners are timetabled in at several points in the process and, at the conclusion of the review, dissemination can be targeted anywhere in the 'whole system' from senior officials to front-line practitioners. As a final example, consider the findings of the review of mentoring programmes. In Chapter 6, these were presented formally and diagrammatically through Figure 6.3. Given their explanatory nature, such formats are not the only output of the synthesis, and in the larger version of the review I also took the opportunity to point the conclusions at the volunteer practitioner in what may well be the very first 'evidence-based pep-talk'.

Welcome to your toughest ever challenge. What we'll attempt to do in this session is to teach you to play 'snakes and ladders', to help you anticipate the ups and downs of our mentoring scheme. Don't expect too many of your charges to make it to the winning square, but please appreciate that surviving at least some of the steps on the way will still be worthwhile.

Expect your relationship to uncoil very slowly. Try to begin with the basic elements of befriending – be a good companion. Start unambitiously by establishing and building upon mutual interests before moving on to the consideration of alternative futures and the means of striving towards them. Build these further plans with caution because we do need to affirm that, as sure as eggs are eggs, your mentee will not stick to the script: s/he will let you down and the partnership will tend to crack. For you both to continue in the programme, you should anticipate having to build and rebuild trust continually. The problems that got your mentees into their present predicaments are still likely to be present, and so your next main aim is that of building up resilience in the face of life's continual knocks.

To get to some sort of equilibrium at this stage will be achievement indeed, but you will find that any further progress is impossible unless other agents and agencies are drawn into the orbit of your partnership. You may have accepted this challenge because of your ability to get on with young people. Success at a one-to-one level ultimately depends, however, on the many-to-many. So-called 'engagement mentoring' is just that, and depends on your ability to know and show the ropes through family and peer ties, into channels of community support and on to education, training and career opportunities.

Don't worry. We appreciate that, at some point in this sequence, your capacity to help and direct your mentee through the appropriate networks will become exhausted. At this point, especially, you should call on the assistance of the programme co-ordinator who will make use of our formal liaisons with allied youth and career schemes. [*Here, our pep-talk takes for granted another lesson learned in the review, namely that the new voluntarism needs to be firmly anchored in old-style service provision.*]

Don't imagine, however, that you hand over responsibility at this point. Volatility does not disappear overnight. You should expect a further round of trust-building, and a further role in fence-mending as your mentee's spleen is vented, and sometimes justifiably so, against this new set of authority figures.

Whilst realist synthesis pursues a radical agenda on the construction of evidence, on the matter of its utilization it is decidedly in the mainstream. The percolation of evidence into policy is protracted and convoluted. We should, therefore, match humility with agility in our attempts to promote it.

Reprise

I have argued for a different vision, a new paradigm, in evidence-based policy. A realist approach has a range of theoretical and practical strengths that can be summarized as follows:

- It has firm roots in the philosophy of science and the social sciences and is confident, therefore, of its scientific credentials.
- It is not a method or formula, but a logic of enquiry that can be applied formatively, summatively, prospectively and retrospectively.
- It adopts an open-door policy on evidence. It can draw in studies using the entire repertoire of research and evaluation approaches, as well as drawing on literature that is more conceptual and critical.
- It seeks not to judge but to explain, and is driven by the question 'What works for whom in what circumstances and in what respects?'
- It learns from (rather than 'controls for') real-world phenomena such as diversity, change, idiosyncrasy, adaptation, cross-contamination and programme 'failure'.
- It engages stakeholders systematically, as fallible experts whose 'insider' understanding needs to be documented, formalized and tested.
- It provides a principled steer away from failed one-size-fits-all ways of responding to problems.
- By taking programme theory as its unit of analysis, it has the potential to maximize learning across policy, disciplinary and organizational boundaries.
- It is inherently creative, producing lessons that apply to programmes *unlike* any already tried.

This chapter has been about influencing the policy community, but in this concluding section, I return to *my* constituency, for methodologists are just as hard to convince. This book has been several years in the making and I am well able to anticipate the objections that will come its way. Let me respond, in advance and with gusto, to just four protestations.

Isn't it all rather intricate and reliant on judgement?

I have to concede a point about what I would prefer to term the 'challenging' nature of the method. Whatever else it maps, Figure 4.3 is not a cakewalk. Realist review requires sustained thinking and imagination to track and trace the initial map of programme theories. It requires shrewdness, experience and the ability to converse with policy-makers in refining the precise questions to be put in the review. It requires know-how in respect of a range of disciplines, methodologies and literatures to be able seek out, digest and assess the appropriate bodies of evidence. It requires considerable finesse in respect of research design and analysis to be able to foster the most productive format and strategy for the review. It demands the skills of an intellectual generalist rather than those of a super-specialist. Whilst it does not require workaday familiarity with the precise intervention or service under review, it does trade on the possession of a general nous about programme implementation. It is not, therefore, a task that can be handed over to newly doctored research assistants, working to an established formula.

Such delivery of realist review thus contrasts sharply with the original motivation for evidence-based medicine. Not only was the clinician's 'personal experience' dismissed as 'anecdotal', equally mistrusted was the idea that reviews and commissions should be left in the hands of 'experts', who were often perceived as interested parties, time-servers and so forth. The solution is a technicist model of evidence-based policy. Protagonists claim that any competent reviewer, armed with a focused question and a set of rigorously developed protocols, can find the relevant papers, develop a robust critique of the evidence, and produce a summary with a clear estimate of effect size and quantified level of confidence.

This deep suspicion of the exercise of judgement not only misconstrues the scientific method but it caricatures what we have seen in this chapter about the nature of decision-making. The research literature on expert decision-making finds it to be a rapid, intuitive and seemingly idiosyncratic process, which incorporates and makes sense of multiple and complex pieces of data including subtle contextual evidence. In grey areas, experts sometimes break the rules judiciously and justify themselves reflectively. Novice decision-making, on the other hand, is rule-bound, formulaic and reductionist. It ignores anything that is seen as 'complicating factors' and makes little concession to context. In grey areas, the novice persists in applying the formula and proves unable to bend the rules to accommodate the unanticipated (Eraut, 1994).

I am not claiming here that the realist approach is inherently 'cleverer' than conventional systematic research synthesis, nor – especially – that the reviewer needs to be all-seeing and all-knowing. What I am claiming is that the team assembled to conduct the review, and the network involved in its commissioning and use, must comprise an experienced and flexible unit. It is because realist review involves so many grey zones (including, but not confined to, grey literature), so much 'off-piste' work, so much contemplation of the subtle and contextual, so much negotiation of meaning with real-world practitioners, that I am wary of the novice and tolerant of the novel.

Aren't the findings just too feeble?

A further limitation of realist synthesis, acknowledged throughout this book, is that even when undertaken well, it promises no certitude in terms of findings or recommendations. It provides no verdicts. It eschews magic bullets. It shuns best buys. It abstains from the goal of achieving a clear demarcation of programmes-that-work from programmes-that-do-not. However it is softened – as in the currently favoured nomenclature of the search for 'best practices' – realism rejects the quest for the unqualified answer. Again, I look to Lindblom for a gritty way of putting the rejoinder to those who seek direct advice from evidence-based policy:

> Best problem solutions, if found at all, are appropriate or best to a time and a place ... The timeless universal solutions sought in some versions of scientific problem solving do not exist. (1990: 224)

Enduring empirical generalization can only be discovered in artificially closed systems, and modern public policy regimes are palpably open systems. With its emphasis on contextual contingency and temporal changes in the ways programmes are implemented, and its stress on how interventions are interpreted and reinterpreted by their participants, realist synthesis sees no opportunity to ponder counterfactual questions. Realism sees programmes and services as a series of decisions and it seeks to offer enlightenment on the key options and how preferences have fared in the past. It can offer reasons for preferring theory A over theory B, and for backing theory A over theory C, but that always leaves open the possibility that a further set of ideas D might be more efficacious. Even at best, its findings are provisional and fallible.

No apology, but only the above explanation about open systems, is offered for the partial and incomplete claims of realist synthesis. Some knowledge is preferable to no knowledge, and is rather more plausible than 'certain' knowledge. We cannot even know where the evidential pointer lies between these two extremes. The point, however, is to keep striving for more knowledge. Evidence-based policy should be seen as a process and an objective rather than a method. Synthesis should continue to be aimed at solving problems but, to paraphrase Marklund (1982), what must be eliminated is the expectation that it will provide *the* solution to *the* problem. Real policy decisions are always made in conditions of scarcity and always face a limited range of potential solutions. There is considerable utility in helping to adjudicate between them.

Aren't the lessons just too complex?

The conclusions of realist synthesis have been described variously as models, as refined theories, as highway codes and as 'context, mechanism outcome configurations'. As the unit of learning drops down to the component processes of interventions and the theories that underpin them, much more dexterity is required in deciphering, utilizing and re-utilizing research results. The expectation is that the same theory A, crops up in interventions B, C, D, and has been interrogated in primary inquiries E, F, G and that synthesis of the evidence thereupon will result in distilled theory A*, which can be used to inform future interventions H, I and J.

This is indeed a more complex vision of research utilization, and one that requires organization, patience and memory to put into practice. As this chapter has shown, these are not the prime characteristics of decision-makers (indeed see Pollitt, 2000, on 'policy amnesia'). Realist synthesis is bullish about the sense-making model as the only viable and reliable vehicle for evidence-based policy, but it remains extremely modest about the timetable. The best hope in the face of intricacy, perhaps, is that we have been there before. In the days before evidence-based policy we had seat-of-the-pants policy navigation. Reasoning went something like this: 'we are faced with implementing this new scheme A but it's rather like the B one we tried at C, and you may recall that it hit problems in terms of D, E and F, so we need to watch out for that again. Come to think of it, I've just heard they've just implemented something rather like A over in the department of G, so I'll ask H whether they've come up with any new issues I, J and K.'

Configurational thinking is thus nothing new (and may be as simple as A, B, C). Not only is realist review equipped to uphold and inform this kind of reasoning (to give it an evidence base, so to speak), it is also well suited to an updated version called organizational learning. Nowadays, this kind of informal knowledge-sharing is being encouraged through such schemes as the Breakthrough quality improvement collaboratives that are part of the UK NHS Modernisation Programme. The goal is to facilitate the transfer of the 'sticky knowledge' that makes for success in complex organizational innovations by bringing policy-makers and practitioners together in informal space (Bate et al., 2002). Realist review supplements this approach to organizational learning by thinking through the configurations of contexts and mechanisms that need to be attended to in fine-tuning a programme. With a touch of modernization, via the importation of empirical evidence, 'thinking it through' may still be the best model.

Why, when you allow for so much intuition, do you say that it's scientific?

Although I have set out a template for realist review in Chapter 4, I have cautioned against treating it as a set of rules which the reviewer should follow faithfully and systematically. I have emphasized that there can be no single and simple procedural formula that provides for synthesizing the labours of thousands of practitioners and dozens of researchers, each tackling different objectives and different hypotheses, in different contexts, with different resources and different methods. The most this (or any other) book can offer are some principles for the complex judgements involved in drawing it all together.

In this conviction, I depart sharply from the most committed advocates of procedural uniformity and protocol in research synthesis (for example, Straus and McAlister, 2000; Green and Higgins, 2004). One of the great themes of the Cochrane and Campbell collaborations is that the validity of reviews stems from their transparency and thus reproducibility. This desideratum is conceived in terms of technical clarity and standardization, so that by following the formula it matters not whether team and A or team B has carried out the review. It is the procedure itself that is considered to furnish certainty. Such a viewpoint has rich echoes of the notion of the reproducibility of experiments, an idea that for many is the cornerstone of empirical science.

My objections to the reproducibility principle are two-fold. The first lies with the sheer impossibility of making transparent every single decision involved in research synthesis. Many years ago Polanyi (1966) taught that the conduct of laboratory experiments is so intricate that they never in fact get fully written up. Yet, physical scientists are able to follow and to build upon each other's work because they rely on tacit knowledge, gained from years of laboratory life.

In the same manner it is impossible for reviews to tell the full story. When one is reviewing the vast literature associated with complex interventions, and if one admits all manner of empirical research, grey literature and even policy thought pieces as potential evidence, one is faced with an endless task that has, at some stage, to be arbitrarily terminated. This requires judgement and I am inclined to believe that it happens in all forms of review (Hammersley, 2002; Briggs, 2005). When faced with search results that have generated a thousand documents, one has to rely on a mixture of experience, sagacity and short-cuts to sift out those with greatest relevance. This inevitably depends on intuition about such matters as to whether one can rely on titles and abstracts to make the cut, or how much effort to put into finding that obscure paper that seems beyond retrieval. We know this, and systematic review is not fatally contaminated by it because the truth lies beyond procedure.

My second rebuttal gets to the deep philosophical roots of the argument. I question whether objectivity in science has ever stemmed from standardization of procedure. My preference is for a model of validity that rests on refutation rather than replication. In the context of research synthesis, this does require showing one's working, laying down one's methodological tracks and surfacing one's reasoning, but clarity on this model is for the purpose of *exposing a developing theory to criticism*. A fundamental principle of realist review is that its findings are fallible. The whole enterprise is about sifting and sorting theories and coming to a provisional preference for a particular explanation. Constant exposure to scrutiny and critique through evidence is thus the engine for the revision and refinement of programme theories.

The same is true for evidence-based policy writ large. What is needed is a dismantling of the oligarchies. What is needed is struggle with the methodological supremacists. What is needed is a system in which reviewers challenge rather than attempt to police each other. In the words of Donald Campbell:

> The objectivity of physical science does not come from turning over the running of experiments to people who could not care less about outcomes, nor from having a separate staff to read the meters. It comes from a process that can be called 'competitive cross-validation' and from the fact that there are many independent decision makers capable of rerunning an experiment ... The resulting dependability of the reports comes from a social process rather than from dependence on the honesty and competence of any single experimenter. Somehow in the social system of science a systematic norm of distrust, combined with ambitiousness, leads people to monitor each other for improved validity. Organized distrust produces trustworthy reports. (Campbell, 1984: 38)

How appropriate that Campbell should have the last word.

References

Ackroyd, S. and Fleetwood, S. (eds) (2000) *Realist Perspectives on Management and Organizations*. London: Routledge.

Adkins, G., Huff, D. and Stageberg, P. (2000) *The Iowa Sex Offender Registry and Recidivism*. Des Moines, IA: Iowa Department of Human Rights, Division of Criminal and Juvenile Justice Planning and Statistical Analysis Center. Available via: http://www.state.ia.us/government/dhr/cjjp/publications/sex_offend.html.

Archer, M. (1995) *Realist Social Theory: the Morphogenetic Approach*. Cambridge: Cambridge University Press.

Archer, M., Bhaskar, R., Collier, A., Lawson, T. and Norrie, A. (eds) (1998) *Critical Realism: Essential Readings*. London: Routledge.

Armstrong, C.J. and Large, A. (2001) *Manual of Online Search Strategies. Volume III: Humanities and Social Sciences*. Aldershot: Gower Publishing.

Ashworth, K., Cebulla, A., Greenberg, D. and Walker, R. (2004) 'Meta-evaluation: discovering what works best in welfare provision', *Evaluation*, 10(2): 193–216.

Ayres, I. and Braithwaite, J. (1992) *Responsive Regulation: Transcending the Deregulation Debate*. Oxford: Oxford University Press.

Bate, P., Robert, G. and McLeod, H. (2002) *Report on the 'Breakthrough' Collaborative Approach to Quality and Service Improvement Within Four Regions of the NHS: a Research-Based Investigation of the Orthopaedic Collaborative Within the Eastern, South and West, South East and Trent Regions*. HMSC Research Report 42. Birmingham: Heath Services Management Centre, University of Birmingham.

Bedarf, A.R. (1995) 'Examining sex offender community notification laws', *California Law Review*, 83(3): 885–940.

Bemelmans-Videc, M.-L., Rist, R.C. and Vedung, E.O. (eds) (2003) *Carrots, Sticks, and Sermons: Policy Instruments and Their Evaluation*. Somerset, NJ: Transaction Publishers.

Bhaskar, R. (1978) *A Realist Theory of Science*, 2nd edn. Brighton: Harvester Press.

Bhaskar, R. (1979) *The Possibility of Naturalism: a Philosophical Critique of the Contemporary Human Sciences*. Brighton: Harvester Press.

Bhaskar, R. (2000) *From East to West: Odyssey of a Soul*. London: Routledge.

Bhaskar, R. (ed.) (2002) *From Science to Emancipation: Alienation and the Actuality of Enlightenment*. Thousand Oaks, CA: Sage.

Braithwaite, J. (1989) *Crime, Shame and Reintegration*. Cambridge: Cambridge University Press.

Briggs, D. (2005) 'Meta-analysis: a case study', *Evaluation Review*, 29(2): 87–127.

Burns, D. (1992) *Poll Tax Rebellion*. Stirling: AK Press.

Cabinet Office (1999) *Modernising Government*, Cm 4310. London: Stationery Office.

Campbell, D.T. (1969) 'Reforms as experiments', *American Psychologist*, 24(4): 409–29.

Campbell, D.T. (1984) 'Can we be scientific in applied science?', in R.F. Connor, D.G. Altman and C. Jackson (eds), *Evaluation Studies Review Annual*, Newbury Park, CA: Sage, pp. 24–48.

Carter, B. and New, C. (2004) *Making Realism Work: Realist Social Theory and Empirical Work*. London: Routledge.

Colley, H. (2003) 'Engagement mentoring for socially excluded youth: problematising an "holistic" approach to creating employability through the transformation of habitus', *British Journal of Guidance and Counselling*, 31(1): 77–98.

Colley, H. (2004) *Mentoring for Social Inclusion: a Critical Approach to Nurturing Mentor Relationships*. London: Routledge-Falmer.

Collier, A. (1994) *Critical Realism: an Introduction to Roy Bhaskar's Philosophy*. London: Verso.

Connell, J.P., Kubisch, A.C., Schorr, L.B. and Weiss, C.H. (eds) (1995) *New Approaches to Evaluating Community Initiatives. Vol. 1: Concepts, Methods, and Contexts*. New York: Aspen Institute.

CRD (Centre for Reviews and Dissemination) (2001) *Undertaking Systematic Reviews of Research on Effectiveness: CRD's Guidance for Those Carrying Out or Commissioning Reviews*. Report 4 (2nd edn). York: CRD.

CSOM (Center for Sex Offender Management) (1999) *Sex Offender Registration: Policy Overview and Comprehensive Practices*. Silver Spring, MD: CSOM.

CSOM (Center for Sex Offender Management) (2001) *Community Notification and Education*. Silver Spring, MD: CSOM.

Davies, H.T.O., Nutley, S.M. and Smith, P.C. (2000) *What Works? Evidence-Based Policy and Practice in Public Services*. Bristol: Policy Press.

de Anda, D. (2001) 'A qualitative evaluation of a mentor program for at-risk youth: the participants' perspective', *Child and Adolescent Social Work Journal*, 18(2): 97–117.

Deshpande, R. (1981) 'Action and enlightenment functions of research', *Knowledge: Creation, Diffusion, Utilization*, 2(3): 134–45.

Dixon-Woods, M., Agarwal, S., Young, B., Jones, D. and Sutton, A. (2004) *Integrative Approaches to Qualitative and Quantitative Evidence*. London: Health Development Agency.

Dobrow, M.J., Goel, V. and Upshur, R.E. (2004) 'Evidence-based health policy: context and utilisation', *Social Science and Medicine*, 58(1): 207–17.

DuBois, D., Holloway, B., Valentine, J. and Cooper, H. (2002) 'Effectiveness of mentoring programmes for youth: a meta-analytic review', *American Journal of Community Psychology*, 30(2): 157–97.

Edgley, R. (1998) 'Reason as dialectic: science, social science and socialist science', in M. Archer, R. Bhaskar, A. Collier, T. Lawson and A. Norrie (eds), *Critical Realism: Essential Readings*. London: Routledge.

Edin, K. and Lein, L. (1997) 'Work, welfare, and single mothers' economic survival strategies', *American Sociological Review*, 62(2): 253–66.

Ekblom, P. (2002). 'From the source to the mainstream is uphill: the challenge of transferring knowledge of crime prevention through replication, innovation and anticipation', in N. Tilley (ed.), *Analysis for Crime Prevention*. Crime Prevention Studies 13. Monsey, NY: Criminal Justice Press, pp. 131–203.

Elster, J. (1999) *Alchemies of the Mind: Rationality and the Emotions*. Cambridge: Cambridge University Press.

English, K., Pullen, S. and Jones, L. (eds) (1996) *Managing Adult Sex Offenders: A Containment Approach*. Lexington, KY: American Probation and Parole Association.

Eraut, M. (1994) *Developing Professional Knowledge and Competence*. London: Falmer Press.

European Commission (2001) *European Governance: a White Paper*, COM(2001) 428 final. Brussels: European Commission.

Evans, C.C. (2003) 'Consultant appraisal', *Clinical Medicine*, 3(6): 495–6.

Exworthy, M., Berney, L. and Powell, M. (2002) '"How great expectations in Westminster may be dashed locally": the local implementation of policy on health inequalities', *Policy and Politics*, 30(1): 79–96.

Farrington, D.P. and Welsh, B.C. (2002) *Effects of Improved Street Lighting on Crime: a Systematic Review*. Home Office Research Study 251. London: Home Office.

Fergusson, D., Glass, K., Waring, D. and Shapiro, S. (2004) 'Turning a blind eye: the success of blinding reported in a random sample of randomised, placebo controlled trials', *British Medical Journal*, 328(7437): 432–4.

Fisse, B. and Braithwaite, J. (1983) *The Impact of Publicity on Corporate Offenders*. Albany, NY: State University of New York Press.

Fox, N. (2003) 'Practice-based evidence: towards collaborative and transgressive research', *Sociology*, 37(1): 81–102.

Freedman, M. (1993) *The Kindness of Strangers: Adult Mentors, Urban Youth, and the New Voluntarism*. Cambridge: Cambridge University Press.

Freeman-Longo, R.E. (1996) 'Prevention or problem', *Sexual Abuse: a Journal of Research and Treatment*, 8(2): 91–100.

Giddens, A. (1984) *The Constitution of Society: Outline of the Theory of Structuration*. Cambridge: Polity Press.

Giddens, A. (2000) *The Third Way and Its Critics*. Cambridge: Polity Press.

Glaser, B.G. and Strauss, A.L. (1967) *The Discovery of Grounded Theory: Strategies for Qualitative Research*. Chicago: Aldine.

Grayson, L. and Gomersall, A. (2003) *A Difficult Business: Finding the Evidence for Social Science Reviews*. London: ESRC UK Centre for Evidence-Based Policy and Practice, Queen Mary, University of London. Available via: http://www.evidencenetwork.org.

Green, S. and Higgins, J. (eds) (2004) *Cochrane Handbook for Systematic Reviews of Interventions*. Available via: http://www.cochrane.dk/cochrane/handbook/handbook.htm.

Greenhalgh, T., Robert, G., Bate, P., Kyriakidou, O., Macfarlane, F. and Peacock, R. (2004) *How to Spread Good Ideas: a Systematic Review of the Literature on Diffusion, Dissemination and Sustainability in Health Service Delivery and Organisation*. Report for the National Co-ordinating Centre for NHS Service Delivery and Organisation. Available at: www.sdo.lshtm.ac.uk/pdf/changemanagement_greenhalgh_report.pdf.

Greenwood, J. (1994) *Realism, Identity and Emotion: Reclaiming Social Psychology*. London: Sage.

Grossman, J. and Tierney, J. (1998) 'Does mentoring work? An impact study of the Big Brothers Big Sisters program', *Evaluation Review*, 22(3): 403–26.

Hammersley, M. (2001) 'On "systematic" reviews of research literatures: a "narrative" response to Evans and Benefield', *British Educational Research Journal*, 27(5): 543–54.

Hammersley, M. (2002) *Systematic or Unsystematic: Is That the Question? Some Reflections on the Science, Art, and Politics of Reviewing Research Evidence*. Text of a talk given to the Public Health Evidence Steering Group of the Health Development Agency, October 2002. Available at: http://www.hda-online.org.uk/evidence/sys_unsys_phesg_hammersley.pdf.

Hanney, S., Gonzalez-Block, M., Buxton, M. and Kogan, M. (2003) 'The utilisation of health research in policy-making: concepts, examples and methods of assessment', *Health Research Policy and Systems*, 1(2): doi:10.1186/1478-4505-1-2. Available at: http://www.health-policy-systems.com/content/1/1/2.

Harré, R. (1978) *Social Being: a Theory for Social Psychology*. Oxford: Blackwell.

Hebenton, B. and Thomas, T. (1997) *Keeping Track? Observations on Sex Offender Registers in the US*. Crime Detection and Prevention Series Paper 83. London: Home Office.

Hedström, P. and Swedberg, R. (eds) (1998) *Social Mechanisms: an Analytical Approach to Social Theory*. Cambridge: Cambridge University Press.

Hemsley-Brown, J. and Sharp, C. (2003) 'The use of research to improve professional practice: a systematic review', *Oxford Review of Education*, 29(4): 449–71.

Henry, G.T., Julnes, G. and Mark, M.M. (eds) (1998) *Realist Evaluation: an Emerging Theory in Support of Practice*. New Directions for Evaluation 78. San Francisco: Jossey-Bass.

Houghton, G. (1992) *Car Theft in England and Wales: the Home Office Car Theft Index*. Crime Prevention Unit Paper 33. London: Home Office.

Hunt, M. (1997) *How Science Takes Stock*. New York: Russell Sage Foundation.

Jekielek, S., More, K. and Hair, E. (2002) *Mentoring Programs and Youth Development: a Synthesis*. Washington, DC: Child Trends Inc. Available at: http://www.childtrends.org/PDF/MentoringSynthesisfinal2.6.02Jan.pdf.

Kestenbuam, A. (1996) *Independent Living: a Review*. York: Joseph Rowntree Foundation.

Kram, K. and Isabella, L. (1985) 'Mentoring alternatives: the role of peer relations in career development', *Academy of Management Journal*, 28(1): 110–32.

Kuhn, T.S. (1970) *The Structure of Scientific Revolutions*, 2nd edn. Chicago: University of Chicago Press.

Lau, J., Antman, E.M., Jimezsilva, J., Kupelnick, B., Mosteller, F. and Chalmers, T.C. (1992) 'Cumulative meta-analysis of therapeutic trials for myocardial-infarcation', *New England Journal of Medicine*, 327(4): 248–54.

Lau, J., Ioannidis, J.P.A. and Schmid, C.H. (1998) 'Summing up evidence: one answer is not always enough,' *Lancet*, 351(9096): 123–7.

Lavis, J.N., Ross, S.E., Hurley, J.E. et al. (2002) 'Examining the role of health services research in public policymaking', *Milbank Quarterly*, 80(1): 125–54.

Lawson, T. (1997) *Economics and Reality*. London: Routledge.

Laycock, G. and Tilley, N. (1995) 'Implementing crime prevention', in M. Tonry and D.P. Farrington (eds), *Building a Safer Society: Strategic Approaches to Crime Prevention*. Chicago: University of Chicago Press, pp. 535–84.

Layder, D. (1998) *Sociological Practice: Linking Theory and Social Research*. London: Sage.

Levi, R. (2000) 'The mutuality of risk and community: the adjudication of community notification statutes', *Economy and Society*, 29(4): 578–601.

Lindblom, C.E. (1990) *Inquiry and Change: the Troubled Attempt to Understand and Shape Society*. New Haven, CT: Yale University Press.

Lipsey, M.W. (1997) 'What can you build with thousands of bricks? Musings on the cumulation of knowledge in program evaluation', in D.J. Rog and D. Fournier (eds), *Progress and Future Directions in Evaluation: Perspectives on Theory, Practice and Methods*. New Directions for Evaluation 76. San Francisco: Jossey-Bass, pp. 7–24.

Lipsey, M.W. (2003) 'Those confounded moderators in meta-analysis: good, bad and ugly', *Annals of the American Academy of Political and Economic Science*, 587: 69–81.

Lipsey, M.W. and Wilson, D.B. (1993) 'The efficacy of psychological, educational and behavioral treatment: confirmation from meta-analysis', *American Psychologist*, 48(12): 1181–209.

Lomas, J. (2000) 'Using "linkage and exchange" to move research into policy at a Canadian foundation', *Health Affairs*, 19(3): 236–40.

Lonbom, K. (1998) 'The Illinois registration and notification system for sex offenders', in *National Conference on Sex Offender Registries: Proceedings of a BJS/SEARCH Conference*. Washington, DC: US Department of Justice, pp. 72–4.

Long, A., Godfrey, M., Randall, T., Brettle, A. and Grant, M. (2002) 'Evidence-based social care policy and practice. Part 3: Feasibility of understanding systematic reviews in social care'. Nuffeld Institute for Health, University of Leeds, pp. 71–5.

Longo, D., Land, G., Schramm, W., Fraas, J., Hoskins, B. and Howell, V. (1997) 'Consumer reports in health care: do they make a difference?', *Journal of the American Medical Association*, 278(19): 1579–84.

Lucas, P. and Liabo, K. (2003) *One-to-one, Non-Directive Mentoring Programmes Have Not Been Shown to Improve Behaviour in Young People Involved in Offending or Anti-Social Activities*. Evidence Nugget. What Works for Children (Barnardo's, City University and University of York). Available at: http://www.whatworksforchildren.org.uk/docs/Nuggets/pdfs/Mentoring230703.pdf.

MacLure, M. (2005) '"Clarity bordering on stupidity": where's the quality in systematic review', *Journal of Education Policy*, 20(4): 393–419.

Majone, G. (1989) *Evidence, Argument and Persuasion in the Policy Process*. New Haven, CT: Yale University Press.

Marchant, P.R. (2004) 'Research note: a demonstration that the claim that brighter lighting reduces crime is unfounded', *British Journal of Criminology*, 44(3): 441–7.

Mark, M.M., Henry, G.T. and Julnes, G. (2000) *Evaluation: an Integrated Framework for Understanding, Guiding and Improving Public and Nonprofit Policies and Programs*. San Francisco: Jossey-Bass.

Marklund, I. (1982) 'The impact of policy-oriented educational R&D', in D.B.P. Kallen et al. (eds), *Social Science Research and Public Policy Making: a Reappraisal*. Windsor: NFER-Nelson.

Marshall, M., Shekelle, E.P., Brook, R. and Leatherman, S. (2000) *Dying to Know: Public Release of Information About Quality of Health Care*. Nuffield Trust Series 12. London: Nuffield Trust.

Matson, S. and Lieb, R. (1996a) *Sex Offender Registration: a Review of State Laws*. Olympia, WA: Washington State Institute for Public Policy.

Matson, S. and Lieb, R. (1996b) *Community Notification in Washington State: 1996 Survey of Law Enforcement*. Olympia, WA: Washington State Institute for Public Policy.

McEvoy, P. and Richards, D. (2003) 'Critical realism: a way forward for evaluation research in nursing?', *Journal of Advanced Nursing*, 43(4): 411–20.

Mennemeyer, S.T., Morrisey, M.A. and Howard, L.Z. (1997) 'Death and reputation: how consumers acted upon HCFA mortality information', *Inquiry*, 34(2): 117–28.

Merton, R.K. (1968) *Social Theory and Social Structure*, 3rd edn. New York: Free Press.

Mintzberg, H., Raisinghani, D. and Theoret, A. (1976) 'The structure of "unstructured" decision processes', *Administrative Science Quarterly*, 21(June): 246–75.

Mitchell, K. (1997) 'Encouraging young women to exercise: can teenage magazines play a role?', *Health Education Journal*, 56(2): 264–73.

NIJ (National Institute of Justice) (1997) *Sex Offender Community Notification*. Washington, DC: US Department of Justice.

Noe, R. (1988) 'An investigation of the determinants of successful assigned mentoring relationships', *Personnel Psychology*, 41(3): 457–79.

Norrie, A. (1993) *Crime, Reason and History: a Critical Introduction to Criminal Law*. London: Weidenfeld & Nicolson.

Norris, C., Moran, J. and Armstrong, G. (eds) (1998) *Surveillance, Closed Circuit Television and Social Control*. Aldershot: Ashgate.

Oakley, A. (2000) *Experiments in Knowing: Gender and Method in the Social Sciences*. Cambridge: Polity Press.

Øvretveit, J., Bate, P., Cretin, S., Cleary, P. et al. (2002) 'Quality collaboratives: lessons from research', *Quality and Safety in Health Care*, 11(4): 345–51.

Øvretveit, J. and Gustafson, D. (2002) 'Evaluation of quality improvement programmes', *Quality and Safety in Health Care*, 11(3): 270–5.

Parra, G., DuBois, D., Neville, H. and Pugh-Lilly, A. (2002) 'Mentoring relationships for youth: investigation of a process-oriented model', *Journal of Community Psychology*, 30(4): 367–88.

Pawson, R. (1989) *A Measure for Measures: a Manifesto for Empirical Sociology*. London: Routledge.

Pawson, R. (2000) 'Middle-range realism', *Archives Européenes de Sociologie*, 41(2): 283–325.

Pawson, R. and Tilley, N. (1997) *Realistic Evaluation*. London: Sage.

Petrosino, A.J. (2000) 'Mediators and moderators in the evaluation of programs for children: current practice and agenda for improvement', *Evaluation Review*, 24(1): 47–72.

Petrosino, A., Boruch, R.F., Soydan, H., Duggan, L. and Sanchez-Meca, J. (2001) 'Meeting the challenges of evidence-based policy: the Campbell Collaboration', *Annals of the American Academy of Political and Economic Science*, 578: 14–34.

Petrosino, A.J. and Petrosino, C. (1999) 'The public safety potential of Megan's Law in Massachusetts: an assessment from a sample of criminal sexual psychopaths', *Crime and Delinquency*, 45(1): 140–58.

Philip, K. and Hendry, L. (2000) 'Making sense of mentoring or mentoring making sense? Reflections on mentoring process by adult mentors with young people', *Journal of Community and Applied Social Psychology*, 10(3): 211–33.

Philip, K., Shucksmith, J. and King, C. (2004) *Sharing a Laugh? A Qualitative Study of Mentoring Interventions with Young People*. York: Joseph Rowntree Foundation.

Polanyi, M. (1966) *The Tacit Dimension*. New York: Doubleday.

Pollitt, C. (2000) 'Institutional amnesia: a paradox of the "information age"?', *Prometheus*, 19(1): 5–16.

Poole, C. and Lieb, R. (1995) *Community Notification in Washington State: Decision Making and Costs*. Olympia, WA: Washington State Institute for Public Policy.

Popper, K. (1972) *Conjectures and Refutations: the Growth of Scientific Knowledge*, 4th edn. London: Routledge and Kegan Paul.

Presser, L. and Gunnison, E. (1999) 'Strange bedfellows: is sex offender notification a form of community justice?', *Crime and Delinquency*, 45(3): 299–315.

Putnam, H. and Conant, J. (1990) *Realism with a Human Face*. Cambridge, MA: Harvard University Press.

Quinsey, V.L., Harris, G., Rice, M. and Cormier, C. (1998) *Violent Offenders: Appraising and Managing Risk*. Washington, DC: American Psychological Association.

Reynolds, M. (1992) *Uncollectable: the Story of the Poll Tax Revolt*. Salford: Greater Manchester Anti-Poll Tax Federation.

Rhodes, J., Grossman, J. and Resch, N. (2000) 'Agents of change: pathways through which mentoring relationships influence adolescents' academic adjustment', *Child Development*, 71(6): 1662–71.

Rich, R.C., Conn, D. and Owens, W.L. (1993) '"Indirect regulation" of environmental hazards through the provision of information to the public: the case of SARA, Title III', *Policy Studies Journal*, 21(1): 16–34.

Ritzer, G. (1975) 'Sociology: a multiple paradigm science', *American Sociologist*, 10(3): 156–67.

Roberts, K. (1997) 'The British Insurance Industry's Criteria for Vehicle Security: a Solution to Escalating Car Crime in the UK'. Paper to the SAE Global Development Conference: Detroit. Available at: http://www.thatcham.org/resources/pdfs/vehiclesecurity.pdf.

Rosenthal, R. (1991) 'Teacher expectancy effects: a brief update 25 years after the Pygmalion experiment', *Journal of Research in Education*, 1(1): 3–12.

Rossi, P. (1987) 'The iron law of evaluation and other metallic roles', in J.H. Miller and M. Lewis (eds), *Research in Social Problems and Public Policy*. Greenwich, CT: JAI Press, Vol. 4, pp. 3–20.

Rossi, P., Berk, R. and Lenihan, K. (1980) *Money, Work and Crime: Experimental Evidence*. New York: Academic Press.

Salaman, L. (1981) 'Rethinking public management: third party government and the changing forms of government action', *Public Policy*, 29(3): 255–75.

Sayer, A. (1992) *Method in Social Science: a Realist Approach*. London: Routledge.

Sayer, A. (2000) *Realism and Social Science*. London: Sage.

Schram, D.D. and Milloy, C.D. (1995) *Community Notification: a Study of Offender Characteristics and Recidivism*. Olympia, WA: Washington State Institute for Public Policy.

Shaftoe, H. (1994) 'Easton/Ashley, Bristol: lighting improvements', in S. Osborn (ed.), *Housing Safe Communities: an Evaluation of Recent Initiatives*. London: NACRO Safe Neighbourhoods Unit, pp. 72–7.

Shaw, S., MacFarlane, F., Greaves, C. and Carter, Y.H. (2004) 'Developing research management and governance capacity in primary care organizations: transferable learning from a qualitative evaluation of UK pilot sites', *Family Practice*, 21(1): 92–8.

Sheldon, T. (1997) 'Introduction', in L. Grayson, *Evidence-Based Medicine: an Overview and Guide to the Literature*. London: The British Library, p. vii.

Shepherd, J. (2003) 'Explaining feast or famine in randomized field trials: medical science and criminology compared', *Evaluation Review*, 27(3): 290–315.

Sherman, L.W., Gottfredson, D., MacKenzie, D.L., Eck, J., Reuter, P. and Bushway, S.D. (1997) *Preventing Crime: What Works, What Doesn't, and What's Promising?* Washington, DC: US Department of Justice, Office of Justice Programs.

Sherman, L.W. with Schmidt, J.D. and Rogan, D.P. (1992) *Policing Domestic Violence: Experiments and Dilemmas*. New York: Free Press.

Shiner, M., Newburn, T., Young, T. and Groben, S. (2004) *Mentoring Disaffected Young People: an Evaluation of 'Mentoring Plus'*. York: Joseph Rowntree Foundation.

Smith, A.F. (1996) 'Mad cows and Ecstasy: chance and choice in an evidence-based society', *Journal of the Royal Statistical Society A*, 159(3): 367–83.

Solesbury, W. (2001) *Evidence Based Policy: Whence It Came and Where It's Going*. Working Paper 1. London: ESRC UK Centre for Evidence-Based Policy and Practice, Queen Mary, University of London. Available via: http://www.evidencenetwork.org.

Spencer, L., Ritchie, J., Lewis, J. and Dillon, J. (2003) *Quality in Qualitative Evaluation: a Framework for Assessing Research Evidence*. Occasional Paper 2. London: Government Chief Social Researcher's Office.

St James-Roberts, I. and Singh, C. (2001) *Can Mentors Help Primary School Children with Behaviour Problems?* Home Office Research Study 233. London: Home Office Research and Statistics Directorate.

Steinmetz, G. (1998) 'Critical realism and historical sociology: a review article', *Comparative Studies in Society and History*, 40(1): 170–86.

Stern, E. (1995) 'Editorial', *Evaluation*, 1(1): 5–9.

Stewart, M. and Taylor, M. (1995) *Empowerment and Estate Regeneration: a Critical Review*. Bristol: Policy Press.

Straus, S. and McAlister, F. (2000) 'Evidence-based medicine: a commentary on current criticisms', *Canadian Medical Association Journal*, 163(7): 837–41.

Stronach, I. (1997) 'Evaluation with the lights out: deconstructing illuminative evaluation and new paradigm research', in L. Mabry (ed.), *Advances in Program Evaluation: Evaluation and the Post-modern Dilemma*. Greenwich, CT: JAI Press, Vol. 3, pp. 21–39.

Walter, I., Nutley, S. and Davies, H. (2003) *Research Impact: a Cross-Sector Review – Literature Review*. St Andrews: Research Unit for Research Utilisation, University of St Andrews.

Weisburd, D., Petrosino, A. and Lum, C. (eds) (2003) 'Assessing systematic evidence in crime and justice: methodological concerns and empirical outcomes', *Annals of the American Academy of Political and Economic Science*, 587, complete issue.

Weiss, C. (1980) 'Knowledge creep and decision accretion', *Knowledge: Creation, Diffusion, Utilization*, 1(3): 381–404.

Weiss, C. (1986) 'The circuitry of enlightenment: diffusion of social science research to policy makers', *Knowledge: Creation, Diffusion, Utilization*, 8(2): 274–81.

Weiss, C. and Bucuvalas, M. (1980) *Social Science Research and Decision Making*. New York: Columbia University Press.

Welsh, B.C. and Farrington, D.P. (2001) 'Towards an evidence-based approach to preventing crime', *Annals of the American Academy of Political and Economic Science*, 587: 158–73.

Whitman, C.D. and Farmer, J.F. (2000) *Attorney General Guidelines for Law Enforcement for the Implementation of Sex Offender Registration and Community Notification Laws*. Trenton, NJ: State of New Jersey Office of the Attorney General.

Whitman, J.Q. (1998) 'What is wrong with inflicting shame sanctions?', *Yale Law Journal*, 107(4): 1055–92.

Williams, M. (2000) *Science and Social Science*. London: Routledge.

Winick, B.J. (1998) 'Sex offender laws in the 1990s: a therapeutic jurisprudence analysis', *Psychology, Public Policy and Law*, 41(1/2): 505–70.

Zevitz, R.G. and Farkas, M.A. (2000a) 'Sex offender community notification: managing high risk criminals or exacting further vengeance?', *Behavioral Sciences and the Law*, 18(2/3): 375–92.

Zevitz, R.G. and Farkas, M.A. (2000b) 'Sex offender community notification: examining the importance of neighbourhood meetings', *Behavioral Sciences and the Law*, 18(2/3): 393–408.

Zevitz, R.G. and Farkas, M.A. (2000c) 'The impact of sex-offender community notification on probation/parole in Wisconsin', *International Journal of Offender Therapy and Comparative Criminology*, 44(1): 8–21.

Index

Indexed by Caroline Eley